CYBERCRIME

How to Avoid Becoming a Victim

H. Thomas Milhorn, MD, PhD

Universal Publishers
Boca Raton, Florida

Cybercrime:
How to Avoid Becoming a Victim

Universal Publishers
Boca Raton, Florida
USA • 2007

ISBN: 1-58112-954-8
13-ISBN: 978-1-58112-954-0

www.universal-publishers.com

Preface

Computers and the Internet can be used almost anywhere. Desktop computers are found in homes, schools, libraries, businesses, and cybercafés. The advent of wireless Internet connection has allowed the use of computers in places not envisioned a few years ago—on a train, on a bus, in a restaurant, or even on a busy street corner. In addition, you can plug your laptop into an outlet in many hotel rooms for a traditional, hardwired Internet connection. And more and more people, including the elderly, are taking the necessary steps to learn how to use computers and the Internet.

In teaching basic computer courses for adults, the most frequent question I get asked is "Is using the Internet safe?" The answer is, "well yes and no." Americans lost more than $336 million to online fraud in 2005, and that doesn't count all the headaches, lost hours spent trying to restore their computers to normal functioning states after they were disrupted by viruses and other intrusive programs, or the money paid to computer experts to fix the problems. In addition, dealing with viruses, spyware, computer theft, and other computer-related crimes cost U.S. businesses $67.2 billion a year, according to the FBI. And the criminals are still out are there just waiting to plant a virus that crashes your whole system, install spyware that keeps track of everything you do on the Internet, defraud you out of money, or steal your personal information, including passwords, Social Security number, bank account number, and credit card number. However, there is good news. There are steps you can take to protect yourself and your computer, and they are spelled out in this book.

My interest in cybercrime began after personally experiencing a modem hijacker (dialer program) and having my browser hijacked by an unethical anti-spyware company, not to mention a multitude of viruses. I've also had bogus charges added to my credit card following online purchases. All this made me very conscious of the need for knowledge of cybercrime and computer security. "Cybercrime: How to Avoid Becoming a Victim" is my attempt to share with fellow computer users what I learned from experience and research on the topic.

I have laid out each chapter in a format consisting of a discussion of the basics of the crime, followed by real-life examples of the particular crime, and then things you can do to avoid becoming a victim of the crime. In addition to the chapters on individual cybercrimes, I have included a chapter on the role of organized crime in Internet fraud and a chapter on Internet hoaxes. Although hoaxes are not crimes as such, some can lead you to damage your own computer if you follow their instructions, and they are a nuisance. In addition, I have included an appendix on where to report various cybercrimes and another appendix on cybercrime terminology.

Being a firm believer that people learn from example, I have used over 200 case reports to illustrate specific crimes. I have no personal knowledge of any of these. They are all taken from various sources, both online and the print media.

I would like to thank Phyllis Millett for proofreading the manuscript and making a number of valuable suggestions.

Tom Milhorn

Meridian, Mississippi

Contents

Chapter 1

Introduction

Computers and the Internet offer great benefits to society. The Internet provides instant access to news, banking, auctions, shopping, reference information, stock trading, travel information, and much more. Chat rooms, emails, and instant messaging have become common methods of communication. Unfortunately, criminals also use the Internet, giving rise to the term *cybercrime*, which refers to any type of activity that uses the Internet to commit a crime. A *cybercriminal*, or *cybercrook*, is defined as a person who uses a computer and the Internet to commit a crime.

The fact is, the more you know about cybercrime the better able you will be to protect yourself and your computer from those out there who wish to do you harm.[1,2]

CATEGORIES OF CYBERCRIME

Cybercrime has been categorized a number of ways. The two presented here depend on (1) the target of the crime and (2) whether the crime occurs as a single event or as a series of events.

Target of the Crime

The target of cybercrime can be (1) persons, (2) property, or (3) organizations.

Persons

When an individual or group is the target of cybercrime, the computer is said to be the tool of the crime. The goal is to exploit human weaknesses, such as greed and naivety. These crimes, including financial crimes, sale of stolen or nonexistent items, child pornography, copyright violation, harassment, and stalking, have existed for centuries. Criminals have simply been given a new tool which increases their potential pool of victims. It also makes it harder to trace and apprehend the criminals.[3,4]

Property

Crimes against property include stealing a laptop; transmitting harmful programs that disrupt the function of a computer, wipes out the hard drive, or spies on the computer's user; and hijacking a computer, a browser, or a modem.[4]

Organizations

Organizations include governments and companies. Cyberterrorism is one distinct kind of crime against government. In this type of crime the Internet is used by individuals and groups to terrorize the citizens of a country or to threaten international governments. The latter form includes breaking into military computers and stealing secret information. More recently, the definition of cyberterrorism has been extended to include attacks against computers and networks of nongovernmental natures. Various companies, including Internet service providers, are often the target of cybercrimes, such as hacking into a computer network to steal information, damage programs or files, or plant programs that allow control of the network.[4]

Single or Series of Events

Single Event Cybercrime

Single event cybercrime is a single event from the perspective of

2

the victim. For example, you unknowingly open an email attachment that contains a virus that infects your computer. Or you might receive an email containing what appears to be a link to well-known company, but in reality is a link to a criminal website whose goal is to still your credit card number. Other examples of this type of cybercrime include hacking, spyware, and fraud.[2]

Series of Events Cybercrime

Series of events cybercrime involves repeated interactions with the target. For example, an adolescent is contacted in a chat room by someone who, over time, establishes a relationship. Eventually, the criminal exploits the relationship to commit sexual asault.[2]

In this book I simply present the various types of cybercrime in alphabetical order to make it easy for you, the reader, to find information about individual crimes.

STEPS TO PROTECT YOURSELF

Attacks against home computer users generally fall into two classes—fraud and crimeware, although other crimes, such as stalking, harassment, prostitution solicitation, and child pornography, do occur and are discussed later in this book.

Fraud is a deception deliberately practiced to secure unfair or unlawful gain, usually monetary in nature. Internet fraud includes auction fraud, identity theft, work at home scams, investment scams, and many others. An online fraud is known as a *dotcon,* which is a take off on *.com. Crimeware* is defined as software designed to steal personal information or perform some other illegal operation. It is malicious software that allows a crime to be committed.

Two special forms of crimeware are warez and malware. *Warez* refers to pirated software distributed over the Internet. *Malware* is a contraction of *mal*icious soft*ware*. It consists of browser hijackers, dialer programs, viruses, worms, Trojans, and spyware, all of which are designed by people who wish to do you or your computer harm.[5,6] Dialers and browser hijackers are discussed in Chapter 12, and viruses, worms, Trojans, and spyware are discussed in Chapter 35.

As we move from dial-up Internet connections (connected to

the Internet only when you connect them to the Internet) to high-speed connections (always connected to the Internet when the computer is on) the risk of becoming a target of cybercrime increases considerably. So, if you have a high-speed Internet connection and leave your computer on for long periods of time when you're not using it, it's a good idea to disconnect it from the Internet.

In addition, there are six basic steps you can take to reduce the risk of becoming a victim of cybercrime. You should (1) create a virtual shield, (2) beware of impersonators (3) avoid taking the bait dangled by cybercrooks, (4) stay away from high-risk websites, (5) download with caution, and (6) keep an eye on your children. In addition, if you have a wireless home network, use computers made available in public places, or travel with a laptop there are some additional steps to take.

Create a Virtual Shield

Online criminals look for easy targets. To thwart them by creating computer security in the form of a virtual shield you should (1) have a firewall, (2) have antivirus software, (3) have anti-spyware software, (4) choose strong passwords, and (5) update your operating system periodically.

Firewall

A *firewall* serves as a digital barrier that shields your computer from the outside world and monitors all out-going and in-coming programs that connect it to the Internet. A firewall's primary purpose is to alert you to unsolicited connection attempts and to block them.[7,8]

Every program on your computer uses ports to connect to other computers on the Internet. Ports are access ways through which information enters and leaves your computer. There are thousands of ports in use today, numbered from 1 to 65,535. They are logical accesses, not physical or hardware ones. Some applications use specific ports. For instance all regular HTTP (web traffic) uses ports 80 and 1080, and all HTTPS (encrypted web traffic) uses port 443. File sharing and instant messaging systems use a variety of ports. Many of these programs use whatever ports

4

are available at the time. Because applications use ports to access computers, one job of a firewall is to monitor the ports that are allowed to communicate with your computer.[5]

If you use a modem (dial-up connection), you are at a much lower risk from Internet attackers, since most hackers don't want to waste their time hacking into computers with slow Internet connections and which are rarely connected to the Internet. However, just because you aren't the most desirable target, doesn't mean you shouldn't run a firewall program.

For high-speed DSL, Cable, and Satellite Internet users, a firewall is essential. You are a primary target for Internet hackers for two reasons. First, hackers are interested in high speed transmission to get their fraudulent schemes out to as many people as possible in a short period of time. Second, many people with high-speed Internet connections leave their computers on for hours, days, or even all the time. With a dial-up Internet connection your Internet service provider assigns your computer a new IP (Internet Protocol) address each time you access the Internet. However, with high-speed Internet connections the IP address stays with your computer until you power down or log off. Leaving your computer on for long periods of time makes it easier for cybercrooks to obtain your computer's IP address and then come back at a later time to do their dirty work. Thus, although it might be convenient to have a ready Internet access, it does increase the risk.

Modern operating systems, like Windows XP and Mac OS X, have built-in firewalls, but you have to make sure they are turned on. Commercial firewalls are also available, including Norton Personal Firewall (www.symantec.com), McAfee Firewall (www.mcafee.com), and PC-cillin firewall (www.trendmicro.com). These and others can be purchased for a reasonable price and updated annually for a smaller fee.[7,8]

Antivirus Software

An *antivirus program* is software designed to detect and delete computer viruses, worms, Trojans, and other malicious software from your computer's email, memory (RAM), and hard drive. Such unwanted intruders can slow your computer down, make it difficult to open programs, such as Microsoft Word or Norton

SystemWorks, and even shut your computer down by crashing your hard drive and deleting everything that is stored there.

You should configure your antivirus program to automatically scan incoming and outgoing email for viruses. Most antivirus programs come with a real-time scanner that checks your files each time you open them. And most antivirus programs can be set to run scans at predetermined intervals. Even so, you should probably do a manual scan at least once a week.[7,8,9]

Unfortunately, antivirus software can't protect you from viruses it doesn't know about. New viruses and other forms of malware get a free pass until the antivirus companies can analyze them, create software to get rid of them, test the software, and distribute it. This usually only takes three or four hours after the outbreak of the virus.[5]

Most new computers come with an antivirus programs installed, but it is up to you to update it annually. Since new virus programs are written and released on a daily basis be sure you have your antivirus program set to automatically update itself. The first year of updates is usually free. Many Internet service providers provide free antivirus programs, but some of them you have to download and install.

Never open emails from someone you don't know or a company you have not agreed to receive emails from. But if you should open these emails, don't open any attachment that comes with them or click on any hyperlinks within the body of the email as these are common sources of viruses. It's best simply to delete the emails unopened.

Examples of antivirus programs include Norton Antivirus (www.symantec.com), McAfee Antivirus (www.mcafee.com), and PC-cillin Antivirus (www.trendmicro.com).[7,8,9]

Anti-spyware Software

Anti-spyware programs offer protection from malicious software codes that track your online activities and may capture everything you type, including passwords, credit card numbers, and bank account numbers. Anti-spyware programs can be purchased commercially, and like antiviral programs they need to be updated automatically.[8]

Commercially available anti-spyware programs include Ad-aware SE Personal (www.lavasoft.com) and Stopzilla (www.stopzilla.com). Also, there are some good freeware/shareware programs available on the Internet, such as Spybot-S&D (www.safer-networking.org). Microsoft has a free beta anti-spyware program called Windows Defender (www.microsoft.com).

A word or two of warning—there are a number of commercial anti-spyware websites on the Internet that offer a free spyware scan. Only after the scan is completed do you find out that you have to buy the software to get rid of the spyware they find. Not only that, but many of them grossly over report the amount of spyware they "find" in an attempt to induce you to purchase their product.

Spyware is often installed as a component of freeware programs, so be careful when downloading anything from the Internet that is said to be free.[8,9]

Strong Passwords

Hackers may try to figure out your passwords to gain access to your computer, your bank account, or your credit card company. You can make it tougher for them by doing the following:

Number of Characters. Use passwords that have six or more characters and include numbers and uppercase and lowercase letters. You can make your passwords even more secure by including symbols.

Common Words. Avoid common words, such as apple or crankshaft. Some hackers use programs that can try every word in the dictionary.

Personal Information. Don't use personal information, such as your name or city, as a password.

Change Passwords. Consider changing your passwords regularly—at a minimum every 90 days.

Different Passwords. Use different passwords for every online account you access. For instance, don't use the same password for your Internet service provider, your bank, your credit card company, and your financial investments. That makes it too easy for cybercriminals.[10]

Update Your Operating System Regularly

Microsoft and Apple, on a regular basis, come out with security fixes for their operating systems to help you stave off cybercriminals. It is extremely important that you download these fixes as they are released. If you have your operating system set to download the fixes automatically then you can put this out of your mind. If not, you will have to access the Microsoft or Apple website and do it manually.[9,10]

Other Measures

Other steps you may wish to take include using (1) an alternative operating system or browser, (2) a popup blocker, and (3) a spam filter.

Operating System and Browser. Some experts suggest that you go as far as using an operating system other than Windows, but I find that a bit extreme, provided you take the necessary precautions. Because 90 percent of the computers in the world use the Windows operating system it is only natural that it should be the primary target of cybercrooks. Other less-popular operating systems, such as Mac OS X and Linux, are much less often attacked. Similarly, Internet Explorer, being the most popular browser in the world, is more often attacked than other browsers. Switching to an alternate browser, such as Firefox (www.mozilla.org) or Opera (www.opera.com), will decrease the number of attacks, at least until these browsers become more popular.[6]

Popup Blocker. Many websites generate popup ads as you visit the site. The popup may appear in front of the webpage or under it so that it shows up only after you close the webpage. These ads are potentially dangerous because spyware, among other methods, uses popup windows as a way of tricking you into installing their programs on your computer.

The current Windows operating system comes with a built-in popup blocker that is enabled by default. If you are using an operating system that doesn't have a popup blocker you can download free tools that do this. For instance, Yahoo (www.yahoo.com) and Google (www.google.com) offer browser toolbars that can block popups.[6]

Spam Filter. Unsolicited commercial email is known as *Spam*. It is junk email messages from people you don't know. It has one purpose—to generate income for the senders or the people they represent. Marketers are increasingly using email messages to pitch their products and services, and cybercrooks bombard your inbox with fraudulent offers and attempt to steal your credit card or bank account number.

Approximately 30 million emails are sent across the Internet each day, and it is conservatively estimated that 50 percent of these are spam, although the actual percentage is probably much higher. Internet service providers, such as AOL, Comcast, and MSN, ensure that you get a fairly clean mail stream; however, they tend to err on the side of letting spam in to avoid blocking legitimate email.[5]

Some computer users find spam annoying and time consuming; others have lost money to bogus offers that arrived in emails. A spam filter is helpful in preventing many of these from reaching your in-box. There are a number of spam filters on the market, such as Spam Killer (www.mcafee.com) and Spam Buster (www.spambuster.com).

Symantec (www.symantec.com) offers a free security check that scans your computer for a variety of vulnerabilities, including ports that may respond to unsolicited requests, the presence of Trojan horses, and whether you have an antivirus program or if your antivirus program is active.[6]

Beware of Impersonators

One of the most common cybercriminal tricks is to get you to click on a link that you think will take you to a desired site (eBay, a video store, a bank, a gaming site, and so forth) but instead connects you to a "spoof" site that appears identical, or similar to, the site you wished to go to. When you type in your user name and password to enter the site or give personal information, such as your credit card number, the criminal steals the information and then can use it to purchase items in your name. So, never click on a link in an unsolicited email, even if it seems to be from your bank, your credit card company, eBay, or another familiar source. Simply delete the email. Legitimate companies don't request personal information via email.[8,10]

Don't take the Bait

It's amazing what greed will cause some people to do. If you receive an email telling you that you have won a contest you didn't enter or a Nigerian banker telling you he wants to transfer a large sum of money to your bank account and is willing to share it with you, don't take the bait. The next encounter will involve a request for an advance fee before you "get" that much larger sum of money. Simply laugh at the email because of its poor grammar, misspelled words, and unusual punctuation and then delete it. And when you get popups telling you that you've won a laptop or a sum of money, or anything else, do the same. Trust me, you haven't won anything. They just want your email address so they can start sending you spam.[8]

There are a number of ways to spot an Internet scam, including the following:

Advance Fee. Beware of great sounding offers in which the details of the offer are kept hidden until you pay a fee. Any offer that requests money upfront most likely is a scam.

Capital Letters and Excessive Punctuation. Be skeptical of ads that shout at you, like "MIRACLE CURE!!!" or "Make BIG $$$$$ MONEY in HOURS A WEEK!!!!!"[11]

Credit Card Number. Don't give your credit card number to anyone when it is requested by email or by website that is linked to an email. Don't give it to what appears to be your bank, the IRS, eBay, or anyone. Legitimate companies don't request this type of information via an email.[11]

Hidden Name or Address. Don't conduct business with someone unless the person reveals his or her name, address, and phone number. Beware of users who try to buy or sell things using an anonymous email address or a post office box.[11]

Money Back. Remember, a "money-back-guarantee" from a stranger may be worthless. By the time you decide you want your money back the website may have disappeared or the "company" may simply refuse to answer your emails or phone calls.[11]

Not a Scam. Scammers say "This is not a scam" all the time. Don't fall for this trick. A legitimate business doesn't spend time trying to convince you of its honesty.[11]

Password. Never reveal your password to anyone online, unless you are required to do so to enter legitimate sites, such as your bank or credit card company. And if someone asks you to change your password to a specific "word" for the purpose of "system testing," be immediately suspicious; this is a well-known trick.[11]

Pyramid. If you are asked to send money to five people, who each send money to five more people, who each send money to five more people, and so on, then you are looking at an illegal pyramid scheme or chain letter. Avoid it. Not only will you lose money, but it is illegal.[11]

References. The ad might state "As appeared in such and such magazine or newspaper." The credentials sound impressive, but you aren't given enough information to look them up.[11]

Secret Method. Beware of ads that say such things as "secret available only to a limited number of people." If it were a secret they wouldn't be advertising it.[11]

Talk about Money. There's too much talk about money and not enough about the deal. Scammers try to blind you with dreams of becoming rich so you won't notice the fine print. Watch out for bogus promises of wealth.[11]

Too Much Knowledge. Beware of emails that know details about you that you have not revealed. Also, if someone you don't know starts asking very personal questions about you, be very suspicious.[11]

Unsolicited Email. If you get an email from a stranger offering to give or sell you something or that leads to a website requesting personal information, treat it with great suspicion. It's best simply to delete it.[11]

Avoid High-risk Websites

Some websites put you at higher risk for getting your computer infected with a virus or spyware than others. Pornography and gaming sites are notorious for this. So the best advice is to avoid them like the plague. Some major Internet companies, including Google, are taking steps to warn computer users if they are about to visit a webpage that could harm their computer. A warning pops up if users click on a link to a page known to host spyware or other malicious programs.[12]

Download with Caution

Be wary of downloading free programs or files over the Internet. Things are seldom completely free. These files or programs may contain spyware, viruses, or other malicious software. Also be wary of floppy, CD, or DVD discs received in the mail if you don't know the sender personally. Buying products online from reputable retailers all but eliminates the threat of an attack in this manner.[13]

Keep an Eye on Your Children

The younger members of your family, if you have children at home, are the most likely to respond to bogus email requests, visit high-risk websites, and use file-sharing programs to download music or other material from the Internet. Music, movie, and software companies take copyright violations very serious. You may find yourself the target of a lawsuit because one of your children downloaded a movie, a song, or a game program.

The following are some guidelines that may keep your children, and you, out of trouble.

Chat Rooms. Be cautious of online chat rooms. Younger children shouldn't be allowed to use them, and the older ones should be allowed to use them only under your supervision. Explain to them that they shouldn't believe everything they are told. A person saying that he is a teenaged girl might actually be an adult male with ulterior motives.[9,15,16]

Comfort. Teach your children to come to you if anything they run across makes them feel uncomfortable, such as inappropriate questions in a chat room, an invitation to a private chat room, or an offensive email.[9,15,16]

Common Area. Put computers in a common area so you can monitor your children's time online. Discuss and set rules with your children for computer use. Post these rules by the computer as a reminder.[9,15,16]

Email and Instant Messaging. When your children are young they should share the family email address rather than have their own. As they get older you can set up separate email addresses, but your children's email should still reside in your account. Tell your children never to respond to emails or instant messaging from strangers.[9,15,16]

Face-to-face Encounters. Never allow your children to meet someone face-to-face that they've "met" online. This is an invitation to disaster. Early on, explain to them that they might get such an invitation, that it is dangerous, and that such a meeting won't be allowed.[9,15,16]

Filtering. Although far from perfect, browsers and search engines, such as Google and Yahoo, can be set to filter some content. In addition, some Internet service providers, such as AOL and EarthLink, provide parental filtering software. There are a number of commercial parental filtering programs available, including Cyber Patrol (www.cyberpatrol.com), CYBERsitter (www.solidoak.com), and Net Nanny (www.netnanny.com). For your younger children you might want to consider using a children's browser, which has some built in safety factors. There are a number of these available, including Garfield's (www.garfieldisland.com) and Junior Net's (www.juniornet.com).[9,15,16]

Limit Online Time. Limit your children's online time as you would television viewing.[9,15,16]

Personal Information. Teach your children not to give out personal information online, such as phone number, address, last name, name of school, passwords, or credit card information (assuming your older children have their own credit cards).[9,15,16]

Signs. Watch for signs that your child may have been approached by a sexual predator online.[6] These are discussed in Chapter 29.

Webcam. If you have decided to let your children have computers in their bedrooms, whatever else you do don't let them have a webcam as well. That is just begging for trouble.[9,15,16]

ADDITIONAL STEPS

If you have a wireless network, are in the habit of using computers made available in public places, or travel with your laptop, there are some additional steps you should consider.

Wireless Networks

Many households have more than one computer. Quite often these are connected to share a common Internet connection. Today a common way of doing this is to use a wireless network, called a Wi-Fi (Wireless Fidelity) or WLAN (Wireless Local Area Network). Although convenient, wireless networks come with a security price. The signals sent out by your wireless devices can be picked up by another device within range of the signal. Attackers know this and use software programs called *sniffers*, which allow them to eavesdrop on unencrypted wireless connections. By doing so they can pick up your passwords, credit card number, and bank account number if you type them into an online form. In addition, another computer within range can connect to your access point and connect to the Internet through your connection.

The risk you face with an unencrypted home wireless network is small because the signal can only travel about 150 feet, so chances are small that crooks would hang around your house trying to capture your wireless traffic. They are more likely to be attracted to corporate wireless networks. Nevertheless, you probably don't want your neighbors monitoring what you do online.[6,17]

There are some steps you can take to prevent others from tapping into your wireless network. You should do as many of these as you feel comfortable doing. If you feel the need for even more security for your wireless connection you may have to get help from a local computer expert.

Encryption. The most effective way to secure your wireless connection from intruders is to encrypt, or scramble, communications. Most wireless routers, access points, and base stations have a built-in encryption mechanism. Most older access points offer only WEP (Wired Equivalent Privacy) encryption; however, newer access points offer a choice between WEP and WPA (Wi-Fi Protected Access). You are better off using WPA than WEP because if someone is able to capture enough data it is possible to decipher WEP.[6,17]

Identifier. Most wireless routers have a mechanism called identifier broadcasting. They send out a signal broadcasting their SSID (Service Set ID) to any device in the vicinity. The SSID is basically just a name that is assigned to the wireless access point. Wireless hardware manufacturers assign the same SSID to every access point that rolls off of the assembly line.

Hackers can use identifier broadcasting to home in on

vulnerable wireless network connections. Even if you aren't broadcasting your access point's identification to the world, it isn't that hard to figure out that you have an access point in your house and that it is using a default SSID name.[6,18]

Change your identifier to something only you know. Better yet, disable the identifier broadcasting mechanism if your wireless router allows it. If not, turn the router off when you're not using it.[6,18]

MAC Address. Every network interface card (including wireless cards) has what is known as a MAC (Media Access Control) address associated with it. Most wireless access points contain a mechanism that allows you to allow only network cards with specific MAC addresses to use your network. So take advantage of this by limiting access only to those computers you choose.[6,17]

Password. The manufacturer of your wireless router probably assigned it a standard default password that allows you easily to set up and operate the router. Hackers know these default passwords, so change your password to something only you know.[6,17]

Public Computers

A cybercriminal secretly installed keystroke monitoring software on the computers of 14 Kinko's outlets that allowed him to capture more than 450 user names and passwords, which he used to access and open bank accounts online. Therefore, it is advisable not to use public computers for transactions which involve passwords or personal information.

Many cafés, hotels, airports, and other public stablishments offer wireless Internet connections for their customers' use. These connections are convenient, but they may not be secure. To be on the safe side, you may want to assume that other people can access any information you see or send over a public wireless Internet connection. Unless you can verify that an Internet connection has effective security measures in place, it may be best to avoid sending or receiving sensitive information.[18]

Laptop

A laptop, like any other small item, can be stolen. That's the old-fashioned way of losing your personal information and any other information that might be available on the hard drive. Your laptop can be stolen from your office while you are on a coffee break, taken from your hotel room while you are out, stolen from your table at a restaurant when you go to the bathroom, or taken from any other location. So, protect your laptop. Don't leave it laying around indiscriminately. Be especially careful when you carry it through the X-ray screening area at an airport. A specific criminal act involves two people—one to distract you and the other to steal your laptop. Laptop theft is discussed in Chapter 23.

IF YOU ARE A VICTIM OF CYBERCRIME

If you believe you have been a victim of cybercrime in the form of crimeware or online fraud, there are a series of steps you can take in each instance to respond to and recover from the incident. In addition, you should report it to the appropriate authorities as discussed in Appendix A.

Crimeware

Disconnect. Immediately disconnect the Internet connection from your computer to prevent data from being sent back to the attacker.[20,21]

Back Up. Back up your critical information. Sensitive data may be disrupted by crimeware, and it also may be inadvertently destroyed or lost during your clean-up effort. Making a copy of installed programs and valuable files, such as your photos and videos, will ensure your information is available after the computer is free of crimeware.[19,20]

Scan. Scan your computer with up-to-date antivirus and anti-spyware programs. These can detect and often remove crimeware that would otherwise remain hidden on your computer. If the threat can be detected but not removed, consult Symantec's free removal-tool listing (www.symantec.com) to see if the crimeware can be removed using a separately downloaded utility.[19,20]

Ground Zero. Consider going back to ground zero. The worst examples of crimeware are sophisticated enough to burrow deep within your system in an attempt to hide from your security. If all else fails, including System Restore and operating system repair, re-install the operating system of your computer and then re-download updates.[19,20]

Online Fraud

Accounts. You should close affected credit card, bank, and other online accounts before they can be accessed by the thief. You might want to call your financial institutions on the phone and discuss any impact the fraud might have on your accounts and the steps you should take if the accounts have been compromised. If charges are made, you may have to dispute them.[19,20]

Notify. Notify one of the consumer reporting agencies: Equifax at www.equifax.com; Experian at www.experian.com; TransUnion at www.transunion.com. Contacting any one of the three companies will set up the alert for all of them. The fraud alert will tell creditors to contact you directly before making any changes to existing accounts or trying to open new ones. This is an essential step to control the amount of damage an identity thief can do with your stolen information.[19,20]

Signs. Look for signs of identity theft. Be on the lookout for odd things with the mail, including credit cards you did not request and bills that you normally receive which have stop being delivered. Being contacted by vendors regarding accounts you are unaware of or by debt collectors for purchases someone else made in your name are clear signs of identity theft. To ensure you're not being victimized and to detect unauthorized charges check your credit card bill at least every month, or more often if you can do so online. Remember, you have 60 days to dispute a charge.[19,20]

Watch. Watch your credit reports closely. Keeping a sharp eye on your accounts from all three credit reporting agencies is essential as information may not be the same across all three. Remember that it may take some time before all of the fraudulent activity appears on your credit reports.[19,20] Identity theft is further discussed in Chapter 20.

References

1. Milhorn, H. Thomas, Crime: Cybercrime, In Computer Viruses to Twin Towers, Universal Publishers, Boca Raton, 2005, Pp 46-70.
2. What is Cybercrime?, Symantec, www.symantec.com/avcenter/cybercrime/index_page2.html.
3. Joseph, Aghatise, E, Cybercrime, Computer Research Center, www.crime-research.org/articles/joseph06, June 28, 2006.
4. Duggal, Paval, Cyberlaw and you, Indiana InfoLine, www.indiainfoline.com/cyva/colu/cybe/padu2.html, July 16, 2002.
5. Crimeware, eEncyclopedia, PCMag.com, www.pcmag.com/encyclopedia_term/0,2542,t=crimeware&i=55434,00.asp.
6. Conry-Murray, Andrew and Vincent Weafer, The Symantec Guide to Home Internet Security, Addison-Wesley, Boston, 2006.
7. Fighting back against email spammers, Internet hackers, and other web thieves, www.infohq.com/Computer/Spam/fight-internet-hackers-email-spammers.htm, January 17, 2004.
8. Moritz, Robert, Protect yourself from cyber crooks, Parade, www.parade.com, June 28, 2006.
9. Take five steps to protect your computer, Take Control, Penn State University, http://its.psu.edu/takecontrol.
10. Top 8 cybersecurity practices, StaySafeOnline.org, www.staysafeonline.info.
11. Barrett, Daniel J., Bandits on the information superhighway, www.quackwatch.org/04ConsumerEducation/BookContents/ban.html.
12. Security Tips, CBSNEWS.com, www.cbsnews.com/htdocs/internet/security/tips.html.
13. Online Predators, Web Aware, www.bewebaware.ca/english/OnlinePredators.aspx#a1.
14. Google warns on 'unsafe websites," BBC News, http://news.bbc.co.uk/2/hi/technology/5251742.stm, August 7, 2006.
15. Feldman, Barbara J., Protecting your kids on the Internet, Surfing the Net with Kids, www.surfnetkids.com/safety.htm#intro.
16. Protect yourself: Safety tips for parents, learnthenet.com, www.learnthenet.com/English/html/10kids.htm.
17. Wireless Security, Onguard Online, Your Safety Net, http://onguardonline. gov/wireless.html, May 2006.
18. Beware using public computers, CBC.Ca, www.cbc.ca/story/news/national/2003/07/23/Consumers/Internet_030723.html, July 23, 2003.
19. If you are the victim of a cybercrime, Office of the Attorney General, State of Utah.

http://attorneygeneral.utah.gov/CA/cybercrimevictim.html.

20. What to do if you are a victim, Symantec, www.symantec.com /avcenter/cybercrime/victim.html.

Chapter 2

Auction Fraud

Online auctions rank as the number one source of fraud on the Internet. There are dozens of online auction sites, including eBay and Yahoo Auction. On these sites you can bid on anything from a comic book to a luxury boat and everything in between. Millions of people are attracted to these sites because of the potential of getting a bargain or the thrill of playing the bidding game.[1,2]

TYPES OF AUCTION FRAUD

There are numerous ways criminals can defraud online auction participants out of money or goods. These are divided into two groups—fraud by the seller and fraud by the buyer.

Fraud by the Seller

Additional Charges

Watch out for additional charges added to your item's cost after the auction has closed. Sellers can add hidden and sometimes inflated charges, including separate fees for postage and shipping and handling. This is called *fee stacking*. Unscrupulous sellers are happy to make money on inflated shipping charges for which they don't have to pay a percentage fee to the auction site[3,4]

Black-market Goods

It is illegal to sell black-market goods on Internet auction sites, but you may still find pirated software, music CDs, or videos.[3]

Counterfeit Goods

In this scam an item is advertised as the real thing, but a counterfeit item is sent. For instance, an item might be advertised as a Rolex watch. The high bidder pays the money and then receives a Timex with a simulated Rolex front.[5]

False Information

If you receive an item which doesn't appear to be exactly what you bid on based on its description or photo, you may be a victim of fraud. For instance, suppose you post the winning bid on a porcelain figurine which is stated to be in pristine condition and appears to be so in the picture, but on arrival it is found to be stained and chipped in multiple sites.[3]

Escrow Fraud

Online auction sites recommend using escrow services for large transactions. An escrow service is a neutral third party which holds your money in trust until an item is delivered. For a small charge they protect you in case something goes wrong. In most cases, escrow services are a good security measure; however, scammers are known to set up fraudulent escrow sites, often located in foreign countries. Posing as sellers, the scammers offer expensive goods, such as cars or boats, for sale in online auctions. When the bidding closes, the winner is asked to send payment to a recommended, but fake, escrow service, which absconds with the money.[3]

Fencing Stolen Goods

Cybercrooks have discovered that online auctions are a great way to get rid of stolen goods. You bid on an item you want, not knowing that it's been stolen. You end up with the winning bid, pay your money, and the item is shipped to you. It arrives and it's perfect, just as advertised. Then the police show up at your front door and confiscate the stolen item. Now you're out the item and the money you paid for it.[6]

Nonexistent Items

In some cases an auction may involve the seller placing an item for sale when, in fact, there's actually no item at all. This is the most common type of auction fraud.[3,7]

Over-valued Items

In this fraud the item is simply advertised as being worth more than it is. For instance, a comic book might be stated as being a very valuable collectible item when in fact it is practically worthless.[7]

Review fixing

One of the ways many auction sites attempt to regulate sales is through a feedback mechanism. When an auction is over, the winner can grade and comment on the seller and the transaction, and the grading is published for all to see. Sellers may attempt to fix their grades by submitting positive feedback about themselves or by getting friends and confederates to provide glowing reports.[4]

Second Chance Offer

Ebay and other auction sites offer a legitimate second chance to buy an item if the high bidder fails to follow through with payment. However, the use of the second chance offer is also a common form of Internet auction fraud. Scammers constantly monitor Internet auction sites for sales of items that fit a specific profile—higher priced items with lots of bids. After the end of the auction, the scammer sends you an email, which appears to come from the original seller, claiming that the high bidder failed to pay or that the seller has more of the same item. The scammer then offers to sell you the item for the amount of your last bid. To complete the transaction, the scammer often directs you to a phony eBay site that has all kinds of information to make it seem like this "second chance" is a legitimate offer. Many phony second chance offers can be identified because the scammer asks you to pay for the item with a wire transfer. This is generally an indication that the offer is a fraud.[8]

Shill Bidding

Shill bidding is a fraudulent action used by sellers to drive up the price of their item. It is done by intentional fake bidding by the sellers themselves or others who are closely related to the seller.[4]

Triangulation

With *triangulation* a seller originally purchases an item from an online merchant using a stolen identity and credit card. The seller then lists the item for sale on an auction site. When the auction closes, the successful buyer pays for the item and receives the merchandise. Later, the item is traced by the police to the buyer and collected for evidence. Meanwhile, the seller has pocketed the money from selling the stolen item and the buyer no longer has the item or his money.[3]

Fraud by the Buyer

Claiming Damages

You ship an item to the winning bidder and it is in the condition as advertised. However, the buyer fraudulently claims that it was damaged during shipment. He or she may even submit a fake bill for damages to repair it. Crooks like this depend on your sense of honesty. So, to do the right thing you send the buyer a check to cover the "damages." However, even if you decide not to send the check you are not in the clear. The buyer can fraudulently claim to his credit card company that the item was damaged and have the company not honor the charge.[6]

Escrow Fraud

Scammers pose as bidders and tell you they'll send their money to an escrow service of their choosing. The phony escrow service notifies you that the money has been received and you send your goods to the scammer. Before the scammer can be tracked, he or she closes the phony site and you are left without goods and money.[3]

Money Back Returns

In this scam the buyer receives your item, states he's not satisfied with it, and wants his money back immediately. Furthermore, he wants you to credit his credit card before he returns the item. So you do what he wants. He either doesn't send the item back or if it's software he makes a copy of it and then sends the original back.[4,6]

Multiple Aliases

Buyers sometimes use multiple aliases in the same auction. For example, to lower the price of an item a buyer may place multiple bids (high and low) on the same item using different identities. The high bids cause the price of the item to escalate, scaring off other bidders. Just before the auction closes, the buyer withdraws the higher bids, leaving one of his much lower bids, allowing him to win the auction and purchase the item. This form of fraud can be avoided by using sites that don't allow withdrawing of bids.[3]

Overpayment

One of the more popular scams today is for a buyer to send you a cashier's check for an amount that is higher than the agreed upon final bid. The buyer then claims it was in error and asks you to return the overage when the item is shipped. You ship the item along with the overage. The cashier's check then turns out to be worthless, so you are out the item and some cash.[9]

EXAMPLES OF AUCTION FRAUD

- **No Fat Boy for Him.** A Marshalltown, Iowa man was duped by a false advertisement on eBay for a used 2003 Harley Davidson 100th Anniversary Fat Boy. The man thought he was getting the motorcycle for about half the normal price when he placed the winning bid and wired his $9,700. The bike's "seller" requested the money go to an escrow account, which would hold it until the purchaser received his prize. A few days later the victim became suspicious and contacted the police, who discovered that the money actually had been wired outside the country and that no motorcycle would be shipped.[10]

- **Stolen Credit Cards.** Two 16-year-old students used stolen credit card numbers as part of their scheme to defraud buyers. Through multiple eBay accounts, the teenagers auctioned cards that could be used to obtain free satellite TV service. The would-be buyers paid as much as $2,000 for sets of cards that did not exist. The fraudulent auctions netted the teens $20,000 in cash and also gave them access to credit card numbers which they used to purchase an array of items online. The defendants enlisted other teenagers to ship and drop off illegally obtained merchandise and used other students and parents to cash their checks and launder funds. In the end, five teenagers pleaded guilty and were sentenced to probation under very restrictive terms. In addition, the youths and their parents were held liable for $23,000 in restitution.[11]

- **If at First You Don't Succeed.** While awaiting trial for auction fraud, Corey Dominique, 22, of Phoenix, Arizona returned to an auction site using names of friends to conduct transactions. After victims agreed to pay for various car parts, he asked them to send the money to his business partner, Corey Kelly. The parts were never shipped. For his illegal activities he was sentenced to three months in jail and three years probation and was ordered to pay restitution totaling $33,075. After his release from jail and while serving his probation sentence, he posted an ad for a non-existent Mercedes convertible on eBay Motors. The online auction received a high bid of $73,000, but the buyer became suspicious and contacted the police. When Kelly went to pick up what he believed was a $73,000 money order for the vehicle, he was arrested. Dominique pled guilty and was sentenced to more than four years in prison.[12]

- **You May Get What You Pay For.** Jake Bisenius, who lived near Gig Harbor, Washington, wanted a Sony Play Station II for Christmas. He found a "deal" on eBay in which he could save $50 and get free shipping—the total cost only $275. But instead of a deal on a Play Station II all he got was a piece of paper with a picture on it. Bisenius was shocked to realize he'd bought a picture, not the real thing. The ad had looked legitimate. Then he went back and re-read the ad. It said "We guarantee the item to be exactly as shown below," and he had gotten what was shown below—a picture.[13]

- **A Shill Game.** In California, Kenneth Fetterman, a former pizza deliveryman, portrayed rummage sale art as masterpieces in online auctions. According to him the "art" ranged from the Renaissance to abstract expressionism. Fetterman, 36, and two accomplices, Kenneth Walton, 36, and Scott Beach, 33, created more than 40 online aliases to falsely drive up bidding on hundreds of paintings. The scam came to light when the trio auctioned a colorful canvas doctored to look like the work of abstract artist Richard Diebenkorn. The painting was said to come from a garage sale in Berkeley where Diebenkorn lived in the 1950s. It contained the inscription RD52, which is similar to the way the artist signed his works. Fetterman and Walton had bought the piece in a junk shop in Southern California and Walton forged the initials. The three crooks placed more than 50 fake bids to send the price skyrocketing before a bidder from the Netherlands won with a $135,805 bid. Fetterman was eventually arrested and sentenced to nearly four years in federal prison, ordered to repay more than $94,000 in restitution to the people he defrauded, to serve three years probation, and be barred from online auctions during that time.[14]

- **Stolen Goods.** In Georgia, David and Mindy Oliver and Marcus Abercrombie pleaded guilty to defrauding Home Depot and Lowe's of more than $200,000 by selling improperly obtained store cards and merchandise on eBay. The five-state scam involved switching bar codes of high-priced items with those from lower-priced items, which allowed them to purchase the expensive items at a reduced price. The three then returned the high-priced items for store credit in the form of store debit cards, and then fenced the cards and merchandise purchased with some of the debit cards on eBay. In addition to prison terms, the Olivers were ordered to pay $229,127 in restitution to Lowe's and Home Depot, and Abercrombie was ordered to forfeit over $186,000 to compensate the two companies.[15]

- **Pirated Software.** Bilal Khan, a 23-year-old trainee accountant, pleaded guilty to five offences under the Trademarks Act for selling pirated copies of Macromedia, Adobe, and Microsoft software through online auction sites. When Khan's home was raided, 236 discs of counterfeit software were found, as well as blank CDs, a laptop, and a CD burner. He was sentenced to 12 months in prison and fined £15,000 for selling counterfeit software. However, after being tried he skipped bail and fled to Pakistan for nine months where he continued his pirate operation.[16]

TIPS TO PROTECT YOURSELF

Even though the vast majority of sellers and buyers are ethical and the vast majority of sales go through without problems, there are enough scams involved to put anyone buying or selling through online auctions at risk. So what can you do to protect yourself against potential fraud? You can:

Delivery, Returns, Warranties. Ask about delivery, returns, and warranties before you pay. Get a definite delivery time and if the item is expensive insist that the shipment be insured. If you're buying electronic goods or appliances, find out if there is a warranty and how to get service.[17]

Escrow Services. Only use escrow services recommended by the auction site. Be wary if a seller or bidder insists on using a specific escrow company. Phony escrow sites are usually copies of legitimate sites. Read the terms and conditions or privacy pages. With a phony escrow site you might find grammatical errors. If anything seems questionable, find another escrow service.[3,17]

Expensive Items. Be wary of claims about collectibles and other expensive items. Since you can't examine the merchandise or have it appraised until after the sale, don't assume that claims about its condition or value are true or that photographs are accurate. Print out and save the description and any photos to document the claims that were made.[17]

How it Works. Learn how the online auction site works. No two online auction sites are exactly the same. Just because you've had a good experience with eBay or another site don't expect the dozens of other sites to work the same. Read the rules on the site and take the site's tutorial if it offers one. Find out if the site provides any buyer protections, such as free insurance or guarantees for items that aren't delivered or aren't as advertised. Understand that many auction sites don't verify whether the advertised item exists or is described accurately.[2,17]

Know about the Item. Know about the item you want to buy. If you are not familiar with it learn all you can about it from other sources. Don't just depend on the seller's photo and the information provided. For products, such as computers, DVD players, cameras, and so forth, which are readily available through commercial sources, do a price comparison to see if the price of the auction product is in fact a good buy.

And be sure to read the fine print. Make sure you understand what all the words mean. For instance, a computer might be listed as "like new" when the small type indicates that it's refurbished. Also if you are interested in buying a product in a field with which you are not familiar, make sure you know what the field's jargon means. If you don't, look it up.[2,18]

Other Countries. When dealing with individuals outside your own country, be cautious. Dealing with someone selling an item in another country is risky because the country will be outside the jurisdiction of U.S. law enforcement agencies.[19]

Overpayment. Never accept an overpayment for an item. Be especially leery if the buyer wants the overage returned with the item. Should you get such a request, be sure the cashier's check is good before paying back the overpaid money and shipping the item. And then do so at your own risk.[9]

P.O. Boxes. Never buy anything from a seller who asks for payment to be mailed to a P.O. Box. The risk of fraud is just too high.[20]

Payment. Pay by the safest method. The large online auction sites accept most payment options—personal checks, credit cards, money orders, cashier's checks, and payments through billing or escrow services. You either pay the auction house or pay the seller directly. If you pay the seller directly using a credit card you can dispute the charges if the item never comes or isn't what the seller represented it to be. For expensive items you might want to consider an escrow service, if the seller accepts such. Be wary if the seller only accepts wire transfers or cash.[2,17]

Personal Information. Protect your personal information. No online auction seller ever has any need for your Social Security number, driver's license number, bank account number, and so forth. A request for personal information should set off alarm bells. At best, your money paid for the item could be at risk, and at worst you could be a victim of identity theft.[1,2]

Private Individuals. Beware of sales from private individuals. Most consumer protection laws don't cover private sales.[1]

Record. Keep a record of everything about the transaction. Run a copy of the seller's listing on the auction site. Keep copies of each email. Make notes on any phone conversations. In other words, record every step in the transaction. Keep those in a safe place until you've received the item and everything is as it should be.[2]

Seller. Before you bid, check out the seller. First, read the feedback forum for the auction site. Feedback forums offer comments and ratings from other people who've used the site and bought items from specific sellers. If a seller has overwhelmingly negative comments written about him or her, you should stop right there. If the feedback is positive, then get the seller's telephone number so you have a way to contact him or her other than through the auction site. It's not a good idea to do business with any seller who won't give contact information, including name, street address, email address, and phone number.[2,19]

Second Chance. Beware of emails telling you that you have a second chance to buy an item that you bid on but didn't win. If you are asked to wire the money, this may be a red flag for a scam.[8]

Shipping and Insurance. Don't forget the cost of shipping and handling and insurance. Will your bid still be a deal after you add these costs to the buying price? Find out what these costs will be before you bid. Also look out for other add-on fees that some sellers and sites sometimes add. If you get a $200 item for $170, it's not a bargain if the shipping and handling charge is $50.[2,17]

References

1. Online auctions number 1 Internet fraud, CNN.com, http://archives.cnn.com/2000/TECH/computing/10/02/i.fraud/i.fraud.sidebar/index.html, October 2, 2000.
2. Sutton, Remar, Buyers Beware! Online Auction Fraud Tops Consumer Internet Complaints, Straight Talk Report from Remar Sutton, www.corningcu.org/StraightTalk/reports/may2003.htm, May 2003.
3. Bidders burned by internet auction fraud, Choice, www.choice.com.au/viewArticle.aspx?id=103557&catId=100405&tid=100008&p=1&title=Bidders.
4. Brownlow, Mark, Online auction fraud, www.ibizbasics.com/ecom061201.htm, June 12, 2001.
5. Milhorn, H. Thomas, Cybercrime, In Crime: Computer Viruses to Twin Towers, Universal Publishers, Boca Raton, 2005, Pp 46-70.
6. Thomes, James T., Dotcons: Con Games, Fraud, and Deceit on the Internet, Writers Club Press, New York, 2000.
7. Internet Fraud, United States Department of Justice, www.internetfraudusdoj.gov, May 15, 2001.
8. Don't be fooled by bogus "second chance offers," July Consumer Alerts, www.law.state.ak.us/pdf/consumer/july06-cpalert-re-second-chance-offers.pdf.
9. Woodward, Steve, Online Auction Fraud, www.macosx.com/articles/Online-Auction-Fraud.html.
10. Slusark, Kate, Des Moines Register, Crime and Courts, http://desmoinesregister.com/news/stories/c4788993/23274357.html, January 16, 2004.
11. Case #3, Protecting Our Kids, http://da.co.la.ca.us/pok/realcases.htm, February 1, 2006.
12. Con Artist Sentenced for Internet Auction Fraud, ConsumerAffairs.com, www.consumeraffairs.com/news04/2005/az_auction.html, May 15, 2005.
13. Knopp, Leslie, DOH! Gig Harbor Man Gets Taken In Sneaky eBay scam, Komo 1000 News, www.komotv.com/news/story.asp?ID=16017, December 21, 2001.
14. Melley, Brian, California eBay scam artist sent to federal prison, www.usatoday.com/tech/news/2004-05-27-ebay-art-fraud_x.htm, June 27, 2004.
15. Roberts, Paul F., Three sentenced in eBay fencing scam, eWeek.com, www.eweek.com/article2/0,1895,1833032,00.asp, June 29, 2005.
16. Internet crime prevention tips, Internet Crime Complaint,

www.ic3.gov/preventiontips.aspx#item-1.

17. Thompson, Ian, Accountancy Age, Accountant trainee arrested over software scam, www.accountancyage.com/accountancyage/news/2033282/trainee-accountant-jailed-software-scam, July 14, 2003.
18. Online Auctions: Deal or Steal?, Scambusters.org, www.scambusters.org/Scambusters43.html.
19. Online Auctions, Internet Fraud Tips, National Consumer League's Internet Fraud Watch, www.fraud.org/tips/internet/onlineauctions.htm.
20. Yaukey, John, How to avoid online auction fraud, USA Today, www.usatoday.com/tech/columnist/2002/05/07/yaukey.htm, May 7, 2002.

Chapter 3

Business Opportunity and Job Scams

BUSINESS OPPORTUNITY SCAMS

Online *business opportunity scams* are numerous. They are often advertised in banners on websites and by emails. They make it sound easy to start a business that will bring lots of income without much work. The solicitations claim unbelievable earnings—$200 a day, $500 a day, $1,000 a day, or more. All you have to do is send $59.95 to get the details. Or they give a telephone number to call for more information. In many cases, you'll be told to leave your name and telephone number so that a salesperson can call you back with the sales pitch, or you will be connected to an overseas area code with an expensive per-minute charge.[1,2]

Examples of Business Opportunity Scams

Business opportunity scams may involve (1) home employment scams and (2) multilevel marketing scams.

Home Employment Scams

Home employment scams cover a wide area. They include

envelope stuffing, assembly work, medical billing, and many more.

Envelope Stuffing. Promoters advertise that, for a small fee, they will tell you how to earn money stuffing envelopes at home. Later you will find out the promoter never had any employment to offer. Instead, for your fee, you're likely to get a letter telling you to place the same envelope-stuffing advertisement in newspapers or magazines or on the Internet. The only way you'll earn money is if people respond to your fraudulent work-at-home advertisements.[2,3]

- Two Hollywood, California men, Russian-born Steve Shklovskiy and Yan Shtok, both 23, pleaded guilty to fraud charges. Authorities said the men devised a way to use personal computers equipped with commercially available software to obtain 50 million email addresses. They then sent a mass emailing asking recipients for a $35 "processing fee" in exchange for a chance to work at home stuffing envelopes. More than 12,000 people were duped. The men received two-year prison terms for a scam that overwhelmed the largest U.S. Internet providers. They also were required to pay more than $100,000 in restitution. The plea agreements required the men to reveal to the Internet service providers how they accomplished their scheme. Two others involved in the scheme were sentenced to probation.[4]

Assembly Work. Assembly-work scams often require you to invest hundreds of dollars upfront in equipment, supplies, or training. In return, the "company" promises to buy the completed products. However, after you've paid the upfront costs and performed the work, the fraudulent operators won't pay you because the work does not meet their "quality standards." Unfortunately, no work is ever "up to standard," leaving workers with relatively expensive equipment and supplies and no income.[2,3]

- A Miami company, National Crafters Corporation, solicited home-based workers to assemble jewelry, bilking 28,000 victims in several states out of $1.4 million. The website advertisements stated "No experience required," and the average assembler would have to work only a few hours to earn $360 to $720 a week. Consumers were asked to send $44 for materials. In return, they received packets of beads and instructions, and were told they would have to submit a sample bracelet for review to make sure the company's quality standards were met. According to the FTC, doing the company's bidding was nearly impossible because National Crafters provided too few beads to assemble the bracelets properly and supplied instructions that were too complicated for novices. After receiving numerous complaints, the FTC filed a restraining order and froze the company's bank accounts. National Crafters agreed to pay $25,000 to settle allegations that its operations bilked consumers, and the owner of the company, Thomas Diaz, Jr., was barred from running any more work-at-home companies.[5]

Medical Billing. Emails for medical billing businesses may inform you that the market for medical billing is wide open. Most often you are urged to purchase unique, specialized software programs and even computers. The price tag ranges between a few hundred and thousands of dollars. Unfortunately, few people who purchase a medical billing business opportunity are able to find clients and generate enough revenue even to recover their investment.[2,3]

- The FTC filed a complaint against Charles Lloyd and his company, Healthcare Claims Network, alleging that for $485 prospective "customers" were promised everything necessary to perform medical billing services from home. The promise included training, a list of doctors in need of home-based medical billers, and the software to perform the work. Instead, they were provided with inadequate training and medical billing software that many consumers were unable to use. In addition, consumers found that the doctors on the provided list had no need for at-home billing services. As a result, consumers were unable to earn any income using the medical billing packages. Health Claims Network was banned from promoting or selling medical-billing work-at-home opportunities. The settlement required that the company be liquidated and that Lloyd pay $10,000. In addition, the settlement prohibited future deceptive claims in connection with the sale of any goods or services.[6]

Other Home Employment Scams. Other home employment scams include assembling wooden calendars, making towel holders, assembling electronic circuit boards, making hair bows, making beaded earrings, assembling holiday decorations, assembling various crafts, testing products, and doing data entry and word processing.[9,10]

Still other work at home scams fall under the heading "Your opinion is worth money" and include taking online surveys, participating in online focus groups, trying new products, and previewing movie trailers. For the service, they offer to pay you anywhere from $5 to $150 per hour. The catch—you have to pay a relatively small fee to join. In addition to the fee, the perpetrators also get to collect your credit card information.[2]

Multilevel Marketing Scams

Legitimate *multilevel marketing* plans are a way of selling goods or services through distributors. These plans typically promise that if you sign up as a distributor you will receive commissions for sales of the plan's goods. If a plan offers additionally to pay commissions for recruiting new distributors, it may be illegal. Most states outlaw this practice, which constitutes a pyramid scheme. State laws against pyramiding say that a multilevel marketing plan should only pay commissions for retail sales of goods or services, not for recruiting new distributors. Mary Kay Cosmetics and Avon are two legitimate and successful multilevel marketing programs which only pay commissions on sales.[7]

- **Internet Malls.** Operators of an Internet-based business opportunity that promised easy income for investors agreed to settle FTC charges that their scheme was an illegal pyramid operation, not a legitimate multi-level marketing program. Bigsmart.com LLC and its principals, Mark and Harry Tahiliani, marketed Internet theme "malls" claiming that individuals would earn substantial income from commissions on products purchased through the Internet. The malls were a collection of links to retail sites maintained by independent third-party merchants, such as MarthaStewart.com, and to a "Superstore" maintained by Bigsmart itself. Traffic was directed to the malls through the personalized Bigsmart "welcome pages" that members bought access to for a $10 application fee and a $99.95 "hosting" fee. The scheme was structured in such a way that realizing continued financial gains depended on the successful recruitment of other participants, not on retail sales of products and services to the public. To settle the charges, Bigsmart and the Tahilianises were to provide up to $5 million in consumer redress. They were also required to post a $500,000 performance bond before engaging in any new multi-level marketing activity.[8]

Another version of the business opportunity scam promises you "the secret to a successful business." After paying a fee, you receive the secret—place ads in emails exactly like the one you answered.[11]

JOB SCAMS

There are many variations of job scams, including (1) overpayment scams, (2) fake check scams, (3) advance fee scams, and (4) mail-forwarding scams.

Examples of Job Scams

Overpayment Scam

There are many variations on the overpayment scam. Many start with an email contact in which a stranger proposes to send you a check and have you wire some of the money in return. It may start with someone offering to buy something you advertised for sale, pay you to work at home, or give you an advance on a lottery you supposedly won. Whatever the set-up, the bottom line is if someone you don't know wants to pay you by check but wants you to wire some of the money back, it's a scam.[12]

Signing Bonus Scam. Individuals and banks have been victimized by the signing bonus scam. This scheme involves online job applications. Prospective clients are sent a check for more than the advertised bonus and asked to cash it and send the difference back to the sender.[13]

* Individuals applied for and accepted jobs through an online job search service advertising "signing bonuses" of $2,000 to $4,000. Each prospective employee then received a check ranging from $19,000 to $50,000 by mail from the prospective employer with instructions to deposit the check, preferably at an ATM. The recipient was further instructed to keep the amount of the signing bonus and return the balance by wire to a location in Europe. The checks were fraudulent. As a result the depositors ended up being responsible for the amounts charged back to their bank accounts resulting from the dishonor of the checks. In some cases, banks suffered losses when customers were unable to cover the overdrafts.[13]

Fake Check Scam

There are many variations of the fake check scam. The bottom line is that someone sends you a check, asks you to deposit it in your bank account, and then wire money in the same amount back to the sender or to someone else. The check, of course, is fake and you are out the money you wired.

Nanny Scam. In the nanny scam a criminal answers an ad for someone wishing to be employed as a nanny. He or she contracts with the person to do the work and sends checks for expenses and salary. Then the nanny gets a letter stating that the criminal will not be able to follow through with the job offer. The nanny is instructed to deposit the checks in her checking account and send the criminal a money order to refund the money. Of course the checks are worthless and the nanny gets stuck for the amount of the deposits.

* A young Pittsburgh woman lost money in a scam after posting her ad to serve as a nanny on www.pittsburghnanny.com. The victim said a man who claimed to be from England responded to her ad stating he needed a nanny to take care of his daughter for three weeks while he was in Pittsburgh on business. He said he would send her money in advance to cover his daughter's food and clothing expenses during her stay. The

woman said she received five travelers' checks totaling $4,625. Soon after the checks arrived, the man claimed that his daughter had become very ill and their trip had been canceled. He asked the woman to send the money back so his daughter could receive medical treatment. The woman told investigators she deposited the checks into her account and, as instructed, wired part of the money to the medical doctor in England who was caring for his daughter and the remainder to his friend in Nigeria. She said several days after wiring the funds via Western Union she learned that the travelers' checks were counterfeit and the bank was holding her liable for the funds.[14]

Charity Job Scam. In another variation of the fake check scam the criminal contacts a potential victim who has posted a resume' online and offers a job working for a charity. The potential victim is to receive checks, deposit them in his or her bank account, and wire money to a third party. Of course the checks the victim receives are worthless.

- After Kathy Paskvan posted her resume´ in the classifieds, she received a job offer from what appeared to be a nonprofit organization, the Elena Foundation. Kathy was told she would be a donations processor. All she had to do was receive cashier's checks and send the money on to different branches of the foundation. She would keep a small percentage of the checks she processed. Then she received a cashier's check for $4600, deposited it in her bank account, and then sent the money out in two Western Union installments to two different addresses as instructed. A few days later her bank informed her that her account was overdrawn by $4600. The cashier's check had been a forgery.[15]

Advance Fee Scam

With the advance fee scam a potential victim applies for a job offered online and is told that he will have to pay an upfront processing, or some other fee, to get the job. These nonexistent jobs include airline jobs, modeling jobs, and many others.

- **Airline Job Scam.** Anthony Peter Remsen pled no contest to six criminal counts of running false advertisements and making false and misleading statements to customers. Remsen was the owner of Air Lynx International, a Santa Monica, California based operation that promised jobs in the airline industry through nationwide Internet and newspaper ads. The ads stated that airlines were "now hiring" and implied that specific jobs were available. Customers paid Air Lynx $165.00 each, but got no jobs. Instead, they were merely sent packets with generic information and job-hunting advice. Remsen was placed on three years' probation and ordered to pay $7,095.00 in restitution to some 43 victims nationwide. As part of his sentence he was forbidden from operating any form of employment agency for the three years.[16]

- **Processing Fee/Identity Theft.** Ottawa police uncovered an Internet-based scam that was used to steal personal information from unsuspecting victims who were applying for jobs. At least 60 victims were identified, but authorities suspected there were many more. Victims were contacted after they applied for a job that was posted online. After being notified that they were a suitable candidate for the $70,000-a-year position, they were asked to fill out a job application form and to send a $20 processing fee. Once the scammers got the application form they used the personal information to apply for credit cards in the victims' names. Of course there were no jobs. About $500,000 worth of merchandise was purchased with the fraudulent credit cards. Police charged a 35-year-old man and a 31-year-old woman with conspiracy to commit fraud.[17]

- **Modeling Scam.** The New Faces Development Center was cited for making deceptive and exaggerated claims about the services it provided to aspiring models and actors. The company claimed it provided talent management services, including industry placement and training, and that it was highly selective in scouting, screening, and reviewing young people for potential as models and actors. However, New Faces principally provided photographic services, and for an additional fee posted photographic images on its website www.gigacomps.com. New Faces' "talent scouts" were said to have approached consumers, usually children, teenagers, and young adults, in public places and led them to believe that they had been scouted because they had a "look" that made them likely to succeed as models and actors. They were told that they would incur no costs and should contact a director at New Faces to schedule an evaluation. Those who met with a director were told that they had to sign a photo shoot agreement and pay hundreds or even thousands of dollars upfront. Under the settlement, New Faces had to pay the State $75,000 in penalties and $2,000 in costs, and up to $500,000 in restitution to aggrieved consumers.[18]

Mail Forwarding Scam

With the mail forwarding scam you are offered a job forwarding packages to an address in a foreign country. Unknown to you the contents of the packages have been obtained illegally, so you unwittingly have become part of the crime.

- **Accused of a Crime.** Being unemployed, Chris Melton was looking for a job—any job. Finally, he got an offer from a firm claiming to be a mail-forwarding company. He was told he would get $70 per package to help a company ship overseas. He took the "job" and began forwarding packages he received in the mail. Soon police showed up at his door threatening to arrest him for online auction fraud. He unknowingly had helped someone steal $12,500. The ad looked real enough, as did the company's website, www.postforward.org. The ad said "We specialize in priority courier service by hand-carrying of your valuable items, both worldwide or nationally."[19]

Other Job Scams

Other job scams include being instructed to dial a 900 charge-per-minute number to discuss the job and a number of advance fee "jobs," including bogus cruise ship jobs, training-required jobs, background check jobs, overseas job scams, post office job scams, and many more. Even college students have been targeted for summer jobs that are claimed to pay thousands of dollars.[10,20]

TIPS TO PROTECT YOURSELF

If you are looking for a job online, be aware of the following:

Advance Fee. Be leery if you apply for a "job" and you are requested to send a processing or any other fee prior to being considered for the job.

Charity. Be leery of any "charity organization" that wants to hire you to receive checks, deposit them in your bank account, and then write checks to other people you don't know. If the checks turn out to be fake you are responsible for your deposits.

Details. Get all the details beforehand. A legitimate company will be happy to give you information about exactly what you will be doing before you invest any money.[21]

Emails. Be cautious of emails offering work-at-home opportunities. Many unsolicited emails are fraudulent. Legitimate companies don't advertise for employees through spam email.[21]

Government Jobs. Government agencies never charge an application fee, nor do they guarantee that an applicant will be hired; and no one can guarantee you a high score on any required Postal or civil service exam. Ads that offer information about hidden or unadvertised federal jobs are fraudulent.[22]

Huge Income. Don't believe that you can make a huge income easily. Operating a home-based business is just like any other business; it requires hard work, skill, good products or services, and time to make a profit. You will not get rich overnight, and you might not make any money at all.[21]

Legal Issues. Be aware of legal issues. To do some types of work you may need a license or certificate, and some things are just plain illegal.

Mail Forwarding. Beware of "jobs" that involve forwarding packages, especially to a foreign country. You could be involved in an illegal activity.

Modeling. Modeling and talent agencies don't discover their talent in a mall or on the street. Be leery of anyone who approaches you and wants you to call and make an appointment. They may just want to sell you an expensive photography package.

Ready Market. If the company says it has customers waiting, ask who they are and contact some of them to confirm.[21]

Send Money Back. If someone you don't know wants to pay you a sign-on bonus by check but wants you to wire some of the money back, beware. The scam that could cost you thousands of dollars because the check most likely is fake and you are responsible for the checks you write.[12,13]

Toll Free Numbers. Ads that refer to a toll-free number may not be offering to employ you directly, only sell you a "valuable" booklet containing job listings, practice test questions, and tips for entrance exams. Avoid answering these ads.[21,22]

Work at Home. Be leery of any work at home opportunity in which you are requested to buy supplies or equipment upfront.

References

1. FTC Names Its Dirty Dozen:12 Scams Most Likely to Arrive Via Bulk Email, Federal Trade Commission, www.ftc.gov/bcp/conline/pubs/alerts/doznalrt.htm, July 1998.
2. Work at home schemes, Fraud, Office of Minnesota Attorney general, www.ftc.gov/bcp/conline/pubs/invest/homewrk.htm.
3. Milhorn, H. Thomas, Cybercrime, In Crime: Computer Viruses to Twin Towers, Universal Publishers, Boca Raton, 2005, Pp 46-70.
4. Fifty Million Fraudulent E-Mails Net Los Angeles Pair Two Years in Prison, Mail Utilities, www.mailutilities.eom/news/archive/l 8/182.html, January 3, 2001.
5. FTC Charges Miami Company Operating a Work-At-Home Business Opportunity with Engaging in Fraudulent Activities, Federal Trade Commission, www.ftc.gov/opa/2001/12/nationalcrafters.htm December 5, 2001.
6. Med Data Defendants Banned from Selling Medical Billing Work-At-Home Business Opportunities, www.ftc.gov/opa/2003/08/meddata3.htm, August 26, 2003.
7. Multilevel marketing plans, Federal Trade Commissions, http://www. ftc.gov/bcp/conline/pubs/invest/mlm.htm, November 1996.
8. Bigsmart Pyramid Promoters Settle FTC Charges, Federal Trade Commission, www.ftc.gov/opa/2001/03/bigsmart.htm, March 27, 2001.
9. Sewah, Sara, Fraudulent work-at-home schemes, schemes, scams, and frauds, Work at Home, www.crimes-of-persuasion.com/Crimes/Telemarketing/Inbound/MinorIn/HowTo/work_at_home.htm, June 13, 2003.

10. Summer employment scams, Your Legal Rights, www.ag.state. mn.us/consumer/ylr/ylr_college_05_ May.htm, May 2005.
11. Fleitas, Amy C., Internet spam spawns scam, Bankrate.com, www. bankrate.com/brm/news/advice/20021025b.asp, March 26, 2003.
12. Fake check scams, National Consumer Leagues' Internet Fraud Watch, raud.org/tips/internet/fakecheck.htm.
13. Fraudulent Bonus Checks For Non-Existent Jobs, Federal Deposit Insurance Corporation, www.fdic.gov/news/news/financial/2002/ fil0230.html, March 28, 2002.
14. Travelers Check Scam Targets Nannies, ConsumerAffairs.com, www.consumeraffairs.com/news04/2006/03/nanny_scam.html, March 1, 2006.
15. Duffy, Ryan, On Your Side: Online Charity Scam, www.wrdw.com/onyourside/2807056.html, May 15, 2006.
16. Man convicted in local airline employment scam, City of Santa Monica, Consumer Protection Agency, http://santa-monica.org/atty/consumer_protection/news/2000/ cao20000501, August 1, 2005.
17. Two charged in Internet-based identity theft scam, CTV.ca, www.ctv.ca/servlet/ ArticleNews/story/CTVNews/20060308/ idtheft_scam_060308/20060308?, March 9, 2006.
18. Long Island talent agency to pay penalties and restitution to would-be models and actors, Office of the New York State Attorney General, www.oag.state.ny.us/press/2006/jan/jan19a_06.html, January 19, 2006.
19. Sullivan, Bob, Online job seeker duped to help con, MSNBC, www.msnbc.msn.com/id/3078470, April 29, 2003.
20. Sabatini, Patricia, Post office job scam highlights the need for caution, Post-Gazette.com, www.post-gazette.com/pg/06183/702558-68.stm, July 2, 2006.
21. Be scam free fro life, www.work-at-home-jobs-iowa.com/ scamfree.html.
22. FTC Continues to "Stamp Out" Job Fraud, www.ftc.gov/opa/2001/03/stampout2001.htm, March 20, 2001.

Chapter 4

Charity Scams

After natural disasters there often are thousands of people in need of shelter, clothing, food, drinking water, and medications. And millions of people answer the call for help. Unfortunately, there also are those who want to take advantage of the situation—often in the form of online charity scams. [1]

In addition to spam emails asking for donations, crooks set up fraudulent websites pretending to be legitimate disaster relief organizations. These sites request charitable donations, but their purpose is to steal financial and personal information so it can be used to make charges on your credit card or empty your bank account. Any contribution you make, of course, goes into the pockets of the scammers rather than helping people who need it.[2]

EMOTIONS

Charity scams play on people's emotions. The emotions most likely to be targeted are:

Caring. Risky or fake business ventures promote investing in companies which produce products the city which suffered the disaster "is going to need." They expect you to contribute because, after all, you're a caring person.

Fear. Crooks exploit people's fears related to disasters. Phony or bad insurance deals exploit fear of loss of life or property, and pushing gold or other "safe" investments exploit fear of economic collapse. Pushing gas masks and other safety measures exploit fear of another attack.

Grief. Crooks take advantage of the grief of the families of victims, firefighters, and other emergency workers involved in disasters to request donations.

Patriotism. Crooks exploit people's patriotism. Phony police or military organizations ask for donations for fake war bonds or for giving flags to children or troops.

Revenge. Phony organizations seek donations purporting to seek revenge for a terrorist attack or to stop terrorism.[3]

TYPES OF CHARITY SCAMS

Hate Websites. Hate websites characterize the disaster as the "wrath of God"—and then ask people to donate to them.[2]

Individual donations. Emails may request that you to help a person's family members. These bogus requests usually say something like "My family lost everything in Hurricane Katrina. Please help by sending money to (mailing address here).[2]

Investment and Security. Investment and security scams include emails that tout specific stocks on the basis of activity related to a natural disaster. For example, after Hurricane Katrina one email said that investors could more than double their money in just days on certain penny stocks because of refinery glitches.[2]

Officials. Scammers posing as officials from government agencies, banks, insurance companies, credit card companies, and so forth claim they will help victims in some way, such as helping process their insurance claims more quickly. However, the goal of these scams is obtain bank, credit card, and other personal information to steal your money.

Unrelated Products. Misleading emails try to take advantage of a disaster to sell unrelated products. This is usually done with a description of the disaster, which includes a hyperlink labeled "Read More." When you click on the link it takes you to a website advertising some unrelated product, such as generic Viagra, which in itself is a scam.[2]

Variants of the Nigerian Fraud. Unsolicited emails were sent with the supposed purpose of retrieving large amounts of money tied up in areas devastated by Hurricane Katrina. This is simply a version of the advance fee fraud. If you agree to help the person, you are then asked for money upfront.[2]

Viruses and Trojans. Spam is sent that includes attached photos of disaster areas or individual survivors, and these attachments contain computer viruses. For example, the Trojan, Cgab, was related to a Hurricane Katrina email that made the rounds. It provided the criminal full access to the victim's computer. The email titles consisted of such things as "Re: Tropical storm flooded New Orleans" and "Re: 80 percent of our city underwater."[2]

EXAMPLES OF CHARITY SCAMS

September 11 Attack

Within hours of the September 11, 2001 terrorist attacks, swindlers had already begun trying to profit from Americans' grief. Unsolicited email messages began circulating that urged people to donate money to the Red Cross, the United Way, the September 11 Fund, and other charities benefiting victims and their families. Clicking on donation links led victims to fraudulent websites where they were requested to give valuable personal information, such as credit card numbers.[4,5] A typical email might appear as follows:

- "From: september11fund@AOL.com
  To: xxxxxxxxx@xxxxxxx.net
  Date: Wednesday, September 21, 2001 03:35:23
  Subject: Help for the Red Cross and the victims of our Nation's tragedy.
  Express Relief Fund: *Click here*
  Victims Survivor Fund. *Click here*
  Thank you for your help.
  september11fund@AOL.com"[5]

Asian Tsunami

- **Mercy Corps.** The FBI arrested Matthew Z. Schmieder, 24, of Carrick, Pennsylvania on charges of flooding the Internet with spam solicitations for a bogus tsunami relief fund. Schmieder admitted to the FBI that he had sent out 800,000 emails purporting to be from the Mercy Corps, an international group of humanitarian agencies. He confessed to lifting images from the Mercy Corps website to use in spam messages in an attempt to fool donors into sending him money through a PayPal account he had established. Immediately upon learning of the scam, Mercy Corps worked directly with federal authorities to help shut down the fraudulent website. When agents arrested Schmieder at his apartment, he initially said he thought it would be okay to keep the funds for his own use if he gave some of the contributions to charity. Subsequently, he stated that he intended to use the money to fix his car and to pay some bills because "everybody needs money."[6]

Red Cross. The following unsolicited email, claiming to be from Red Cross International, asked recipients to donate money to tsunami victims by arranging a money transfer. Note the poor grammar, spelling, and punctuation.

- "Subject: please help tsunami victims, help tsunami victims, help tsunami victims, help tsunami victims.
  The Red Cross International Amsterdam, the Netherlands zone (b) hereby appealling to you friends,public,families and companies, to help us with online fund raising to enable us treat over 1.5 million children affected with quake/tsunami desaster across Asia. Visit www.cnn.com/tsunami to see why your help/money is highly needed. Help the needy,poor and sick,no amount is small for god loves a cheerfull giver. In order to expedite the sending of the relief funds to the needy urgently, you are advised to send us your donation/contribution in holland by express moneygram transfer services (www.moneygram.com) or Western Union money transfer (www.westernunion.com) through the name of our financial officers Mrs (Lilian David) and Mr (Robert John) respectively. You are advised to respond back to us through this email address and provide us with the transfer details including your contact address on our official e-mail address: Donators from 100 to 4500 euros will only have their names appeared in our relief magazines and websites while

those donations above (5000 euros) to any amount will have a space for their fotos,names and business adverts in our magazines and websites as does in the past years.for the later (vip)s please send us your fotos and business details. We await your urgent response and thanks for your co-operations and generosity to mankind.
Yours sincerely.
Jensen hall, Relief Coordinator."[7]

Hurricane Katrina

Fraudulent Website. After hurricane Katrina, fraudulent websites soliciting funds appeared on the Internet.

- In Florida, Gary S. Kraser pled guilty to fraudulently soliciting charitable donations, supposedly intended for Hurricane Katrina relief. According to the indictment, Kraser falsely claimed in conversations on the Internet, and ultimately via the website at www.AirKatrina.com, that he was piloting flights to Louisiana to provide medical supplies to the areas affected by Hurricane Katrina and to evacuate children and others in critical medical condition. Kraser further claimed that he had organized a group of Florida pilots to assist him in his relief efforts. He reportedly claimed that he personally paid for these fictitious relief flights, and that he approved the creation of the website to solicit donations to purchase the fuel for his humanitarian aid missions. According to the website, "every dollar, every nickel, will go directly into the tanks of these pilots planes on their mission of mercy." The website allowed for donations to be made directly into Kraser's PayPal account, a service that allows customers to send and receive money online for transactions conducted over the Internet. In addition, Kraser provided instructions for wiring contributions directly into his bank account. In just two days, he received almost $40,000 in donations from 48 different contributors from around the world.[8]

Identity Theft. After Hurricane Katrina, spam emails sent out by the thousands gave a plea for help and then gave a link that took potential victims to a bogus website. Once there, the people were asked to fill out a form about personal and financial information. The goal was to steal Social Security numbers, bank account numbers, and credit card numbers. The following is such an email:

* "Please donate to Hurricane Relief Efforts. We have seen the horrible destruction this past week that was caused by natural causes. Our hearts and prayers go out to those affected by Hurricane Katrina. If you'd like to help we encourage you to make a generous donation to the American Red Cross. Thank You for your compassion. www.americanreddcross.com"[2]

Notice that in the website address, "redcross" is spelled "reddcross" and the suffix is .com instead of .org so that the potential victim is taken to the fraudulent website, www.reddcross.com rather than the actual one, www.redcross.org.

TIPS TO PROTECT YOURSELF

Disasters. Be especially cautious when there are natural or other disasters. Fraudulent "charities" take advantage of those situations to trick people who want to help the victims.[9]

Emails. Be cautious about emails seeking charitable contributions. It's best simply to delete unsolicited emails that request money because virtually 100 percent of them are fraudulent.[9]

Emotion. Be wary of appeals that are long on emotion. Emails that are long on emotion but short on describing what the charity will do to address the needs of victims and their families should raise a red flag.[10]

How Used. Ask how donations are to be used. One of the most important things to consider is how much of your money goes to fundraising and administrative costs, rather than to the charitable work itself. Be leery if you can't get a specific response.[9]

Personal Information. Do not give your credit card number or other personal information. Fraudulent emails have been use in identity theft. Ask the caller or sender to provide you with written information on the charity's programs and finances.[10]

Police or Firefighters. Be wary of requests to support police or firefighters. Some fraudulent fundraisers claim that donations will benefit these groups, when in fact little or no money goes to them. Contact your local police or fire department to find out if the claims are true and what percentage of donations, if any, they will receive.[9]

Runners. Be wary of any request to send a "runner" to your front door to pick up your contribution. This is almost always a sign of fraud.

Sound-a-Likes. Beware of sound-a-likes. Some criminals try to fool people by using names that are very similar to those of well-known charities (Redd Cross rather than Red Cross).[9]

Spelling, Grammar, and Punctuation. Many fraudulent emails contain erroneous spelling, bad grammar, and poor punctuation. They often have phrases in upper case letters to focus your attention on the message of these phrases.

References

1. Beware the online "charity" scam, Defending the Net, www.defendingthenet.com/Articles/OnlineCharityScams.htm.
2. Hurricane Katrina Scams, ScamBusters.org, www.scambusters.org/hurricanekatrinascams.html.
3. Barry, Patricia, Scams Swiftly Follow Terrorist Attacks, Beware of Cons Tied to Tragedy, AARP Bulletin, www.aarp.org/bulletin/consumer/a2003-07-01-scams_terr.html, November 2001.
4. Milhorn, H. Thomas, Cybercrime, In Crime: Computer Viruses to Twin Towers, Universal Publishers, Boca Raton, 2005, Pp 46-70.
5. Sieberg, Daniel, FTC exposes top 10 web scams, CNN.com, www.cnn.com/2000/TECH/computing/10/31/ftc.web.scams, October 31, 2000.
6. Torsten, Ove, Carrick man charged in tsunami relief scam, Post-Gazette.com, www.postgazette.com/pg/05014/442096.stm, January 14, 2005.
7. Christensen, Brett M., Red Cross Tsunami Scam Email, www.hoax-slayer.com/red-cross-tsunami-scam.html, 2006.
8. Aventura man sentenced on hurricane Katrina internet scam. United States Department of Justice, Southern District of Florida, http://miami.fbi.gov/dojpressrel/pressrel06/mm050806.htm, May 8, 2006.
9. Charity Scams, Internet Fraud Tips, National Consumer's League Internet Fraud Watch, www.fraud.org/tips/internet/charity.htm.

10. Tips on disaster relief funds, Give.org, www.give.org/news/ disaster_tips.asp.

Chapter 5

Child Pornography

Child pornography is defined as the visual or audio depiction of a child for the sexual gratification of the user and involves the production, distribution, or use of such material. Child pornography as a cybercrime involves using the Internet for the production, manufacture, or distribution of child pornography.[1]

Computer technology has provided child pornographers with powerful new tools for victimizing children. The result is an explosive growth in the production and distribution of illegal child pornography.

EXAMPLES OF CHILD PORNOGRAPHY

- **Pornography Ring.** Federal officials broke open a global Internet child pornography ring that was thought to have had tens of thousands of paying customers in the United States alone. FBI agents arrested 15 people in New Jersey, including a pediatrician, a minister, and a high school bandleader. The individuals were charged with downloading graphic child pornography images onto their home computers. Those arrested had used credit cards to pay for memberships on about 50 pornography sites run out of Belarus and Latvia. Three of the four executives of the Belarusian company, Regpay, were arrested in Spain and France where they were held while the United States sought to extradite them. An American credit card processing company, Connections USA of Hollywood, Florida, helped process payments for Regpay. An executive with that company acknowledged knowing about the child pornography and pleaded guilty to money laundering. Regpay and Connections USA processed 270,000 credit card transactions in one year on Visa and MasterCard alone. About 100,000 of these transactions involved American customers.[2]

• **Texas A&M Student Indicted.** Corey Armstrong, a 21-year-old Texas A&M University student, was indicted on 17 counts of possession of online child pornography. An Internet service provider alerted the National Center for Missing and Exploited Children that Armstrong was posting sexually explicit images of children on the Internet. The center then referred the case to the Texas Attorney General's Cyber Crimes Unit, which searched Armstrong's dorm room and confiscated two computers and external devices. Forensic analysis of the computers revealed the pornographic images. Child pornography is a third-degree felony punishable by two to 10 years in prison and a fine of up to $10,000. Armstrong, a junior geography major from Brandon, Florida, posted $10,000 bail.[3]

• **Company CEO.** Former Newsday publisher, Robert Johnson, pleaded guilty to collecting child pornography on his office computer and then trying to destroy the evidence when officials caught up with him. Johnson, a 60-year-old married father of two grown children, admitted he downloaded at least two child-pornography movie files, including one called "Real Child Rape," in the headquarters of the Manhattan financial publishing firm where he was CEO. He faced 30 years in prison.[4]

• **27 People Arrested.** An Internet chat room that streamed video of live child molestations over the Internet was shut down and 27 people charged with online child pornography. An undercover sting operation also shut down an associated website called "Kiddypics & Kiddyvids." One of the seven molestation victims was younger than 18 months. Four minors under the age of 12, including a 7-year-old girl, also were shown being molested. The host of the chat room used the screen name "G.O.D." Another, using the screen name "Big_Daddy619," allegedly distributed live videos of himself molesting the four under-age-12 children. Brian Annoreno, of Bartlett, Illinois, was accused of producing video of himself molesting and performing oral sex on the infant, officials said. Thirteen of the people charged were from the United States, nine from Canada, three from Australia, and two from England.[5]

- **150 Years.** A Virginia man, Gregory John Mitchel, was sentenced to 150 years in prison for sexually exploiting minors and operating child pornography websites. Mitchel, 39, pleaded guilty to the production, distribution, sale, and possession of child pornography. He was reported to have assisted in the daily operation of child pornography websites and filmed videos of minors engaging in sex acts. Mitchel was implicated by Justin Berry, 19, who for five years starred in his own webcam child pornography business and had testified before Congress about Internet child pornography.[6]

- **Variations of Well-known Websites.** A 56-year-old Florida man, John Zuccarini, pleaded guilty in federal court to charges that he used misspelling or variations of well-known websites to direct minors and other unwitting users to pornographic content. He owned at least 3,000 Internet addresses. He admitted to 49 counts of using domain names to direct minors to nudity or sexually explicit content. Prosecutors said many of the Internet addresses he owned resembled websites of interest to children. One example was www.dinseyland.com. Prosecutors said the man made between 10 cents and 25 cents for every viewer led to the pornographic sites he worked with. He earned as much as $1 million annually, according to the U.S. attorney. He was sentenced to four years in prison with three years supervised probation.[7]

- **His Own Web Cam.** Thirteen year old Justin hooked up a Web camera to his computer, hoping to use it to meet other teenagers online. Instead, he heard only from men who chatted with him by instant message as they watched his image on the Internet. They seemed like friends, ready with compliments and always offering gifts. Then one member of his online audience offered to pay him $50 to sit bare chested in front of his Webcam for three minutes. The man helped Justin open an account on PayPal so he could make the payment. So Justin removed his T-shirt. From that point on the soccer-playing, honor-roll student was drawn into performing in front of the Webcam—undressing, showering, masturbating, and even having sex—for an audience of more than 1,500 people who paid him hundreds of thousands of dollars over five years. Justin eventually fell into the trap of meeting some of the men offline, which led to a series of molestations. The New York Times persuaded Justin to abandon his business and, to protect other children at risk, assisted him in contacting the Justice Department. Arrests and indictments of adults he identified as pornography producers and traffickers began. Investigators also focused on businesses, including credit card processors that aided illegal sites. Anyone who created, distributed, marketed, possessed, or paid to view pornography was subject to being criminally charged.[8]

TIPS TO PROTECT YOURSELF

To avoid websites with child pornography you should be leery of spam emails that direct you to such sites. Should your browser become hijacked and lead you to a child pornography site, immediately take whatever steps are necessary to correct the problem, even if you have to pay a computer expert to eliminate the software causing the problem. If you are fairly good with computers you may be able to do a Google or Yahoo search for the offending agent and find instructions on how to eliminate it.

References

1. Milhorn, H. Thomas, Cybercrime, In Crime: Computer Viruses to Twin Towers, Universal Publishers, Boca Raton, 2005, Pp 46-70.
2. Powell, Michael, Child Porn Operation Busted, FBI Says, Washington Post, January 16, 2004.
3. Welch, Arena, A&M student faces 17 child pornography charges,

The Eagle, www.tamu.edu/upd/am_stud_faces_17_child_porno_ charges.htm, March 28, 2006.

4. Soltis, Andy, Porn exec smack, The New York Post, www.nypost.com/news/regionalnews/porn_exec_smack_regionalne ws_andy_soltis.htm, August 5, 2006.
5. 27 charged in child porn sting, Law Center, CNN.com, www.cnn.com/2006/LAW/03/15/childporn.arrests/index.html, March 16, 2006.
6. Va. man gets 150 years for child pornography, USA Today, www.usatoday.com/news/nation/2006-07-15-child-porn_x.htm, July 16, 2006.
7. Bray, Chad, Florida man pleads guilty to directing kids to porn sites, Detroit News. December 11, 2003.
8. Eichenwald, Kurt, Through His Webcam, a Boy Joins a Sordid Online World, The New York Times, December 19, 2005.

Chapter 6

Copyright Violation

Copyright is the legal right granted to an author, composer, playwright, publisher, or distributor to exclusive publication, production, sale, or distribution of a literary, musical, dramatic, or artistic work.[1,2] *Copyright violation* is the use of copyrighted material without the right to do so, whether the use is for profit or not. Copyrighted material includes the written word, music, movies, videogames, software, and anything else that is subject to copyright laws. *Piracy* is the unauthorized use or reproduction of copyrighted or patented material.[3]

Warez is the name given to commercial software that has been pirated and made available to the public via the Internet. Typically, the pirate has figured out a way to deactivate the copy-protection or registration scheme used by the software. The use and distribution of warez software is illegal.[4]

PLAGIARISM

Copyright for authors is the legal right granted to an author for the exclusive publication, production, sale, or distribution of a literary work. Original works are copyrighted and protected the moment they are written, whether they have a copyright notice or not. The same rules apply to any written work published on the Internet as to physically published material.[2]

Plagiarism is presenting someone else's words as though they are your own. It includes (1) quoting someone else's exact words without documenting the source, (2) modifying or summarizing someone else's words without documenting the source, and (3) failing to get permission to use someone else's work.[5]

Information considered to be common knowledge does not need to have its source documented. Common knowledge is information generally known by everyone. For example, that George Bush was elected to a second term as president of the United States in 2004 is common knowledge.[3]

Example of Plagiarism

Website Plagiarism

- Kent Aoki Lee, 37, of Honolulu, was charged with copying the authorized website of the Honolulu Marathon Association, a non-profit organization which organizes an annual marathon. The Honolulu Marathon Association maintains a website at www.honolulumarathon.org, which provides race information and allows residents of the United States, but not Japan, to register for the race on-line. The indictment charged that Lee copied the authorized website and created his own website at www.honolulumarathon.com. Note that the authentic sites ends with .org, whereas the fraudulent site ends with .com. Lee included the Honolulu Marathon trade name and the King's Runner logo, both of which are registered trademarks of the Honolulu Marathon Association. Claiming the pirated website was the official Honolulu Marathon website, he included a Japanese language section which claimed to offer Japanese runners the chance to register on-line. The fraudulent website charged a registration fee of $165, which was $100 more than the true registration fee, and offered to provide runners with a course tour, transportation, and a pre-race meal. Fourteen people in Japan were said to have sent emails to Lee as a result of his actions.[6]

OTHER COPYRIGHTED MATERIAL

Other copyrighted material includes music, movies, and software.

Examples of Other Copyrighted Material

Music

- **Failed to Delete.** A federal appeals court refused to overturn a $22,500 judgment against a Chicago woman, Ceclia Gonzalez, who was caught downloading music illegally. The court compared her actions to shoplifting. She argued that she downloaded the songs to decide which ones she would buy later. However, she never deleted the songs she didn't buy. The court pointed out she could have been sued for over 1,000 songs found on her computer rather than the 30 the RIAA (Recording Industry Association of America) accused her of downloading. The music industry had wanted to settle for $3,500, but Gonzalez refused. A federal judge later ordered her to pay $750 for each downloaded song named in the accusation ($22,500), which Gonzalez had appealed.[7]

Movies

- **Grandson Did It.** In Wisconsin, Fred Lawrence, 67, who said he doesn't even like watching movies, was sued by the film industry for copyright infringement after a grandson downloaded four movies on a home computer. The Motion Picture Association of America sought as much as $600,000 in damages for downloading the four movies over the Internet file-sharing service, iMesh. The suit was filed after Lawrence refused an offer to settle the matter for $4,000. He said he didn't do it, and he wouldn't do it, but he thought it was an innocent mistake his grandson had made. Lawrence said his grandson, who was 12 at the time, downloaded "The Incredibles," "I, Robot," "The Grudge," and "The Forgotten" without knowing it was illegal to do so. Lawrence and the movie companies finally settled when he agreed to work with them and the Milwaukee Bar Association to develop a program to teach local families and school children about copyright laws.[8,9]

- **Secretly Taped.** Curtis Salisbury, 19, of Missouri was the first person to be indicted under a federal law that prohibits people from secretly videotaping movies when they are shown in theaters. Salisbury was reported to have used a camcorder to make copies of recent releases, "The Perfect Man" and "Bewitched," and then distributed them through illicit computer networks that specialized in piracy. Camcorder piracy accounts for over 90 percent of movies that turn up on the Internet while they are still in theaters. Warez networks, as they're commonly known, distribute movies, music, and software for free, often before they are released to the public. Salisbury was charged with conspiracy and copyright infringement, along with two violations of the camcorder law. He faced up to 17 years in prison.[10]

Software

- **Video Games.** Sean Michael Breen, 38, of Richmond, California was charged with copyright infringement for his leadership role in establishing the first computer-game piracy ring on the Internet. He was the leader of the Internet-based piracy group known as "Razor 1911." The group cracked the codes of the most popular software games and illegally distributed them before they were publicly released. Group members, known as suppliers, often obtained early versions of the game software from company insiders or by posing as game reviewers for bogus online magazines, authorities said. Members of the Razor 1911 group concealed their illegal activities by identifying themselves online only by screen nicknames and communicating with each others in encrypted emails. Breen was sentenced to 50 months in prison.[11]

- **Computer Software.** Kishan Singh, 33, of Lanham, Maryland was convicted of distributing pirated copies of software over the Internet. He had earlier pleaded guilty to a charge of copyright infringement. Singh operated a pay-for-access website through which he offered pirated copies of business software from which copyright protection devices had been removed. The software included programs produced by Adobe, Autodesk, Macromedia, and Microsoft. Evidence revealed that thousands of pirated software programs had been downloaded from Singh's website by users from around the world during a six-month period. The value of the software was estimated to be between $70,000 and $120,000. Singh was sentenced to 18 months in prison and ordered to forfeit his computer equipment.[12]

TIPS TO PROTECT YOURSELF

The Written Word

There are a number of things you can do to avoid plagiarism.

Internet Use. All information on the Internet is not free to use as you see fit. If you use material from an article on the Internet you must treat it just as if you were using it from a printed source.[13]

Permission. Permission must be obtained when using a substantial amount of material from any source. In the case of printed material it's not a bad idea to request permission from both the publisher and the author. You must wait until you receive confirmation of this permission before publishing your work. Having said this, does it mean that if you wish to use as little as a single sentence from a source you have to obtain permission? The answer is no. So how much material can you quote without getting permission? Most authorities agree that you can quote up to 300 words, as long as you put it in quotations and give the source credit.[13]

Quotation Marks and Source. If you are including word-for-word material from another source, you need to put quotes around it and then list the source, either in brackets at the end of the quoted material or as a superscripted numeral that refers the reader to a reference at the end of the chapter or book. For instance "Sam Author said that writers should be aware of the rules to prevent plagiarism" (Sam Author, Writer's Weekly Magazine, 2006) or "Sam Author said that writers should be aware of the rules to prevent plagiarism."[13] The superscripted 14 refers the reader to the list of references of which the Sam Author source is the 14th in the list.[13]

What if you are merely summarizing material in your own words instead of quoting? Do you still have to get permission? The answer is no; however, you do have to give your source credit.[3]

Music, Movies, Software

Copies. Avoid making copies of music, movies, or software. To do so is illegal, whether you sell it, give it away, or simply do it for your own use.

Downloading. Any material—music, movies, software—that normally sells for monetary compensation is illegal to download and use or sell without paying for it.

Purchase. Don't buy illegal copies of copyrighted music, movies, or software.

Video Camera. Don't make videos of movies with your video camera. To make videos in a movie theater with a video camera is illegal.

References

1. Copyright, Answers.com, www.answers.com.
2. Copyright, United States Copyright Office, http://www.copyright.gov/, December 5, 2005.
3. Milhorn, H. Thomas, Cybercrime, In Crime: Computer Viruses to Twin Towers, Universal Publishers, Boca Raton, 2005, Pp 46-70.
4. Warez, ISP glossary, Internet.com, http://isp.webopedia.com/ TERM/W/warez.html.
5. What is plagiarism? Adam's State College, http://www2.adams.edu /library/plagiarism_definition/plagiarism_definition.php.
6. Kent Aoki Lee charged by federal grand jury with wire fraud, trademark violations, and selling Viagra over the Internet without a prescription, U.S. Department of Justice, www.usdoj.gov/criminal/ cybercrime/kaokilee.htm, December 9, 1999.
7. Oswald, Ed, Woman loses appeal against RIAA, BetaNews, www.betanews.com/article/Woman_Loses_Appeal_Against_RIAA/ 1134402326, December 12, 2005.
8. Movie Industry Sues Grandfather Over Grandson's Downloads, Technology, FoxNews.com, www.foxnews.com/story/ 0,2933,174283,00.html, December 2, 2005.
9. Purvis, Bob, To settle lawsuit, grandfather will speak against film piracy, Milwaukee Journal Sentinel, www.jsonline.com/story/ index.aspx?id=378950, December 19, 2005.
10. U.S. charges man in camcorder-piracy crackdown, Reuters, http://news.com.com/U.S.+charges+man+in+camcorder-

piracy+crackdown/2100-1030_3-5819976.html, August 5, 2005.

11. Lee, Henry K., Richmond man gets 50 months for piracy Convicted of leading ring that stole popular online video games, San Francisco Chronicle, February 11, 2004.

12. Software pirate jailed for 18 months, Fairfax Digital, www.smh.com.au/news/Breaking/Software-pirate-jailed-for-18-months/2005/01/10/1105206014797.html January 10, 2005.

13. Barrett, Krista, Plagiarism: What it is and how to avoid it, Writing101.com, http://www.write101.com/plag.htm, 2005.

Chapter 7

Cramming and Slamming

Cramming is the illegal and unexpected adding of charges to a person's telephone service. *Slamming* is changing a person's long-distance carrier without his consent. *Domain slamming* is changing a person's website domain service company without his or her consent. *Credit card cramming* is the illegal and unexpected adding of charges to a person's credit card. Credit card cramming is discussed in the next chapter.[1,2]

CRAMMING

With cramming you get billed for optional telephone services you never wanted or received. The crammers hope you won't notice the change and that you proceed with payment of the bill. These extra charges—typically listed under such services as paging, voice mail, or a personal 800 number—are commonly billed through a local phone carrier. Long distance calls are normally targeted because most people are not familiar with long distance rates. Sometimes a one-time charge for entertainment services will be crammed onto your telephone bill; other times it may be a recurring monthly charge.[3]

Examples of Cramming

Long Distance Number

Promised a free service, such as a free date line, psychic line, or adult entertainment, you call an 800 number as instructed in the email. A recording prompts you to give your name and to say that you want the free service. The phone number from which you call is captured and billed, and you often never get the "free" service you called for. Sometimes a recorded voice directs you to press one or more specific keys on your telephone to be transferred to the desired service. When you do you are connected to the service of your choice, but when the charge for the service appears on your bill it is an international long-distance call billed by the minute.[4]

- **Psychic Hotline.** Miss Cleo's psychic hotline, which had been in hot water for fraud, harassment, and questionable billing practices, reached a settlement with the FTC. Miss Cleo herself wasn't targeted in the action. The FTC investigated the tarot-card reader for fraud after receiving about 2,000 complaints from irate consumers. In commercials, the heavily accented, supposedly Jamaican psychic promised free consultation on matters of life and love. But when callers dialed in they unknowingly were hit with a $4.99-per-minute charge. In the settlement the hotline had to cancel $500 million in customer bills. Two companies, Access Resource Services Inc. and the Psychic Readers Network Inc., also had to pay a $5 million fine. Additionally, the companies were instructed to return all uncashed checks to customers.[5]

Direct Mail Sweepstakes. You receive a lottery promotion in an email that tells you to dial an 800 number to enter or to claim your prize. When you call, a recording follows an automated script to enroll you in a club or service program. The phone number from which you call is captured and billed. Once again, the disclosure on the lottery mailer is very difficult to comprehend because it is in very fine print or is a "negative option" billing, which means that unless you respond to refuse the offer they sign you up.[4]

Call Immediately. You get an email which says there's been an accident or sickness in your family or outstanding bills you owe are past due. The message then gives a name and number in the 809 area code and asks you to call immediately for further information. When you make the call you get a lengthy recorded message or a person who pretends not to understand what the call is about. The intended result is that you are kept on the phone as long as possible. You are actually being billed for the call at a rate of anywhere from $6.99 to $25 per minute.[4]

Order Received. You receive an email informing you that your order has been received and processed and that your credit card will be billed for charges. The trouble is you haven't ordered anything. The email advises you that if you have questions about your "order" or want to speak to a representative you should call a telephone number in area code 767. You call expecting to speak to a representative about the erroneous "order" but are connected to an adult entertainment audiotext service with sexual content. Later you receive telephone charges for the international, long-distance call billed at $25 a minute. You hadn't realized that the area code is for Dominica West Indies because no country code is required to make the call.[4]

Contest Entry Forms

You fill out a contest entry form that arrived in your email, thinking you're entering to win a prize. In fact, some unscrupulous promoter is using the contest to get your phone number, enroll you for a calling card or some similar service, and bill you on your phone bill. The disclosure on the entry form, which is very difficult to comprehend or is in very fine print, says that by completing the form you agree to pay $4.95 a month for the company's services.[4]

Internet Service Provider

- The FTC sued defendants and their parent company, Epixtar Corporation, alleging that they deceptively marketed a free, 30-day trial of Internet services to small businesses and non-profit organizations. The complaint alleged that the defendants crammed a charge of $29.95 per month on the telephone bills of those businesses that did not cancel the service during the trial period, and did so without obtaining consumers' permission to bill them. The FTC obtained a temporary restraining order that froze the defendants' assets. The terms of a preliminary injunction (1) prohibited the defendants from making further misrepresentations, (2) required them to notify current customers that they were being billed for a Web service, and (3) required them to permit these consumers to cancel if they never authorized service. The injunction also stipulated that some of the frozen funds would be used for refunds to consumers who claimed that unauthorized charges had been added to their telephone bills.[6]

Webpage

Webpage scam involves fraudulently billing small businesses and non-profit organizations for services not approved. The prospective victim gets an email or phone call offering free website design and free hosting for 30 days. The email advises that unless you cancel the website you will be billed monthly after the trial period has passed, or it states that that you won't be billed at all unless you call to continue the service after 30 days. You are asked for your company details for inclusion in the website, such as address and telephone number. The charge is then billed to your telephone service. The description of the charge in the bill is usually vague, referring to some nonspecific service. These charges are often overlooked on a lengthy business telephone bill. To add insult to injury, if the website is developed at all it is usually of very poor quality.[2]

- A defendant, Web Valley, Inc., called potential victim companies offering to design and host a webpage for a free 30-day trial period. The defendants did not disclose to the consumers that, to avoid a monthly charge of $19.95 or $24.95, the consumers would need affirmatively to cancel the service. Once a company accepted the free webpage, the defendant began charging the business' telephone accounts monthly without authorization.[7]

SLAMMING

Slamming is switching your telephone or domain service to another company without your permission or knowledge.

Examples of Slamming

Telephone Slamming

Telephone slamming is when your phone service is switched without your knowledge or permission. Although slamming most frequently impacts long distance service, it can also occur as a change to local service.[8]

- **Quest.** Carrole Huber was contacted by someone claiming to be with Qwest Communications. They told her she could get all of her calls on one phone bill so she wouldn't have more than one statement coming each month. But when she got her phone bill for the month, her long distance charges totaled more than $300—nearly five times her normal bill. So when Huber called Qwest to ask about it, they told her nobody from the company had called her. Because she reported the scam quickly – well before the 90-day limit – Huber was able to get her charges reversed. Huber said that from now on she would call a company to switch her service, not do it when someone calls her.[9]

Domain Slamming

Domain slamming is borrowed from an aggressive tactic used by phone carriers to persuade subscribers to transfer their service without realizing they are doing so. If you click through the links that are provided in the email you've received, it will give you a one button choice to change domain registrars. The wording deceptively makes it seem like this is required or advised. You will of course be billed for the new and unneeded registration. Consider the following email:

- "From: "Domain Registry of America" <info@transfer-approval.com>Subject: Domain transfer Request for

CCRH.ORG
Date: Mon, 03 Mar 2003 11:03:11 -0800
Dear customer,
You are receiving this notice because you are listed as one of the contacts for the domain name CCRH.ORG. We have received a transfer request to move this domain to Domain Registry of America from a different registrar. Please click on the following URL link and let us know if you approve OR disapprove this domain transfer: PLEASE NOTE: if the link below is broken you will need to copy and paste everything between < > into your browser <http://www.transfer-approval.com/universal.asp?id=XXXXXX>. The deadline for responding to this request is: Mar 09, 2003. Thank you for your time and attention regarding this matter. If you have any questions please reply to this email.
Sincerely,
Domain Registry of America"[10]

TIPS TO PROTECT YOURSELF

Area Codes. Use caution if you don't recognize the area code of a telephone number you are about to dial, such as **888** or **900** numbers. Check your phone book for the list of area codes to find out where the number is. If you make the call, hang up if the message on the other end sounds suspicious. Be especially wary of following instructions to "enter activation code numbers" or answering "yes" to questions that might unwittingly result in authorizing unwanted services.[1,8]

Awareness. Be aware that your local telephone company may bill for services provided by other companies. Your local phone bill may include charges for long distance telephone calls, information or entertainment services accessed through 900 numbers, club memberships, and non-basic telecommunications services like voice mail or paging.[4]

Bill. Carefully read your telephone bill every month to make sure you have the services you originally signed up for and are being billed only for those services. Many consumers don't catch the charges until they've overpaid for services, often months later.[1]

Domain Name. Be suspicious of any request you get about switching your domain name. If in doubt, call your Web hosting company and check out the honesty of the request.

Fine Print. Read all the fine print on any contest form, coupon, email, or website offer before you fill it out and sign it. Some long-distance carriers may use these offers as a way to get you to switch service.[1]

Freeze your Service. Consider having your local telephone company "freeze" your long-distance service, which prevents anyone but you from switching or adding onto your existing carrier.[1]

Your Rights

Up to 30 Days. You do not have to pay anyone for service up to 30 days after being slammed. This means you do not have to pay either your authorized telephone company (the company you actually chose to provide service) or the slamming company.[1]

Beyond 30 Days. You must pay any charges for service beyond 30 days to your authorized company, but at that company's rates, not the slammer's rates.[1]

Valid Charges. If upon investigation the reported unauthorized company charges are found valid, you may be liable for unpaid charges and will be re-billed for unpaid charges.[1]

Invalid Charges. If a state commission or the FCC makes a finding that a slam has occurred, the slamming company must pay your authorized company 150 percent of the charges it received from you. Upon receipt of the money, your authorized company will then reimburse you 50 percent of the charges you paid to the slammer. For example, if you were charged $100 by the slamming company, that company will have to give your authorized company $150, and you will receive $50 as a reimbursement.[11]

References

1. Hedding, Judy, Avoid slamming and cramming fraud, Slamming and cramming scams, About.com, http://phoenix.about.com/od/scam1/a/slamming.htm.
2. Milhorn, H. Thomas, Cybercrime, In Crime: Computer Viruses to Twin Towers, Universal Publishers, Boca Raton, 2005, Pp 46-70.
3. Telephone scams, http://aatld.com/scams.htm.
4. Cramming Scams, Schemes, Scams, Fraud, www.crimes-of-persuasion.com.

5. Keller, Judy, Feds crack down on Miss Cleo, Eonline, www.eonline. com/News/Items/0,1,10849,00.html, November 15, 2002.
6. FTC Creates a Consumer Hotline to Assist Victims of Alleged Epixtar Web Cramming Scam, Federal Trade Commission, www.ftc.gov/opa/2004/01/epixtar.htm, January, 15, 2004.
7. Sieberg, Daniel, FTC exposes top 10 web scams, CNN.com, www.cnn.com/2000/TECH/computing/10/31/ftc.web.scams, October 31, 2000.
8. Phone cramming and slamming scams, The San Diego Better Business Bureau, www.sandiego.bbb.org/alerts/phonescams.html.
9. Dukart, Todd, Quest warns customers of 'slamming' scam, KOBTV.com, http://kobtv.com/index.cfm?viewer=storyviewer&id= 20184&cat=CONSUMER, July 2, 2005.
10. Gregory, Mark A., Domain slamming scam, www.lists.pdx.edu/netmgrs/current/0040.html, March 3, 2003.
11. Slamming and cramming, Southeast Telephone, www.southeast telephone.com/customer_care/telephone_information/slamming.php.

Chapter 8

Credit Card Fraud

Credit card fraud is the unauthorized and illegal use of a credit card to purchase goods or services or the adding of charges to a card for goods or services not received. The latter is known as *credit card cramming.* The definition of credit card fraud can be expanded to include bogus credit card offers and fraudulent credit card protection scams.

Credit card scams have been around since the advent of credit cards, but the Internet and email have allowed these scams to reach a far greater audience and potentially cause even more damage than in the past. Some of these credit card scams have two goals: (1) to obtain valid credit card numbers and (2) to harvest email addresses for future spam and scam purposes. In the case of fraud, if a consumer claims he did not make a purchase, the charge may not be paid by the credit card company and the online merchant suffers the loss.[1]

EXAMPLES OF CREDIT CARD FRAUD

Credit Card Cramming

Credit Card Cramming is billing card owners for unauthorized purchases. Because the charges are often small, they may go unnoticed for months at a time. The account to which charges are made just as easily could be a debit card or possibly even a checking account.[2]

- **Proof of Age.** The owners and operators of playgirl.com, highsociety.com, and scores of other adult entertainment websites were charged by the FTC with illegally billing consumers for services that were advertised as "free," and billing other consumers who never visited the websites at all. The "free tour" websites claimed that consumers' credit card numbers were required solely to prove that they were of legal age to view the adult material, and that the credit cards would not be billed. Consumers complained, however, that their cards were billed despite the representations. Thousands of consumers were charged recurring monthly membership fees ranging from $20 to $90, the complaint alleged. Consumers who tried to dispute the charges were met with a variety of barriers designed by the defendants to thwart their efforts. According to the complaint, the defendants used billing names different than the names of the websites so consumers often had no idea who was billing them or why. The defendants were required to pay $30 million to settle the charges.[3]

- **Website Crammer.** In Minnesota, a U.S. District Court halted the operation of a website hosting company. The suit named Bryan Kruchten who was doing business as Page Creators and Trinity Host, L.L.C. The defendants were accused of using the Internet to advertise discount Web hosting services (such as domain name registration, webpage design, and technical support) for monthly service fees of $10 to $15. Consumers provided credit card numbers so they could be billed. Without their knowledge or approval the defendants were said to have charged many of their customers huge additional fees, in amounts sometimes as large as $20,000, for such things as excess bandwidth use. Computer server logs showed that the customers did not actually use anywhere near the amount of bandwidth for which they were billed. In fact, the defendants were said to have charged excess bandwidth fees to consumers who had not yet constructed their websites, to consumers who had already canceled their services, and to consumers who had signed up to receive unlimited bandwidth. In some cases the defendants billed individual customers for allegedly using more bandwidth than all their customers combined. The court order halted the illegal billing, froze the defendants' assets, and appointed a receiver to oversee the business pending trial.[4]

Other Types of Credit Card Fraud

Credit Card Creation

Criminals go online and download "credit card account generators" to create counterfeit cards. Anyone can download these generators. The programs are derived from the Luhn formula—the same formula credit card companies use to generate 13 to 16 digit card numbers. From just one legitimate credit card number these account generators can produce as many as 999 usable numbers.[5]

Emails

Criminals use spam emails to obtain credit card numbers from unsuspecting victims. A typical email might state that a relatively large amount of money has been charged to your credit card. It then asks for either verification or denial of the charge. If the charge is denied, the email requests your credit card number.[6]

Site Cloning

Criminals set up websites that are identical to online merchant sites so that shoppers believe they are giving their credit card information to a legitimate company when they order merchandise. Often times these sites even send a confirmation email to make you feel your order was filled.[1]

Triangulation

In a process known as *triangulation* a fraudster sets up a website offering merchandise that will be shipped before payment must be made, but a credit card number is required. The fraudster then orders the specific merchandise from a legitimate entity using a false credit card number and uses your card number to purchase other goods to perpetuate the fraud.[1]

Spyware

A hacker "breaks into" your computer and plants software known as a keystroke logger that captures information you type using the keyboard. When you order something online, your credit card number is stolen and used to purchase other items. Keystroke loggers are discussed in Chapter 35.

- **Turned the Tables.** In Scotland, a schoolgirl named Danielle Athi managed to turn the tables on a criminal who had stolen her father's credit card details. She helped the police track down a teenaged computer criminal who had plundered an estimated £2,000 through Internet-related credit card fraud. The police had been searching for months to identify "Gafferboy," whose stock in trade was breaking into computers and stealing confidential details. Gafferboy and Danielle, then 12, first made contact in August 2000. The pair exchanged emails before he sent her a photograph of himself. The email contained a Trojan horse, which compromised the Athi family's home computer. A month later, Danielle's father, Ravi, was shocked when he received a bank statement containing a number of fraudulent transactions. Gafferboy had searched through the computer, found Mr. Athi's credit card details, and used them to make 15 different transactions, mainly in the United States. In 2001 Gafferboy began flirting with Danielle again. This time she set a trap. She sent him a quiz saying she wanted to get to know him better. Her questions included asking him his favorite color, his favorite pop group, and then his name. Gafferboy replied back with a full list of answers—even volunteering his mobile phone number and his name—Andrew Edgar. Danielle passed this information on to the police who were able to track him down. Edgar was arrested in June 2001, and his computer, which provided evidence of his crimes, seized. Using stolen credit card information, Edgar had set up a website, hackersonline.net, containing tips for fellow criminals and stolen details of 60 credit card accounts. Edgar, then 18, pleaded guilty to seven charges of Internet fraud. Three of the charges related to fraudulent transactions that ran up on Ravi Athi's credit card account. A first offender, Edgar was sentenced to 100 hours of community service.[7]

Stolen Credit Card Information

Individuals with no hacking skills have the ability to physically steal credit card information from banks, credit unions, and so forth.

- In Sacramento, California, Curtis Lawrence Luckey, 26, unlawfully obtained credit card information from a credit union employee. Luckey admitted to masterminding a scheme to defraud Priceline.com, Southwest Airlines, the Hotel Reservations Network, a credit union, and the credit union's credit card holders by making fraudulent Internet credit card purchases for hotel and airline reservations that totaled more than $116,000. Luckey was sentenced to 27 months in prison. He also was ordered to pay restitution in the amount of $116,869.30 and serve a three-year term of supervised release following his incarceration.[8]

Bogus Credit Card Offers

You get an email that states:

- *"YOU ARE APPROVED* FOR A PREMIER CREDIT CARD $2500.00 Immediate Line of Credit - Guaranteed!!! Get sponsorship for your very own Master Card – Regardless of your credit situation!!
  YOU ARE APPROVED - YOU CANNOT BE TURNED DOWN!!
  Call xxx xxx-xxxx"[9]

You respond to the ad by calling the telephone number listed. The "sales person" continues to claim that you have been approved to receive a credit card and a $2,500 line of credit regardless of your credit history. You are asked to pay a $149.95 fee for the credit card. You pay the money and finally receive a package, but you don't receive a major credit card in the package. Instead, you receive a mail-order catalog together with a charge card, good only for ordering items from the catalog. You are informed that you will receive an application for a major credit card only if you first purchase $400 worth of merchandise from the catalog. The $2,500 line of credit, calculated at extremely high rates of interest, applies only to items purchased from their catalogue, and the card cannot be used in ATM machines. After you've ordered and paid for grossly overpriced, low quality merchandise from the catalogue you find out that the sponsorship for a major bank card consists only of a form to request a regular application for a VISA or MasterCard, which you must send to a bank along with the good credit history that banks require.

In an alternative scheme, the phone number listed in the email is a 900 number so that when you make the call, unknowing to you, you are charged an exorbitant amount per minute which appears on your next telephone bill.[9]

Credit Card Protection

All credit card protection plans are fraudulent. These people are trying to exploit your ignorance of the law. Under federal law $50 is the maximum you would have to pay on bogus credit card charges, provided you report the charges within 60 days. The fine print of credit card protection plans usually offers to report the misuse of your card and then states the federal law. If a dispute over credit card charges doesn't work out in your favor, don't expect the protection plan to pay the charges. It won't.[10]

In another type of credit card protection fraud, seniors have been targeted and told that their credit information is posted on the Internet and that for a fee they can get it removed. Of course they have to have your credit card number so they can charge you the fee.

- **Information on the Internet.** The Better Business Bureau warned about a company known as R & R Financials which appeared to be targeting senior citizens, claiming that their credit card information was on the Internet and that the company would be able to take it off for a fee. The company asked for credit card numbers and expiration dates to do so.

Consumers were supposed to receive a packet explaining how it was done. In reality, victims were charged $289.00 for a book, which, although it did have useful information in it, also warned consumers to beware of companies that were doing the very thing that R & R Financials was doing. When consumers called the company they were prompted through a series of selections, but callers reported they were never able to actually talk to a live person. Some consumers reported the company was identifying itself as being with a government agency.[11]

TIPS TO PROTECT YOURSELF

Apply Directly. Apply for credit cards directly from the issuers. It isn't necessary to pay another company to help you get a credit card, nor will it improve your chances of obtaining one.[12]

Bad Credit. Don't fall for promises that you'll get a credit card even if you have bad credit. Fraudulent credit card offers often target people who are having credit problems and haven't been able to get cards elsewhere. If your credit history is bad, your best bet is to get a "secured" credit card. This requires you to place a deposit in an account at the issuing bank equal to your credit limit. If you don't pay your credit card bill, the bank will use your deposit to cover it. It's a good way to start rebuilding your credit.[12]

Bills. Check your credit card bills carefully as soon as you receive them, or more often if you can do so online. Follow the instructions on your bill for questioning or disputing charges. Make copies of any forms or letters that you send your credit card issuer about the dispute, and be sure to pay the rest of your bill on time.[13]

Card Color. Sometimes fraudulent credit card offers promise "gold" or "silver" cards from major card issuers. What you receive – if you get anything at all—is a gold or silver-colored charge card that can only be used to buy overpriced goods from the company's own catalogue.[12]

Emails. Be cautious of emails offering to get you a credit card. Many unsolicited emails are fraudulent. It's best to just delete them.[12]

Extra Protection. Your credit card issuer may offer extra protection for free. If you're not sure what your issuer's policy is, ask.[13]

Imposters. Watch out for imposters. Someone may claim to be connected with your credit card issuer and ask to "verify" your account number to make sure you're protected. Your real credit card issuer doesn't need your account number; it already has it.[13]

Rights. Know your rights. Under federal law, you're not responsible for any charges if you report your card missing before someone else has used it, and you are not liable for more than $50 if it has been used, as long as you report the problem promptly, usually within 60 days.[13]

Upfront Payment. Legitimate credit card issuers don't usually ask for a fee upfront. If there is an application or processing fee, it should be very small, not the hundreds of dollars that con artists request.[12]

References

1. Connelly, Jennifer, Colleen O'Reilly, and Darin Beffa, Credit card fraud online, www.pubpol.duke.edu/centers/dewitt/course/internet/fraud/ccfraud.html.

2. Consumer Alert: Watch Out for Credit Card Cramming, http://cageyconsumer.com/credcram.html, March 9, 1999.

3. Playgirl.com Operators to Pay $30 Million to Settle FTC Charges, Federal Trade Commission, www.ftc.gov/opa/2001/11/crescentstlmt.htm, November 5, 2001.

4. FTC Halts Web Crammer, Federal Trade Commission, www.ftc.gov/opa/2001/04/page.htm, April 3, 2001.

5. How do they do it?, Ziff Davis Smart Business, www.findarticles.com/p/articles/mi_zdzsb/is_200104/ai_ziff8453, April 2001.

6. Email credit card scams, About.com, http://antivirus.about.com/od/emailscams/l/blccscams.htm.

7. Leyden, John, Schoolgirl turns tables on email credit card fraudster, www.theregister.co.uk/2003/02/20/schoolgirl_turns_tables_on_emai l, February 20, 2003.

8. Twenty-Seven Month Sentence In Internet Fraud Scheme To Defraud Priceline.Com And Others Seventh Conviction Concerning Fraudulent Disclosure and Use, U.S. Department of Justice, United States Attorney, Eastern District of California, www.cybercrime.gov/LuckeySent.htm, May 17, 2002.

9. Fraudulent and Misleading Credit Card Offer Scams, Schemes, scams, frauds, crimes-of-persuasion.com, www.crimes-of-persuasion.com/Crimes/Telemarketing/Inbound/MinorIn/MoneyPro

bs/card_offers.htm.
10. Thomes, James T., Dotcons: Con Games, Fraud, and Deceit on the Internet, Writers Club Press, New York, 2000.
11. Campbell, Nan, South Plains senior citizens targeted by credit card protection scam, Better Business Bureau, Lubbock, Texas, www.lubbock.bbb.org/newsrelease.html?newsid=13&newstype=1, April 11, 2001.
12. Bogus credit card offers, National Consumer League's Internet Fraud Watch, www.fraud.org/tips/internet/boguscredit.htm.
13. Credit card loss protection, National Consumer League's Internet Fraud Watch, www.fraud.org/tips/internet/protection.htm.

Chapter 9

Credit Repair Scams

Your credit is shot, and you haven't been able to make any payments on your cards in over a year. Then you receive an email promising that the sender can repair your credit, so you jump at the opportunity. Problem solved? Don't count on it.[1]

Credit repair scams have been around for years. Thousands of people fall victim to these rip-offs each year. The Internet is the latest tool used by phony credit repair companies to target unsuspecting consumers.[2]

Emails state things like: "Repair your credit rating— guaranteed!" or "Remove bad information from your credit file— immediately and forever!" For a fee, they claim to be able to clean up your credit report, which, in turn, will allow you to be able to get a loan, whether it's for a car, a home, or anything else.[3]

The "Credit Repair Organizations Act" prohibits making false claims about credit repair. It makes it a crime for companies to collect credit repair fees from an individual prior to services being rendered. And it requires that these companies inform you about your legal rights and requires that a credit repair company provide information about these rights in a written contract.[4]

No one can erase negative information from your credit record if it's accurate. Only incorrect information can be removed. Accurate information stays on your record for seven years from the time it is reported (10 years for bankruptcy). Even information about bills you fell behind on but now are paid will remain on your report for this time period. However, you can correct mistakes on your credit report yourself. To do so follow the instructions provided by the credit bureaus. The major credit bureaus are Equifax (www.equifax.com), Experian (www.experian.com), and TransUnion (www.transunion.com). Contact all three, as the information each has may vary.[5]

The FTC has jurisdiction over credit repair organizations located inside the USA. They are highly regulated and will be prosecuted for cheating the public. To get around the FTC's jurisdiction, many criminals operate credit repair websites and sell credit repair information or services from outside the United States. If you are cheated by one of these companies, there is nothing the FTC or your state attorney general's office can do to help you get your money back.[6]

EXAMPLES OF CREDIT REPAIR SCAMS

Advance Fee

- Enrique Sanchez and his wife had some issues that he wanted to clear up on his credit report. So he and his wife paid $500 upfront to enlist the help of Credit Connection—$250 for each of them. They waited for several months, but didn't get any reports about their credit having been repaired. After six months of calling Credit Connection, Sanchez finally received a credit report, but nothing had been cleared up. When he tried to complain to the company he discovered that it no longer existed.[7]

Claim Information is False

Once you sign up for the service the scammers send letters to the various credit reporting agencies stating that all the negative information on your credit report is false. The credit reporting agencies generally remove the negative information while investigating the claim. You are shown your cleaned-up report and believe your credit history has been fixed. However, once the credit reporting agencies discover that the negative information is correct, it is placed back on your credit report. And many credit repair services that claim to be nonprofit charge hefty fees and cause more debt problems.[1,8]

File Segregation

Another technique used by fraudulent credit repair companies is called "file segregation." Those who have filed bankruptcy are the most frequent target of this scam. It promises to hide unfavorable credit details and information by creating a new credit identity. You are advised to apply for an IRS Employer Identification Number (EIN), which has the same number of digits as a Social Security number. You are then told to provide the EIN as your Social Security number when applying for credit. Because the new number isn't linked to your old credit report, that report and any negative information it contains won't show on a credit check. What the credit repair company doesn't tell you is that anyone who has two identification numbers and uses them simultaneously is committing a felony under federal law and could end up facing fines and jail time.[4,9]

- In the U.S. District Court in Odessa, Texas, the FTC settled charges with Clifton W. Cross who was the operator of a website that sold credit repair advice and promised "perfect credit instantly." Cross allegedly sold instructions about how consumers could substitute federally-issued, nine-digit Employer Identification numbers for Social Security numbers and use them illegally to build new credit profiles that would allow them to get credit they might otherwise be denied based on their credit histories. The settlement bared future deceptive claims about file segregation (including claims that it is legal) and prohibited Cross from using or selling his customer lists. Cross was sentenced to 49 months in federal prison and ordered to pay nearly $171,000 in restitution.[10]

Attorneys and Accountants

Many attorneys and accountants have come to the realization that they can make some quick, easy money offering credit repair services. Usually, their marketing literature falsely leads one to believe that they have specialized skills, training, or knowledge to perform credit repair. Be aware that if you pay an attorney or accountant to do your credit repair work, he will spend a few minutes filling out some paperwork, or an assistant will actually fill out the paperwork, and you will be billed hundreds of dollars for work you could easily and quickly have done yourself. Although this may be deceptive, it is not illegal.[6]

TIPS TO PROTECT YOURSELF

Advance Fee. Be careful of any company that wants money upfront to repair your credit. Credit repair scams are infamous for taking money upfront and disappearing with it. By law, credit repair companies can only require you to pay for services after they have been received. A similar scam is to require you to pay a specific amount each month until your credit is improved. You can be sure the service is going to stretch out the process as long as possible to collect as much as they can from you.[4,6]

Blanket Dispute. Avoid anyone who recommends that you dispute all information contained in your credit report, not just items that might be incorrect.[4,6]

Don't Contact. Be leery of anyone who offers to repair your credit but suggests that you don't contact a credit bureau directly.[4,6]

EIN. Remember that creating a new credit identity by obtaining an Employer Identification Number from the IRS is illegal.[4,6]

Emails. In general, be leery of any email offering to repair your credit. They almost always will be promoting fraudulent activity. It is best simply to delete them.[4,6]

Guarantee. Anyone who guarantees that he or she can repair your credit should be viewed with a skeptical eye. No one, not even you, can eliminate truthful information contained in a credit report. [Credit3]

Legal Rights Avoid anyone who doesn't inform you that if your credit report is in error you can get it repaired on your own or who doesn't advise you of your legal rights and the laws that protect you.[4,6]

Special Software. Avoid anyone who claims that his or her software can delete negative information from your credit report.

This is, of course, blatantly false.[4,6]

References

1. FTC exposes top 10 Web scams, CNN .Com, Mob accused of $200 million phone fraud, New York Times, February 11, 2004.
2. Brown, Ann, Battling online credit repair scams - Brief Article, FindArticles.com, http://findarticles.com/p/articles/mi_m1365/is_4_30/ai_573887 14, November 1999.
3. Fisher, Jeanette Joy, Free Credit Repair Advice: How to Spot a Credit Repair Scam, Enzine Articles, http://ezinearticles.com/?Free-Credit-Repair-Advice:-How-to-Spot-a-Credit-Repair-Scam&id=110409.
4. Credit Report Repair, Credit repair scams, CreditReportRepair. net, www.creditreportrepair.net/credit_repair_scams.html.
5. Credit Repair, Internet Fraud Tips, National Consumer League's Internet Fraud Watch, www.fraud.org/ tips/internet/creditrepair.htm.
6. Credit Repair Scams, BCSAlliance.com, www.bcsalliance.com/ z_creditrepairscams~ns4.html.
7. Credit repair scam, Local News 9, www.ktsm.com/story_news.sstg?c=1494, January 23, 3006.
8. Milhorn, H. Thomas, Cybercrime, In Crime: Computer Viruses to Twin Towers, Universal Publishers, Boca Raton, 2005, Pp 46-70.
9. Jimenez, Daniel, Credit repair scams, BankRate.com, www. bankrate.com/brm/news/advice/19980720c.asp, April 9, 2003.
10. FTC settles with alleged credit repair scammer, DirectMag.com, w.directmag.com/news/marketing_ftc_settles_alleged/index.ht ml, June 22, 2001.

Chapter 10
Cyberbullying

Bullying is defined as the tendency for some children to frequently oppress, harass, or intimidate other children—verbally, physically, or both. It occurs in and out of school. Cyberspace has created a whole new world of social communications for young people who use email, websites, instant messaging, chat rooms, and text messaging to stay in touch with friends and make new ones. While most interactions are positive, increasingly young people are using these communication tools to antagonize and intimidate others. They say things online they would never say face-to-face because online they feel removed from the person at the receiving end. Such activity has become known as *cyberbullying*.[1]

Cyberbullying is a form of harassment that is limited to problems between school-age children. Cyber-harassment and a special form of cyber-harassment, cyberstalking, involving adults are discussed in Chapter 12.

The point of cyberbullying is to humiliate, threaten, and terrify other students. Because bullies tend to harass their victims away from the watchful eyes of adults, the Internet is the perfect tool for reaching others anonymously. This means that for many young students home is no longer a refuge from the cruel peer pressures of school. Nearly 60 percent of students who have been bullied don't tell their parents or another adult.[1,2]

TOOLS OF THE CYBERBULLY

There are several tools the cyberbully uses to harass other young people online. These include:

Emails. Some students send emails or instant messages containing cruel, vicious, and sometimes threatening insults. Another version of this is breaking into a person's email account, pretending to be the account owner, and sending vicious or embarrassing material from the account to others.[1,3,4,5]

School Bulletin Boards. Some students spam an online school bulletin board with name-calling posts that spread vicious rumors about a student.[1,4,5]

Websites. Some students create websites that have cruel stories, cartoons, pictures, and jokes ridiculing another.[1,4]

Pictures. Some students take an unflattering picture of a person in the locker room using a digital phone camera and email that picture to others within minutes. The perpetrator might ask other students to send vicious comments about the person in the picture. This has been carried a step further—posting doctored pornographic pictures with the original person's head replaced with the student's.[1,4,5]

Instant Messaging. Some students steal a person's password and instant messages another student's close friend, pretending to be the one the password is stolen from. The one who initiated the instant messaging then asks personal questions. Once the questions are answered confidentially the perpetrator then posts the answers online or emails them to classmates.[1,4,5]

Text Messaging. An increasing number of children are being bullied by text messages through their cell phones.[1,4,5]

Depending on the state, a person guilty of cyberbullying can be charged with cyberstalking, which is a relative felony; that is, a judge can decide if it is a misdemeanor or a felony crime. It's punishable with a $2,000 fine or one-year imprisonment.[6]

EXAMPLES OF CYBERBULLYING

- **Love Spurned.** When Chad, a seventh grader, found out his old girlfriend was saying bad things about his new girlfriend, he headed straight for the computer and sent instant messages to an extensive buddy list threatening to kill his old girlfriend. Several friends became alarmed and told their parents, who called the school. The school, in turn, contacted the police. Ultimately, Chad was banished to another middle school and had to go to juvenile court where a judge sentenced him to 25 hours of community service.[7]

- **Attack on Sexuality.** In Louisiana, three Loranger High School students were arrested for cyberbullying. The situation started when a 15-year-old female student created a website called "Loranger'sBiggestQueer.com." The website featured pictures of a 14-year-old male student. He responded with his own website, which investigators said included a list of students and graphically violent poems that were said to have crossed the line. After seeing the boy's website, a concerned parent alerted the sheriff's office. Authorities confiscated the students' computers. Both students were arrested, as well as 18-year old Joseph Sanchez who was charged with contributing to the delinquency of a minor. Authorities said Sanchez had helped the younger male set up and maintain his website. The school system considered whether to expel the three students for the remainder of the year. All of the students were honor students.[6]

- **Overweight.** Greg (not real name), an obese high school student, was changing in the locker room after gym class. Matt took a covert picture of him with his cell phone camera. Within seconds, he sent it by email to classmates. Soon the picture was flying around to cell phones at school. By the time Greg left the locker room, all the students were laughing at him.[8]

- **Make Fun of Dave.** David Knight's life at school was hell. He was teased, taunted, and punched for years. Then someone set up an abusive website about him. On the website David discovered a photo of him and the words "Welcome to the website that makes fun of Dave Knight." There were pages of hateful comments directed at him and everyone in his family. The website creator asked others to join in, and they did— posting lewd, sexual comments. David was accused of being a pedophile and using a date rape drug on little boys. There were nasty emails too. One said "You're gay, don't ever talk to me again, no one likes you, you're immature and dirty, go wash your face." When David's parents learned of the website, they tried to find out who was behind it so they could have it removed, but the site stayed up. Finally, his mother contacted Yahoo, which was the website host. It took seven months of emails, phone calls, and, the family thinks, the threat of legal action before the website was finally removed.[9]

TIPS TO PROTECT YOURSELF

Contact Information. To prevent some forms of cyberbullying you should guard your contact information. Don't give people you don't know your instant messaging name or email address.[1]

Complaint. Cyberbullying is a violation of the "Terms of Use" of most Internet service providers and cell phone companies. File a complaint by providing the harmful messages or a link to the harmful material and ask that the account be terminated and any harmful material removed. If the material appears on a third-party website or a website with its own domain name, go to the host company's website and file a complaint.

Block. Block or filter all further communications through email and instant messaging contact lists. Avoid going to the site or group where you are being attacked. Change your email address, account, and user name if need be.[8]

Parents. Involve your parents. They can send the cyberbully's parents a letter that includes the downloaded material and request that the cyberbullying stop and all harmful material be removed.

Police. If the bullying rises to the level of criminality it should be reported to the Police. The bullying is definitely criminal if it involves any of the following:

- Encouraging or suggesting that a person kill himself or threatening to harm a person, a person's property, a person's pet, or anybody else.
- Posting private information, such as names, addresses, phone numbers, or email addresses in a public forum, chat room, or on a website when a reasonable person would know that doing

so would put the target at risk or open him or her up to new harassment.

- Repeated or excessive bullying with or without threats of harm.
- Threatening to commit a crime.[3]

School Officials. Involve school officials. If the cyberbully is a student at your child's school, meet with school officials and ask for help in resolving the situation.[8]

Tell an Adult. The target should tell an adult he trusts—a teacher, parent, older sibling, or grandparent. Ask for advice.[8]

Tell the Cyberbully to Stop. The target should send one and only one non-emotional, assertive message to the cyberbully telling him or her to stop.[8]

Review. You should review "Keep an Eye on Your Children" in Chapter 1. That section gives some guidelines that might help keep your children out of trouble, or at least help you, as a parent, keep up with what's going on online with them.

Attorney. If all else fails, contact an attorney. An attorney can send a letter to the cyberbully's parents. Often this will resolve the problem.[8]

References

1. Challenging Cyber Bullying, Web Aware, www.bewebaware.ca/english/CyberBullying.aspx.
2. 'Cyber bullying' on the rise, say experts, ABC News, http://abcnews.go.com/GMA/story?id=395270, January 8, 2005.
3. Hardcastle, Mike, Teen advice on Cyber Bullies, About.com, http://teenadvice.about.com/od/schoolviolence/a/cyberbullying1_3.htm.
4. Mobilizing educators, parents, students, and others to combat online social cruelty, Cyberbullying, http://cyberbully.org.
5. Standing Committee on Social Development Second Report of the Third Session Sixty-second General Assembly Cyberbullying and Violence Prevention Initiatives Among Youth, April 7, 2006.
6. Students arrested for cyberbullying, WAFB, www.wafb.com/global/story.asp?s=2774728.
7. Lisante, Joan E., Cyber bullying: No muscle needed, Connect for Kids, www.connectforkids.org/node/3116, June 6, 2005.
8. Willard, Nancy, An Educator's Guide to Cyberbullying and

Cyberthreats, Center for Safe and Responsible Use of the Internet, 2005.
9. Leishman, Joan, Cyber-bullying, www.cbc.ca/news/background/ bullying/ cyber_bullying.html, CBC News, October 2, 2002.

Chapter 11

Cyberextortion

Cyberextortion is a criminal offense which occurs when a person uses the Internet to demand money or other goods or behavior (such as sex) from another person by threatening to inflict harm to the person, the person's reputation, or the person's property.[1] Malicious software that is secretly downloaded to a user's computer that then holds that person's files hostage until a ransom is paid has become known as *ransomware.*

EXAMPLES OF CYBEREXTORTION

Online extortionists have been known to demand a number of things, including credit card details, money, sex, and the purchase of drugs.

Credit Card Details

Threat to Send Child Porn. Spam sent by a group called Shadowcrew claimed that potential victims were going to receive child pornography in the mail and that their credit cards would be billed unless they cancelled the order by sending credit card details to the group. The scammers relied on the automatic revulsion most people feel about child pornography, which would cause them to cancel the fictitious order.

- "Subject: Child Porn Order.
  Nude boys under 16!!! Nude girls under 16!!!! Daddy and
  daughter!!! We have it all!!! Your credit card will be billed at
  $22.95 weekly and a free 3-pack of child porn CD is being
  shipped to your billing address. To cancel, just email back full
  credit card details and the nasty subscription will go away."[2]

Money

Money by far is the most common thing demanded by
cyberextortionists.

- **Threat to Expose Flaws in Their Computer System.**
  Twenty-five-year-old Thomas E. Ray III from Jackson,
  Mississippi allegedly used the email name, Jamie Weathersby,
  in an attempt to extort $2.5 million from Best Buy Co., Inc. by
  threatening to expose flaws in the company's computer system.
  He was charged in a federal indictment with two felony
  extortion charges—extortion-threats to damage property or
  reputation and extortion-threats to damage computers. If
  convicted, Ray faced a maximum penalty of two years in
  prison and/or a $250,000 fine for extortion-threats to damage
  property or reputation and up to five years in prison and/or a
  $250,000 fine for extortion-threats to damage computers.[3]

- **Threat to Let Everyone Use Their Software Free.** In Florida,
  Michael Pitelis, 39, faced charges of attempted extortion of
  more than $1 million from a Waltham, Massachusetts computer
  company, Parametric Technology Corporation. He threatened
  to post data that would grant users access to the company's
  software without paying for it. The company is a developer of
  3D mechanical design software. Pitelis allegedly sent emails
  from a computer at a public library to top officials at the
  company.[4]

  Threat to Bring Down a Gambling Website. A *denial of
  service (DoS) attack* is an assault on a network, such as AOL,
  BellSouth, and Comcast, that floods the network with so many

additional emails that regular traffic is either slowed or completely interrupted. Unlike a virus or worm, which can cause severe damage, a denial of service attack simply interrupts network service for some period of time. When it's over, the network functions normally. A distributed denial of service attack (DDoS) uses multiple computers throughout the network that it previously has infected. The computers act as "zombies" and work together to send out bogus messages, thereby greatly increasing the amount of traffic flow.[5]

• Three ringleaders, ages 21, 22, and 24, of an extortion racket threatened to bring down British gambling websites with DDoS attacks unless a ransom demand for around £10,000 to £30,000 was paid. The three were arrested in St. Petersburg, Saratov, and Stavropol Russia. They faced charges of money laundering, blackmail, and extortion under Russian cybercrime laws. One UK betting firm was advised to pay the ransom to help the police establish a trail that went from the UK to the Caribbean, Latvia, and Russia. The men were arrested after police tracked the payment.[6]

Holding Files for Ransom. In an online attack, extortionists remotely encrypt user files. The attack occurs after a user visits a website containing code that exploits Microsoft's Internet Explorer to download and run a malicious program that, in turn, downloads an application that encrypts files on the victim's computer and network drives. The malicious program, Trojan.Pgpcoder, is a form of ransomware. It searches a victim's hard disk drive for 15 common file types, including images and Microsoft Office files. It then encrypts the files, removes the originals, and drops a ransom note asking $200 for the encryption key.[7]

Threatening Click Fraud. Click fraud is an illegal practice that occurs when individuals repeatedly click on website click-through advertisements to increase the payable number of click-throughs to the advertiser. The more clicks, the more the advertiser has to pay the website operator. The illegal clicks could either be performed by having a person manually click the advertising hyperlinks or by using automated software that is programmed to click the banner ads.[8]

- Michael Anthony Bradley, 32, of Oak Park, California was arrested and charged with attempting to defraud and extort money from Google by developing a software program that automated fraudulent "clicks" on "cost-per-click" advertisements utilized by Google. These fraudulent clicks, in turn, were designed to cause Google to make payments that were supposed to be made only for "clicks" made by legitimate Web surfers. Bradley allegedly stated that he would sell it to top spammers if Google did not pay him $100,000 and that Google thereby would lose millions. The maximum statutory penalty for each violation was 20 years imprisonment and a fine of $250,000. Bradley was released on a $50,000 appearance bond, and on the conditions that he refrain from using any computer or the Internet and avoid all contact with Google and its employees until his preliminary hearing.[9]

Sex

- **Threat to Destroy Reputations.** Robert Harvey Alexander was a pillar of his Florida community and a deacon in the First Baptist Church, but his secret hobby was assembling email addresses of high school and college students across the country. He targeted vulnerable young women, many of whom were at college and away from home for the first time, and threatened to destroy their reputations with online postings if they didn't engage in Internet sex conversation and telephone sex with him. To hide his identity, he logged in on computers at public libraries to send the emails to his targets. In one case, he told the girl if she didn't do what he demanded he would digitally alter a photograph of her face, paste it on a nude body, and post it on the Internet to ruin her reputation. After being arrested at a computer terminal in a public library he pleaded guilty to six counts of extortion. The U.S. District Judge ruled that the crimes were so morally reprehensible that the man deserved a longer sentence than the federal sentencing guidelines recommended. The 21-month sentence handed down was more than double the 10 months recommended by the sentencing guidelines.[10]

Purchase Drugs

- **Another Ransomware Problem.** Aaron Richardson stored everything on his computer, including pictures of his new puppy, his resume', Word documents, spreadsheets that had financial data, music files, and email. This practice made him the perfect target for ransomware. A hacker got into his computer and installed the software through an email attachment or an infected website. All his files seemed to disappear, and then a new file popped up showing a message that told him how to get his files back. The hacker demanded that he go to a pharmaceutical website in Russia and order some questionable pharmaceuticals.[11]

TIPS TO PROTECT YOURSELF

Tips to protect yourself and your computer against unwanted intrusion (and resulting cyberextortion) were given in chapter 1 under "Create a Virtual Shield." Be sure to report any attempt at cyberextortion to the proper authorities.

References

1. Milhorn, H. Thomas, Cybercrime, In Crime: Computer Viruses to Twin Towers, Universal Publishers, Boca Raton, 2005, Pp 46-70.
2. Iwan, Christine. Surfers beware. Internet spawns new age of scam, Battle Creek Inquirer, January 25, 2004.
3. Mississippi Man Indicted for Attempted Extortion of $2.5 Million from Best Buy Co., Inc., United States Department of Justice, www.cybercrime.gov/raylndict.htm, January 6, 2004.
4. Stone, Martin, Florida Man Faces Online Extortion Charges - Company Business and Marketing, Newsbyte News Network, www.findarticles.com/p/articles/mi_m0NEW/is_2000_August_24/ai _64528354, August 24, 2000.
5. Denial of Service Attack, Answer.com, www.answers.com/topic/ denial-of-service-attack.
6. Roberts, Paul, The Standard, UK, Russia break up online extortion ring, www.thestandard.com/article.php?story=2004072115524497,

July 21, 2004.

7. Evers, Joris, Trojans used for online extortion, http://news.zdnet.co. uk/ internet/security/0,39020375,39199958,00.htm, May 25, 2005

8. Olsen, Stephanie, Exposing click fraud, CNETtNews.com, http://news.com.com/Exposing+click+fraud/2100-1024_3-5273078.html, July 19, 2004.

9. Computer programmer arrested for extortion and mail fraud scheme targeting Google, Inc., U.S. Department of Justice, Northern District of California, www.usdoj.gov/criminal/cybercrime/bradleyArrest. htm, March 18, 2004.

10. Cyber-Extortion Results in Prison Sentence, Net4TV Voice, www.net4 tv.com/voice/story.cfm?storyid=2 931, October 8, 2000.

11. Earhardt, Ainsley, MySA.com, Hackers using ransomware to hold computer files hostage, www.mysanantonio.com/business/stories/ MYSA070706.ransomware.KENS.378654a3.html, July 7, 2005.

Chapter 12

Cyber-harassment and Cyberstalking

CYBER-HARASSMENT

Cyber-harassment includes unwanted behavior that demeans, threatens, or offends a victim and results in a hostile environment for him or her. The harassment can be sexual, racial, religious, or other. Cyber-harassers target their victims through chat rooms, message boards, discussion forums, and emails. The hostile environment can be created through persistent misbehavior or a single incident.

Cyberstalking is a special form of cyber-harassment which always consists of a series of events and never a single incident. Additionally, cyberstalking most often arises from interpersonal relationships, whereas cyber-harassment does not necessarily do so.

As discussed in Chapter 10, when the harassment is of a school-age individual by another school-age individual the behavior is referred to as cyberbullying.

Examples of Cyber-harassment

- **Death Threat**. Carl Edward Johnson, 49, of Bienfait, Saskatchewan, Canada was convicted on four felony counts of sending threatening email messages to federal judges and others. He anonymously posted a message on the Internet suggesting that specific sums of money would be paid for the deaths of a Federal Magistrate Judge in Tacoma, Washington and Treasury agents involved in another investigation. He also issued a death threat to several Judges of the United States Court of Appeals for the Ninth Circuit, again through an anonymous email message. His lawyer contended that the statements constituted free speech protected by the First Amendment. The judge disagreed and ruled that the messages were serious expressions of intention to do harm, and thus clearly over the line of protected speech. The retaliation and threatening communication counts each carried a maximum penalty of five years in prison. An obstruction of justice count carried a maximum penalty of 10 years in prison.[1]

- **Claimed She Was a Lesbian.** A high school assistant principal, Anna Draker, at Clark High School in San Antonio, Texas sued two 16-year-old students and their parents, alleging that the teens had set up a webpage on MySpace.com in her name and posted obscene comments and pictures. She claimed defamation, libel, negligence, and negligent supervision. Draker claimed the two students created the page using her name and picture and wrote it as though Draker herself had posted the information. The site falsely identified Draker as a lesbian. Draker, who is married and has small children, was said to have been devastated. MySpace.com removed the page when Draker told them it wasn't hers. The suite was for an unspecified amount for damages for emotional distress, mental anguish, lost wages, and court costs. One of the students also faced criminal felony charges involving retaliation and fraudulent use of identifying information. Both are third-degree felonies.[2]

CYBERSTALKING

The interpersonal relationships involved in cyberstalking include (1) an individual trying to leave a volatile domestic situation or ending a dating or intimate relationship, (2) an individual rejecting an intensely persistent admirer, or (3) a random acquaintance becoming obsessively fixated.

Cyberstalkers target their victims through chat rooms, message boards, discussion forums, and emails. Similar to stalking off-line, online stalking can be a terrifying experience for victims, placing them at risk of psychological trauma and possible physical harm. Many cyberstalking situations do evolve into off-line stalking and involve abusive and excessive phone calls, vandalism, threatening or obscene mail, trespassing, and physical assault.

The two common elements of stalking are: (1) repeated and unwanted behaviors whereby one individual attempts to contact another individual and (2) the behavior causes the second individual to feel threatened or to feel some sense of fear or dread. Most definitions do not require explicit threats of harm or violence, nor is there any requirement that the stalker intends to cause the victim to feel threatened. As with offline stalking, the majority of cyberstalkers are men and the majority of their victims are women, although there have been reported cases of women cyberstalking men and of same-sex cyberstalking.

In most cases, the cyberstalker and the victim had a prior relationship, and the cyberstalking begins when the victim attempts to break off the relationship. However, there also have been many instances of cyberstalking by strangers. Whereas a potential stalker may be unwilling or emotionally unable to confront a victim in person or on the phone, he or she may have little hesitation sending harassing or threatening Internet communications.

A cyberstalker may dupe other Internet users into harassing or threatening a victim by using Internet bulletin boards or chat rooms. For example, a stalker may post a message on a bulletin board under your name, phone number, or email address, resulting in subsequent responses being sent to you by strangers.[3]

EXAMPLES OF CYBERSTALKING

- **I Hope You Get Raped.** In Chicago, Angela Moubray loved to chat about wrestling and soap operas with others in an Internet chat room. Then one day a regular participant sent her a menacing email—and then another. Soon she was barraged with a stream of threats, such as "I hope you get raped." Over nearly two years she received unrelenting messages from a person whom she had never met in person, culminating in a missive that he would kill her, "and he meant it." Terrorized, she started carrying pepper spray and wouldn't go anywhere alone. Her father bought her a gun. After the perpetrator was visited one time by a policeman the cyberstalking ended.[4]

- **Solicited Her Rape.** In Los Angeles, a 50-year-old former security guard, Gary Steven Dellapenta, used the Internet to solicit the rape of a woman who rejected his advances. Dellapenta terrorized his 28-year-old victim by impersonating her in various Internet chat rooms and online bulletin boards, where he posted, along with her phone number, address, and instructions for disarming her home-security system, messages that she fantasized of being raped. On at least six occasions, sometimes in the middle of the night, men knocked on the woman's door saying they wanted to rape her. Dellapenta pleaded guilty to one count of stalking and three counts of solicitation of sexual assault. He faced up to six years in prison.[5]

- **Two 16-year-olds.** Jacksonville, Florida, police charged 16-year-old Racheal Zickafoose with two counts of cyberstalking. Zickafoose, who had split up with her husband, allegedly sent a harassing email, and then another, to the 16-year-old girl who started dating him after the break-up. In the email, Zickafoose was said to have threatened bodily harm. The victim reported it to the police who determined the IP (Internet Protocol) address of the computer from which the emails had been sent. From there it was an easy matter to determine Zickafoose's physical address by subpoena of the Internet company. Zickafoose was arrested, charged with a misdemeanor, and released on a $1,000 unsecured bond.[6]

- **Retaliation for Being Rebuffed.** In Macon County Georgia, Robert Dustin Carpenter, 20, was charged with misdemeanor cyberstalking for harassing a female acquaintance over the Internet. After being rebuffed several times by the victim, Carpenter was alleged to have repeatedly made harassing and obscene contacts with the victim over AOL Instant Messenger. If convicted on the class-two misdemeanor, Carpenter faced as much as six months in jail and/or a $500 fine.[7]

- **Talked to Him through the TV.** For more than a year WFLD-Channel 32 news anchor in Chicago, Tamron Hall, was bombarded with emails, phone messages, and letters from an Indiana fan who urged her to marry him. He sent her sexually explicit messages, and then became angry when she didn't respond. Eventually, Tonny Horne, 32, of South Bend, Indiana was arrested and indicted for cyberstalking Hall and trespassing on Fox property. He said Hall talked to him through the TV. Relatives said Horne had a history of mental illness. He was arrested when he showed up outside the Fox studios. A security guard recognized Horne as he was being taped for a man-on-the-street interview for "Fox News in the Morning." Hall was the host of the show. The guard, an off-duty Chicago police officer who was moonlighting as a security officer, had been given a photograph of Horne and told to keep an eye out for him.[8]

TIPS TO PROTECT YOURSELF

Anti-abuse Procedures. Learn what kind of anti-abuse procedures are in place in the chat-room community. IRC (Internet Relay Chat) channels usually have two or more operators around who have the power and authority to ban abusive users from the channel. If there is no operator on a channel, contact the IRCops of your IRC server. These names are given when you first sign onto the server.[3,9]

Change Email Address. If you are being continuously harassed you may want to consider changing your email address, Internet service provider, and even your home phone number. You should examine the possibility of using encryption software or privacy protection programs. You should learn how to use the filtering capabilities of email programs to block emails from certain addresses.[3,9]

Continued Harassment. If the harassment continues, you may wish to file a complaint with the stalker's Internet service provider, as well as with your own Internet service provider. Many Internet service providers offer tools that filter or block communications from specific individuals.[3,9]

Document. You may want to document how the stalking is affecting your life and what steps you have taken to stop the stalking.[3,9]

Don't Meet Face to Face. Under no circumstances should you agree to meet with the stalker face to face to work it out or talk. Meeting a stalker in person can be dangerous.[3]

File a Report. You may want to file a report with local law enforcement or contact the local prosecutor's office to see what charges, if any, can be pursued.[3,9]

Known Offender. If you know the offender you should send him or her a clearly written warning, stating that the contact is unwanted and asking the stalker to cease sending communications of any kind. You should do this only once. Then, no matter what the response, you should under no circumstances ever communicate with the stalker again.[3,9]

Passwords. Use nonsense passwords that have no relation to you as a person. In doing so, use a combination of numbers and uppercase and lowercase letters and even symbols, and make sure it is six or more characters long. Change your password frequently and never give it out. Try not to keep it written down. Avoid using the same password for multiple accounts.

Personal Information Websites. Check websites that provide information about people, like Four 11 and WhoWhere, to see what information is available about you. Ask that any entries about you be deleted or edit them to give only a P.O. Box as an address. You may want to visit one of the meta search engines (Dogpile, Metacrawler) and search for your name as well.[8]

Personal Information. When using the Internet be very careful to whom you give personal information and where you post such information.[3,9]

Save Evidence. You should save all evidence and document all contact made with the stalker. Save all email or other communications in both electronic and hard-copy form. Record the dates and times of any online contact with the stalker.[3,9]

Under Age 18. If you are under the age of 18 you should tell your parents or another adult you trust about any stalking or threats that occur online.[3,9]

User Names. Avoid user names that give away your sex. If you are a woman, you may want to avoid usernames that are obviously female. Your first initial and last name combine to make a good, easy-to-remember, and gender-neutral user name. This recommendation includes email, chat rooms, bulletin boards, and so forth [3,9]

References

1. Man convicted of threatening federal judges by Internet e-mail, U.S. Department of Justice, ,http://permanent.access.gpo.gov/lps9890/lps9890/www.usdoj.gov/criminal/cybercrime/johnson.htm, April 21, 1999.
2. Official sues students over myspace page, associated press, http://hosted.ap.org/dynamic/stories/m/myspace_principal?site=flta m&section=us, September 23, 2006.
3. Cyberstalking, The National Center for the Prevention of Crime, www.ncvc.org/ncvc/main.aspx?dbName=DocumentViewer&Document Action=ViewProperties&DocumentID=32458&UrlToReturn=http%3a %2f%2fwww.ncvc.org%2fncvc%2fmain.aspx%3fdbName%3dAdvanc edSearch#4.
4. Johnson, Dirk, and Hilary Shenfeld, E-mail: Before clicking 'send' ... , Newsweek, May 19, 2003.
5. 1999 report on cyberstalking: a new challenge for law enforcement and industry, www.usdoj.gov/criminal/cybercrime/cyberstalking. htm, U.S. Department of Justice, February 7, 2003.
6. Papandrea, Roselee, 'Net bullies taking toll among young, The Jacksonville Daily News, www.jdnews.com/SiteProcessor.cfm? Template =/GlobalTemplates/Details.cfm&StoryID=34602& Section=News, August 29, 2005.
7. Lewis, Michael, Man charged with cyberstalking, The Franklin Press, www.thefranklinpress.com/articles/2006/06/07/news/04news.txt, 2006.
8. Sadovi, Carlos, Indiana man charged with cyberstalking Ch. 32 anchor, Chicago Sun-Times, www.findarticles.com/p/articles/mi_qn4155/is_20030712/ai_n12514 423, July 12, 2005.
9. Hartman, Rachel R., Cyberstalking and Internet safety FAQ, Science Fiction and Fantasy Writers of America, Inc., www.sfwa.org/gateway/stalking.htm.

Chapter 13

Cyberhijacking

Cyberhijacking involves hackers who hijack (1) computers, (2) browsers, (3) webpages, (4) instant messaging and email, and (5) modems. Cyberhijacking software is part of malware, which also includes viruses, worms, Trojans, and spyware (discussed in Chapter 35). *Malware* is a contraction of *mal*icious so*ftware*.

EXAMPLES OF CYBERHIJACKING

Computer Hijacking

Bot, short for robot, is a generic term used to describe an automated process. Bots are used legitimately by search engines to crawl the World Wide Web and index websites and webpages by following the hyperlinks within the pages. They also are used in actions such as forwarding email and responding to newsgroup messages. When computers are hijacked they are turned into robots. Bots also are known as *spiders* and *crawlers*.[1]

Malicious bots spread themselves across the Internet searching for vulnerable, unprotected computers to infect. When they find an exposed computer, they quickly infect it, creating a *zombie computer*, and then report back to the botmaster. Bots stay hidden until they are awakened by their master to perform a task. Bots are so silent that sometimes the victims first learn of them when their Internet service provider tells them that their computer has been spamming other Internet users. Bots may be downloaded by a Trojan, installed by a malicious website, or emailed directly to a person from an already infected machine.

Each one of the zombie computers is controlled by a master computer called the *command and control server*. From this server, the cybercriminals instruct the army of zombie computers, known as a *botnet*, to do their bidding. A botnet is typically composed of a large number of victim computers that may stretch across the globe. Some botnets might have a few hundred to a couple thousand computers, but others have tens and even hundreds of thousands of zombies at their disposal.[2,3]

Pornographic Websites

- **Zombie Servers**. More than a thousand unsuspecting Internet users around the world had their computers hijacked by hackers who used them as zombie servers to send out pornographic websites. The hijacked computers, chosen by the hackers because they were linked by high-speed connections to the Internet, were secretly loaded with a software program that made them transmit explicit webpages that advertised pornographic sites and offered to sign up website visitors as customers. The program was invisible to the computer's owner. It did not harm the computer or interfere with its normal operation. The hackers operating the ring directed traffic to each hijacked computer in their network for only a few minutes at a time, quickly rotating through a large number of computers. Some of the computers also were used to send spam email messages to drum up traffic to the sites. By hiding behind a ring of machines the senders greatly reduced the possibility of being caught.[4]

Distributed Denial of Service Attacks

Because of the large numbers of computers involved, hackers are able to use bots to launch *distributed denial of service* (DDoS) attacks in which a multitude of compromised systems attack a single target. The flood of incoming email messages to the target system, such as an Internet service provider, essentially forces it to shut down, thereby denying service to the system by legitimate users.[3]

- **To Buy a BMW.** In California, James Ancheta, 20, was convicted of using a network of zombie computers to rake in tens of thousands of dollars and buy himself a BMW. He built and controlled a network of more than 400,000 zombie computers by using commands sent over Internet Relay Chat (IRC) to instruct the bot machines to infect other vulnerable computers and launch coordinated distributed denial of service (DDoS) attacks on behalf of customers who rented access to the botnet to distribute spam and pay-per-click adware. The FBI built a case against Ancheta that included reams of IRC and instant message exchanges between him and his customers and records of his efforts to keep his botnet operating by moving his IRC servers between various Internet hosting companies to avoid being shut down. He was sentenced to 57 months imprisonment, followed by three years of supervised release.[5]

Browser Hijacking

You want to read the news on the Internet—you see porn. You want to check the stock market on the Internet—you see porn. You want to check the weather report—you see porn. Your browser has been hijacked. Browser hijacking software is aggressive advertising software that is downloaded to your computer when you visit a website that contains the malicious software. It alters your browser settings without your knowledge. Collectively, browser hijacking software has become known as *hijackware*.[6,7]

Browser hijacking software typically (1) changes the browser's home page address so that when you click on your homepage icon you are directed to a website you had no intention of going to; (2) creates search bars, tool bars, desktop shortcuts, Favorites, and intermittent advertising popups; (3) causes an inability to navigate to certain webpages, such as anti-spyware and other security software sites; and (4) causes sluggish computer operation.[8]

Browser hijacking can do more than just annoy you. In one case a man claimed that a browser hijacker sent him to jail after compromising images of children were found on his work computer by an employer who then reported him to law enforcement authorities.[9]

Although there are a number of browser hijacking programs, CoolWebSearch is the most well know. It is used to redirect users to coolwebsearch.com and other sites affiliated with its operators. Variants of CoolWebSearch, including About:Blank, have increasingly gotten more difficult to get rid of. The problem is thought to be due to security holes in Internet Explorer. Microsoft has issued a patch in an attempt to solve the problem.[10]

- **Turned to the Virgin Mary for Help.** Maria DelGiorno, a 67-year-old grandmother, gave up. She unplugged her laptop and carefully placed it underneath a statue of the Virgin Mary. It was the only thing she could think of doing. According to her, the computer was filled with filthy things. Dozens of bookmarks for porn websites had appeared, and ads for porn were popping up every few minutes. Her homepage had been switched to a porn webpage. She was embarrassed by the fact that her grandchildren kept asking her why she was looking at so much pornography. DelGiorno's grandson retrieved the computer and examined it. With some help from a computer-savvy friend he discovered that a browser hijacking program called CoolWebSearch had turned his grandmother's computer into a XXX-rated adventure.[11]

Webpage Hijacking

Known as *pagejacking*, webpage hijacking is stealing content from a website and copying it into another website to siphon some of the original site's traffic to the copied webpage. The owners of websites that the users are diverted to are thereby able to earn money from advertising.

Pagejackers rely on search engines to spider the contents of the illegitimate site and index the results so that the copied site will appear in the search result rankings along with the original site's rankings. Internet users are diverted from material they want to view to other pages from which they can't escape without rebooting their computers. New browser windows, usually with porn content, pop up faster than they can be closed down. The sites often are set up in such a way that users can't leave the sites by clicking on the "back" or "home" button. When they do so they may be connected to another pornographic site, a practice which has been dubbed *mouse-trapping*.

The term pagejacking is a combination of the words web*page* and hi*jacking*, indicating that a webpage has been hijacked.[7]

- **25 Million Affected.** The president of a company that produces a popular Internet game site for teenagers was horrified when he tried to call up his website but instead got a screen full of pornography. When he tried to escape the sites by clicking the "back" or "home" button, he was instead directed to other pornography sites (mouse-trapped). He was held captive and couldn't escape. It turns out that his website was not the only one victimized. Some computer users searching for the Harvard Law Review, or trying to find sites about "Oklahoma tornadoes," "news about Kosovo," "child car seats," or other topics had the same experience. As many as 25 million webpages may have been affected. Investigators blamed it on a Portuguese hacker, Carlos Pereira, and an Australian pornography company working together. Investigators raided the offices of the pornography company and obtained an American court order to stop it. The scheme involved the cloning of legitimate webpages, including such sites as Audi, Paine Webber, and the Japanese Friendship Gardens. When computer users tried to reach those sites using the Alta Vista search engine, they were pagejacked to the site run by the Australian company.[12]

Instant Messaging and Email Hijacking

Instant messaging, often shortened to simply IM, is the exchange of text messages in real-time. Users are able to see whether a chosen friend or "buddy" is online and connected through the selected service. Instant messaging differs from ordinary email in the immediacy of the message exchange. It also makes a continued exchange simpler than sending email back and forth.

- **Microsoft.** A problem in the way that Internet Explorer handled cookies was exploited to allow an attacker to hijack

MSN Messenger. The attacker was able to see the user's MSN contact list and cookies and read files on vulnerable machines. It then could send spoofed messages to those contacts and take files off the local drives. The vulnerability was corrected by Microsoft.[13]

- **AOL.** Hackers exploiting a loophole in America Online's signup process began taking their pick of AOL Instant Messenger (AIM) accounts, hijacking them virtually at will. By manipulating AOL's signup form with tools long available on the Internet, hackers set the value of a two-character variable that is sent immediately prior to the screen name in the signup process. The signup process ignores that variable while checking the screen name for a conflict. But the process later attaches the variable to the beginning of the screen name when actually creating the account. A hacker exploits this by setting the two character variable to say "Jo" when establishing an account with the screen name "hn Doe." If "hn Doe" Is available on both AOL and AIM, then the system will set up the account for "John Doe," even if "John Doe" is already in use. The hacker then uses the new AOL account to access John Doe's personal "buddy list," or to change John Doe's password and take over the AIM account, masquerading as the real owner.[14]

Recently there have been reports of hijacking of free online email accounts, such as MSN Hotmail, refusing to cede control unless the user pays them a ransom. The hackers gain access to the email accounts by infecting Internet cafe computers with a keystroke logger, allowing them to obtain the username and password of each person that logs in.[15] Keystroke loggers are discussed in Chapter 35.

Modem Hijacking

Dialers are software programs that have the ability to make telephone calls from your computer without your knowledge. The programs are automatically downloaded from malicious websites without your knowledge. They are only effective if you have a dial-up Internet connection. DSL, cable, and wireless Internet connections are not subject to this scam because they don't use a dial-up modem.

Dialer programs connect through your telephone line to websites that usually are pornographic in nature. The numbers are pay-per-minute calls, so you get charged for the amount of time your computer is connected to it, which can be substantial.[16]

Typical signs of modem hijacking include: (1) You can hear your modem disconnect and dial-up again; (2) you receive an unexpectedly high telephone bill, which lists an unknown international telephone number or premium rate number; (3) an unfamiliar shortcut icon appears on your desktop; and (4) you are online but cannot send emails (the pay-per-minute connections don't have email servers).[17]

- **Adult Entertainment.** Charges were brought by the FTC against a major billing aggregator, Integretel, Inc., and its subsidiary, eBillit, for their role in an illegal scheme—misusing the international telephone billing system. The group charged consumers for Internet-based adult entertainment that the consumers never purchased nor authorized. Through the scheme, thousands of consumers were billed an average of $127 apiece. Unknown to the computer users, dialer software had been downloaded from adult websites. Once the dialer software was downloaded, it disconnected the consumer's modem from its usual Internet service provider, dialed an international telephone number to Madagascar, and reconnected the modem to the Internet at that overseas location. The line subscribers then began incurring charges on their telephone bills for the remote Internet connection at the rate of $3.99 per minute.[18]

TIPS TO PROTECT YOURSELF

Malicious Software Removal Tool. Get Microsoft's Malicious Software Removal Tool. This tool checks computers running Windows XP and Windows 2000 for infections by specific, prevalent malicious software, including Blaster, Sasser, and Mydoom, and helps remove any infection found.

Modem Hijacking. To avoid modem hijacking you should (1) turn up the volume on your modem so you can hear if it disconnects and attempts to re-dial, (2) remove any icons on your desktop that are unfamiliar, (3) turn off your computer and modem when not in use, (4) check you phone bill diligently each month for questionable charges, and (5) if your modem is hijacked, immediately unplug the modem.[19,20]

Popup Windows. To close popup windows without clicking on "No" or the "X" in the upper-right corner, press Alt-F4. This safely closes the window without allowing any downloads.[19]

Questionable Websites. Be aware of the possibility of your computer getting infected when visiting sites of questionable content, primarily pornographic and gamming sites, or better yet avoid such sites entirely. Monitor your child's use of the Internet. Consider using blocking software to keep children from questionable sites.

Security Windows. Be aware of *Security Warning Windows*. Normally hijacking software is installed when you consent to a security warning window that appears over a secure webpage. The

Security Warning Window contains the following or similar text: "Do you want to install and run <name of program> signed on <date and time> by <name of software vendor or advertiser>."

By clicking "Yes" on a malicious Security Warning Window, the malicious software may be integrated into your browser system. The software changes the behavior of your Web browser to suit the desires of the aggressive advertiser. To prevent this from happening, never click "Yes" on Security Warning Windows that appear with webpages that you are suspicious of.[6]

Specific Programs. Download and run specific programs, such as Trend Micro's CWShredder (www.trendmicro.com) and HijackThis (www.Merijn.org.) as needed to get rid of specific hijacking programs. Even with these it may still be impossible to get rid of the software, requiring a reinstallation of your operating system.

Virtual Shield. Hijacking can only happen when a hijacker's software finds its way into your computer. So the best way to protect yourself is to not let the hijacker in. To achieve this you need to carry out the steps outlined in Chapter 1 under "Create a Virtual Shield."

References

1.   High-tech Dictionary, Computer User, www.computeruser.com/

resources/dictionary.

2. Crimeware: Bots, Symantec, http://sarc.com/avcenter/cybercrime/ bots_page1.html.

3. Distributed denial-of-service attack, SearchSecurity.com Definitions, http://searchsecurity.techtarget.com/sDefinition/0,,sid14_gci557336, 00.html, July 10, 2006.

4. Swartz, John, Porn sites sent from hacked PCs, Contra Costa Times, Ring Scam, www.drcomputer.com/news.html, July 11, 2003.

5. Roberts, Paul F., Botmaster gets five years in prison, www.infoworld.com/article/06/05/09/78136_HNbotmasterancheta_1 .html, May 9, 2006.

6. HP and Compaq PCs - About Spyware, Adware, and Browser Hijacking Software, Hewlitt-Packard, http://h10025.www1.hp.com /ewfrf/wc/document?lc=en&cc=us&dlc=&product=59375&docnam e=c00206121.

7. US acts against 'page-jack' fraud, Sci/Tech, BBC News, http://news. bbc.co.uk/2/hi/science/nature/456287.stm, September 24, 1999.

8. Browser hijacking: How to help avoid it and undo damage, Microsoft, www.microsoft.com/athome/security/online/ browser_hijacking.mspx#EPB, November 15, 2005.

9. Delio, Michelle, Browser hijackers running lives, Wired News, www.wired.com/news/infostructure/0,1377,63391,00.html, May 11, 2004.

10. The CoolWebSearch Chronicles, http://cwshredder.net/cwshredder/ cwschronicles.html, September 20, 2005.

11. Delio, Michelle, Nasty malware fouls PCs with porn, Wired News, www.wired.com/news/infostructure/0,1377,63280,00.html, April 30, 2004.

12. Labatron, Stephen, Millions of websites sabotaged for profit, investigators reveal, The New York Times, www.sfgate.com/cgi-bin/article.cgi?file=/chronicle/archive/1999/09/23/MN51775.DTL&t ype=tech_article, September 23, 2009.

13. Fisher, Dennis, MSN Messenger vulnerable to hijacking, eWeek.com, www.eweek.com/article2/0,1895,1657628,00.asp, February 11, 2002.

14. Poulsen, Kevin, Hijackers take AIM accounts, Security Focus, www.securityfocus.com/news/119, November 29, 2000.

15. Moses, Asher, Cyber hijackers demand ransom, The Sidney Morning Herald, www.smh.com.au/news/security/cyber-hijackers-demand-ransom/2006/12/13/1165685743135.htmlhttp://www.smh. com.au/news/security/cyber-hijackers-demand-ransom/2006/12/13/ 1165685743135.html, December 16, 2006.

16. Understanding spyware, browser hijackers, and dialers, BleepingComputer.com, www.bleepingcomputer.com/tutorials /tutorial41.html, March 25, 2004.

17. How to protect yourself against "modem hijacking," RomTelecom, www.romtelecom.ro/en/services_and_products/internet_services/dial-up_internet_access/how_to_protect_yourself_against_modem_hijacking/the_internet_users_guide_against_modem_hijacking.html.
18. Companies That Billed Consumers for Adult "Videotext" Internet Services Settle FTC Charges, Federal Trade Commission, www.ftc.gov/opa/2002/11/integretel.htm, November 26, 2002.
19. How to protect against computer hijacking and against theft of your personal data (with potential to be used in Identity Theft), SOHO Data Defense, www.sohodatadefence.com/MainContent/hijacking%20personal.htm.
20. Tips to prevent modem hijacking, www.oag.state.ny.us/internet/tips%20to%20prevent%20modem%20hijacking.pdf.

Chapter 14

Cyber Snake Oil

Illegal Internet operations involving the field of medicine include (1) false claims about dietary supplements; (2) selling unapproved home laboratory tests that don't work; (3) providing prescription medications with little or no physician involvement; (4) providing fake medications; (5) selling all kinds of quack treatments to enlarge women's breasts or grow hair on any head; and (6) providing cures for illnesses for which there are no cures, such as arthritis, AIDS, and many cancers. And then there's always the one treatment that cures almost every thing from dandruff to lumbago.

EXAMPLES OF CYBER SNAKE OIL

Dietary Supplements

The array of dietary supplements—vitamins and minerals, amino acids, enzymes, herbs, animal extracts—present a confusing picture. While some have been tested and found to be safe and effective for the ailments they profess to treat or cure, most have not. Unlike prescription medicines, the companies that make dietary supplements are not required by the federal government to obtain such data.

Websites that make false claims about dietary supplements tend to use phrases like "secret remedy," "scientific breakthrough," "miraculous cure," "exclusive product," "secret ingredient," or "ancient remedy." Or they use meaningless scientific-sounding terms like "oxidative phosphorylation," "hunger stimulation point," or "thermogenesis."[1]

- **Seasilver.** The FTC charged two companies (Seasilver USA, Inc. and Americaloe, Inc.), their owners, the principal distributor, and a purported "expert" with promoting the dietary supplement Seasilver with false and unsubstantiated medical claims about the health benefits and safety of the supplement. Seasilver was said to be safe and effective for the treatment or cure of 650 diseases, including AIDS, diabetes, Lyme disease, various cancers, and chronic obstructive pulmonary disease. In addition, it was claimed that the product enabled post-heart attack patients to reduce their heart medication, eliminated high blood pressure, caused substantial and permanent weight loss, and was 100 percent safe for pregnant and lactating women, senior citizens, children, and infants. Finally, the complaint alleged that the defendants provided deceptive advertisements and promotional materials to distributors for use in their marketing and sale of Seasilver. A 32-oz. bottle of the supplement sold for $39.95.[2]

Home Test Kits

Medical tests, like prescription medication, must be approved by the Food and Drug Administration (FDA) before they can be marketed and used.[1]

- **HIV Home Test Kits.** In Newark, New Jersey, Stanley Lapides, 56, pleaded guilty to fraud charges. He admitted that from October 1997 through March 1999 he mailed approximately 628 HIV home test kits to U.S. customers, yet neglected to advise them that the medical device had not received FDA approval. Lapides was a principal in NERCO Associates Ltd. and IHT Ltd., which were Bahamian companies that distributed the kit to test human saliva for HIV antibodies. He had solicited orders through three websites which claimed that the kit yielded results in five minutes with more than 99 percent accuracy. The FDA conducted testing on a small number of the home test kits and determined that none of them yielded accurate results. At a cost of $49.95 each, Lapides generated about $31,368 in revenue through sales of the kits.[3]

- **DNA Home Test Kits.** Federal investigators said home tests that claim to analyze consumers' DNA for genes that play a role in diseases, such as cancer, heart disease, high blood pressure, and diabetes, were misleading. The kits were said to provide results that were medically unproven, ambiguous, or both. Ads for such genetic test kits are common on the Internet, ranging in price from less than $100 to about $400. Investigators bought kits from three businesses—Suracell of Montclair, New Jersey; Genelex of Seattle, Washington; and Sciona of Boulder, Colorado—all of which advertised that the kits sampled four to 19 genes to provide consumers with personalized diet and lifestyle recommendations. While genetic science has great potential, the claims for these kits were said to have represented a fraudulent mutation of that promise.[4]

Medications

Internet customers can buy a vast array of painkillers, antidepressants, stimulants, steroids, and other prescription medications with virtually no medical monitoring. The doctors involved are veritable script-writing machines. Some of them have financial problems and histories of substance abuse or medical incompetence.[1]

- **Prescription Mill.** In Pennsylvania, two doctors, Ranvir Ahlawat, 42, and Steven Klinman, 57, were charged with helping peddle millions of dollars' worth of diet drugs through an online pharmacy by approving thousands of prescriptions without seeing anyone in person. By signing off on the orders, they helped RxMedicalOne.com take in $33.6 million in nine months. Most of the orders were for highly-addictive controlled drugs, such as Phentermine and Adipex. Ahlawat and Klinman reviewed the questionnaires customers sent in with their orders.

Ahlawat alone was said to have reviewed 1,000 to 1,500 a day at times. The indictment also charged pharmacy operator Michael Bezonsky; pharmacist Alexander Atchildiev, who was accused of shipping the drugs without ensuring the prescriptions were valid; and Thomas Beaulieu, who helped Bezonsky run the business.[5]

Cosmetic Scams

Penis Enlargement Pill

Advertisements for penis enlargement pills frequently find their way into email inboxes. And many people actually fall for the scam, sending off good money and getting nothing of value in return.

- **Stop at 8 or 9 Inches.** In Arizona, authorities seized over $30 million in luxury homes, cars, cash, jewelry, and bank accounts from individuals operating a company that primarily sold "penis enlargement" pills over the Internet. The individuals named in the civil forfeiture action were Michael A. Consoli, Vincent J. Passafiume, and Geraldine Consoli (Michael's mother). Operating as C.P. Direct, Inc. from a Scottsdale office building, the business sold capsules or pills called Longitude, which were claimed to open up erectile tissue chambers to permanently enlarge the penis 1 to 3 inches, or larger if taken for a longer time, netting permanent results within months. Users were warned to stop at 8 or 9 inches because, "Any longer of a penis would be too large for most women to handle." The website offered testimonials, purported before-and-after photographs, and endorsements from magazines and nationally syndicated radio host Howard Stern. The company also offered to refund 100 percent of customers' money, including shipping fees, if customers were not satisfied. A one-month bottle of Longitude cost $59.95 plus shipping and handling for the first month, and then $39.95 thereafter. The company only paid about $2.50 per bottle for the pills. Many customers complained that they did not receive requested refunds and that the company had continued to ship products and charge for further shipments after being asked to stop.[6]

Weight Loss

Many diet websites engage in misleading "bait-and-switch" billing practices in which a user is promised a free sample, but then finds that he has been automatically subscribed to an expensive monthly service. Other websites advertise weight loss products and deliver the pill or lotion they advertise. The problem is—they don't work.

Some sites claim you can eat all you want and lose weight effortlessly. If you believe that I have some ocean front property in Arizona I'd like to sell you. The fact is, if you want to lose weight your caloric intake must be less than your caloric output. This can be accomplished by three and only three methods: (1) Eat less, (2) exercise more, or (3) eat less and exercise more. Anyone who wants to sell you a weight loss product that doesn't center about these principles is trying to take advantage of you.[7]

Cellulite Treatment

Cellulite is a name advertisers use for the dimpled fat that some people accumulate around their thighs, buttocks, and stomachs. Before you buy products advertised to dissolve cellulite, you should be aware that no amount of rubbing, wrapping, massaging, scrubbing, taking mineral supplements or vitamins, or applying creams will get rid of fat deposits. The best way to reduce fat deposits is by following a sensible diet to lose weight and exercising to improve muscle tone.[7]

Breast Enlargement

A Google search for "breast enlargement" turned up 2,640,000 hits. This tells you that breast enlargement fraud is a very profitable business.

- **One of Many.** J. Michael Ernest touted a "breast enhancement" product marketed as "The Isis System," which consisted of a dietary supplement and a topical cream that was purported to increase a woman's breast size. The FTC alleged that Ernest made unsubstantiated claims that The Isis System

119

significantly increased breast size by stimulating breast cells to regenerate the growth process. The Isis product was advertised on the Internet and through print, radio, and TV. The FTC order required Ernest to have competent and reliable scientific evidence before making any claims about the benefits, performance, efficacy, safety, or side effects about Isis or any dietary supplement, food, drug, cosmetic, or device. [8]

Baldness Cure

Scams for selling baldness cures are an ever popular source of income. Having been around for hundreds of years, they've found new life on the Internet.

- **Hair Restorer Kits.** Two Canadians, Philip P. West and Wayne P. Kreklewich, made more than $3 million during four years of peddling a phony hair restorer. The two were corporate officers of Westmaster Distributing, also known as Anglo-American Cosmetics and MJS Distributors. They were charged with operating companies that produced and sold kits of unapproved hair restorer products. A 4-ounce plastic bottle each of Westmaster Follicle Cleanser, Westmaster Hair and Scalp Lotion, and Westmaster Natural Source Formula Shampoo cost $210 plus shipping charges. If convicted, the two men were to make full restitution to their victims. [9]

Reverse Aging

Ponce De Leon's fountain of youth is alive and well on the Internet, or so some scammers would like you to believe.

- **HGH Knock-off.** In Chicago a federal court issued an order halting deceptive product claims and froze the assets of Creaghan A. Harry, a resident of Boca Raton, Florida. Harry sold bogus "human growth hormone" products over the Internet through millions of illegal spam messages. The messages contained hyperlinks to various websites that marketed the products "Supreme Formula HGH" and "Youthful Vigor HGH." The websites claimed that the products stopped or reversed the aging process, causing a veritable laundry list of effects, like weight loss, muscle gain, hair regrowth, wrinkle removal, and higher energy levels. Harry charged $79.95 for a one-month supply of the bogus products. Experts for the FTC concluded that Harry's products had no discernible effect on the body and alleged that the false products defrauded thousands of consumers of hundreds of thousands of dollars.[10]

Treatments and Cures

Internet scammers claim to provide cures for a multitude of disorders, including arthritis, AIDS, and cancer.

Arthritis

The Arthritis Foundation estimates that $1 billion is spent annually on unproven arthritis remedies. Many dietary and natural "cures" have been sold for arthritis, a number of them on the Internet. These include herbs, mussel extract, vitamin pills, desiccated liver pills, honey and vinegar mixtures, and copper bracelets. [7]

AIDS

An Herbal Cure. The following email, supposedly from a doctor from India who used a UK-based email address, promised a cure for AIDS. The email was actually sent from an ISP in Nigeria. The "doctor" had discovered an herbal cure and used lots of vitamins to boost the immune system. According to the FDA, no herb, either by itself or in combination with other ingredients, will cure any form of arthritis. Notice the typical misspellings, unusual punctuation, and poor grammar.

- "Dear Sir/Madam,
  I am Dr.Sadiq Harrison, a Trado Medical practitioner,From India. I have over the years carried out extensive research to find a definite cure for Acquired Immune Deficiency Syndrome (AIDS), which has eluded scientific research. I am happy to announce that i have Succeeded in finding a permanent cure for the dreaded AIDS, through natural Herb. Clinical test Carried out with some of the patients i treated

showed Significant improvement after one month and after one Year of treatment, there was no trace of the virus found in them. We therefore encourage victims or their relations to get in touch with us for treatment and cure. I want to assure you that we will treat your identity with the highest level of confidentiality, Please don't hide your face in shame due to the social stigma, it could happen to any body. A trial will convince you and If after one month of treatment you did not record an overwhelming improvement, feel free to take legal action. You can reach me through our alternative email: drsadiq_harrison@yahoo.co.uk
Regards,
Dr.Sadiq Harrison"[11]

- **Cause of AIDS Explained**. The Massachusetts attorney general obtained a temporary restraining order against Marjorie Phillips who was accused of posting an advertisement on her website claiming that she would provide a cure for AIDS to those who purchased a $24 book written by Dr. Hulda Clark. Clark claimed to have discovered the true cause of AIDS. The ad stated that "In six weeks you are HIV negative!" Callers were asked to listen to a nine-minute recording on a 900 number that cost $17.91 to hear in its entirety. For another $12 consumers could send emails to receive the full details explaining the exact cause and cure for HIV/AIDS. Dr. Clark also claims to have found a cure for cancer and other difficult to treat illnesses (www.drclark.net).[12]

Cancer

Cancer Quackery will be around as long as many forms of cancer remain untreatable. Most people who fall prey to these scammers do so as a last hope for recovery. Others simply believe the quacks have a better idea.

- **Cures Almost All Cancers.** In Olympia, Washington, a judge ordered David L. Walker, the owner and operator of DLW Consulting, to permanently shut down an Internet website he used to promote a cancer treatment that had no proven record of success. Consumers paid between $2,436 and $5,220 for a treatment called "CWAT-Treatment: BioResonance Therapy." Walker claimed that all but 15 of the 745 cancer patients who had undergone the treatment were cured. However he was unable to substantiate that claim. His treatment used a combination of an oral herbal mix known as Indian Mud, coffee enemas, a variety of dietary supplements, and the use of an electrical device called a bioresonance oscillator (also known as a molecular enhancer) that patients were instructed to use each day. Walker was accused of providing false hope, phony cures, and fraudulent fees. He was ordered to pay attorney fees and make $230,000 in restitution to 127 consumers nationwide who had purchased his treatment. He was barred from promoting the cancer treatment in print or in seminars. State attorneys were seeking $500,000 in civil fees.[13]

Snake Oil of All Snake Oils

If it cures one thing, why not more than one—or even everything? And people actually fall for these scams.

- **Comfrey.** Norman and Ruth Bacalla of Springfield, Utah marketed and sold a variety of products containing an herbal substance known as "comfrey" on the Internet and through distributors, retail stores, and health care practitioners. They stated in their advertising and promotional materials that their products were safe to take orally, as suppositories, or applied to open wounds, and that even pregnant women, infants, and children could safely use the products internally. They also claimed their products were effective in treating and/or curing asthma, colds, coughs, lung congestion, sore throats, emphysema, bronchitis, tuberculosis, broken bones, curvature of the spine, polio, multiple sclerosis, and spinal cancer. In addition, they claimed their suppository products were effective in treating prolapsed bowel and uterus, yeast infection, and herpes simplex. Their herbal antiseptic, recommended for application to open wounds or taken internally, was claimed to be effective in treating, preventing, and/or curing thrush infection, pyorrhea, sore throat pain, and toothaches. The FTC said that comfrey was not safe for internal use because it contains compounds known to be toxic to the liver, and that taken internally it can lead to serious illness or death. The court order prohibited the defendants from making specific health claims or any unsubstantiated representations about the safety, health benefits, performance, or efficacy of any food, drug, dietary supplement, or other health-related product or service. The order further required them to notify distributors of their products that unsubstantiated claims violated the law and that the defendants were to terminate distributors who made false or unsubstantiated claims.[14]

Other Cyber Snake Oil Scams

Other fraudulent online treatments and cures include candidiasis hypersensitivity treatment, chelation therapy for a variety of disorders, hair analysis, oxygen pills, paralysis cures, and almost anything you can think of.[1]

TIPS TO PROTECT YOURSELF

Conspiracy. The manufacturer may claim the government, medical profession, or pharmaceutical companies have conspired to suppress the treatment. Don't believe it.[1]

Gullibility. The surest way to protect yourself against false claims of treatments and cures advertised on the Internet is don't be gullible. If a treatment or cure is outside mainstream medicine, it is by that fact suspect. Be leery of guarantees and claims of cures for illnesses that mainstream medicine has had little or no success treating. The American Medical Association is not trying to hide anything from you. If there were a cure for arthritis, AIDS, all cancers, multiple sclerosis, and any number of serious conditions, your doctor would be more than glad to tell you about it.

Jargon. Fraudulent advertisements rely on impressive-sounding, yet incomprehensible, medical jargon to disguise the lack of scientific research supporting the product—like these for a weight loss product: "hunger stimulation point," thermogenesis," or "natural product."

No Risk. Promises a money-back guarantee, such as "If after 30 days you have not lost 30 pounds we will refund your money." Don't bet on it.[1,7]

One Source. Advertised as being available from only one source, be in limited supply, or require payment in advance. The product is sold outside normal commercial distribution channels, such as only on the Internet. It is not available through your local physician or pharmacies.[1,7]

Permanent Results. Promises permanent weight loss without exercise. You only have to take their pill or use their lotion. You can even lose weight while you sleep.[6]

Questionable Studies. They say things like "A Harvard study showed that the ingredient in Product X may be effective. The key words here are "may be." This of course means that the treatment or cure hasn't been proven to be effective or ineffective. There's a lot of difference between "definitely is" and "may be."[7]

Quick and Easy Cure. Promises a quick and easy cure of illnesses that mainstream medicine is unable to cure.[7]

Specific Words. Promoter use words such as "miraculous cure," "exclusive product," "secret remedy," "scientific breakthrough," "ancient remedy, "revolutionary innovation," "natural ingredients," "alternative medicine," and so forth.[1,7]

Testimonials. Promoters of fraudulent treatments or cures use case histories that sound too good to be true. "After using product X for only 30 days I was able to get out of my wheelchair and walk again." And remember, a white coat and a stethoscope around a person's neck does not make that person a physician.[15]

Wide Range of Ailments. The product is advertised as effective for a wide range of ailments. One pill does it all— cures arthritis, infections, prostate problems, ulcers, cancer, heart trouble, dandruff, and more.[1,7]

References

1. Milhorn, H. Thomas, Cybercrime, In Crime: Computer Viruses to Twin Towers, Universal Publishers, Boca Raton, 2005, Pp 46-70.
2. No Silver Lining for Marketers of Bogus Supplement; Federal Agencies Crack Down on Health Fraud, Federal Trade Commission, www.ftc.gov/opa/2003/06/seasilver.htm, June 19, 2003.
3. Kenilworth, Man Admits Distributing Unapproved HTV Home Test

Kits, United States Department of Justice, www.usdoj.gov/
usao/nj/publicaffairs/releases/2000/lal025_r.html, October 25, 2000.

4. Appleby, Julie, GAO pounces on home DNA tests to predict
   disease, USA Today, www.usatoday.com/tech/science/2006-07-27-
   genetic-tests_x.htm, July 27, 2006.
5. Internet pharmacy doctors charged, NewsMax.com,
   www.newsmax.com/archives/articles/2006/8/2/232237.shtml?s=he,
   August 3, 2006.
6. Barrett, Steven, Bogus Penis Enlargement Pills Seized;
   Defendants Forfeit over $35 million, Quack-Watch,
   www.quackwatch.org/02ConsumerProtection/AG/AZ/longitude.
   html, May 29, 2002.
7. Health claims: Separating fact from fiction, Facts for consumers
   from the Federal Trade Commission, http://consumerlawpage.com
   /brochure/46.shtml, 1992.
8. Developer of Purported Breast Enhancement. Federal Trade
   Commission, www.ftc.gov/opa/2003/01/evd.htm, January 22,
   2003.
9. Bald-faced hair scam, www.findarticles.com/p/articles/mi_m1370/
   is_n2_v23/ ai_7485433, March 1989.
10. FTC sues Florida man for illegal spam and false "human growth
    hormone" product claims, Federal Trade Commission,
    www.ftc.gov/opa/2004/07/creaghan.htm, July 29, 2004.
11. The Nigerian cure for AIDS (Dr Sadiq Harrison),
    www.joewein.de/sw/419-aids-cure.htm.
12. Aguilar, Rose, Fraud case could set precedent for Net, CNET
    News, http://news.com.com/Fraud+case+could+set+precedent+
    for+Net/2100-1023_3-208903.html, April 4, 1996.
13. Judge shuts down online cancer cure Site, Office of the Attorney
    General, www.atg.wa.gov/releases/rel_walker_071202.html.
14. Latest FTC Case in "Operation Cure.All" Focuses on Safety Risks
    of Comfrey Products Promoted Via Internet, Federal Trade
    Commission, www.ftc.gov/opa/2001/07/chrisenter.htm, July 6,
    2001.
15. McGran, John, 6 ways to sport a diet scam,
    www.ediets.com/news/article.cfm/3/cmi_1303771/cid_6/code_240
    45/, July 12, 2006.

Chapter 15

Cyberterrorism

Cyberterrorism is the convergence of terrorism and cyberspace. It is generally understood to mean unlawful attacks against information stored in computers and networks with the purpose of intimidating or coercing a government or its people to advance political or social objectives. More recently, the definition has been extended to include attacks against computers and networks of nongovernmental natures. Attacks that disrupt nonessential services or that are mainly a costly nuisance usually are not considered terrorism.[1]

TERRORISM AND THE INTERNET

All terrorist groups designated as such by the U.S. government have at least one website, and many have more than one. Hezbollah, for instance, currently operates 55 websites. A group with more than one website typically designates one for other terrorists, one for non-terrorists they want to influence, and one for children they wish to indoctrinate. They may even have the same website in a number of different languages.

Terrorists use websites for psychological warfare (such as the execution of Daniel Perle), propaganda (advancement of their political and ideological agenda), networking with other terrorists, planning attacks, training (such as how to make and execute a car bomb), and recruiting new members.[2]

The Internet is attractive to terrorist groups because it has no boundaries—no mountains or desert barriers to cross—and no paperwork to present to customs officers. Armed only with a home computer, terrorists can use cyberspace to access extremely sensitive information and to spread their doctrine around the world. In the future, terrorists may be able to do such things as take control of the stock market, alter White House security codes, or change the formulas for prescription drugs.

Cyberterrorism does not seem to pose an imminent threat, but this could change. The next generation of terrorists will have grown up in a digital world, with ever more powerful and easy-to-use hacking tools at their disposal. They might see greater potential for cyberterrorism than the terrorists of today, and their level of knowledge and skill relating to hacking will be far greater. Future terrorists might try remotely to hijack systems that control dams, airplane routes, or power grids. They also might combine the use of the Internet with classical terrorist tools. For example, they might try to block emergency communications or cut off electricity or water in the wake of a conventional bombing or a biological, chemical, or radiation attack. Individuals and groups already have tried to attack computer networks, and to some extent they have been successful.[1]

EXAMPLES OF CYBERTERRORISM

Denial of Service Attack. A *denial of service (DoS) attack* is an assault on a network, such as AOL, BellSouth, or Comcast, that floods it with so many additional emails that regular traffic is either slowed or completely interrupted. Unlike a virus or worm, which can cause severe damage, a denial of service attack simply interrupts network service for some period. A *distributed denial of service (DDoS) attack* uses multiple computers that a hacker has previously infected. The computers act as "zombies" and work together to send out messages, thereby greatly increasing the amount of traffic flow. The FBI's cybersecurity agency has issued an advisory warning that increased Distributed Denial of Service (DDoS) attacks are possible by terrorists.[3]

- **Michigan DDoS Attack.** In Michigan, Jason Salah Arabo, 18, was arrested on a federal charge that he hired a New Jersey juvenile to conduct highly disruptive DDoS attacks on competitors of his online sportswear business, including a web-based New Jersey company. Arabo ran two web-based companies, customleader.com and jerseydomain.com, that sold sports apparel. The complaint alleged that the attacks caused widespread harm and disruption to Internet and computer services far beyond the online businesses that Arabo targeted. The Internet service providers that hosted the targeted websites also provided website hosting and other Internet services to a number of unrelated businesses, which, as a result, were also harmed by the attacks. The attacks were said to have affected businesses as far away as Europe, and caused disruption to the operations of major online retail businesses, banks, and companies that provide communications, data backup, and information services to the medical and pharmaceutical industries.[4]

- **Kosovo Conflict.** During the Kosovo conflict in 1999 NATO computers were overwhelmed by emails sent by hackers protesting the NATO bombings. In addition, businesses, public organizations, and academic institutes received virus-laden emails from a range of Eastern European countries. Website defacements also were common. After the Chinese Embassy was accidentally bombed in Belgrade, Chinese hackers posted messages on U.S. government websites such as "We won't stop attacking until the war (Kosovo) stops!"[1]

- **MSN TV Attack.** In Louisiana, FBI agents arrested David Jeansonne, 43, and charged him with cyberterrorism for allegedly tricking a handful of MSN TV users into running a malicious email attachment that reprogrammed their set-top boxes to dial 911 emergency response. According to prosecutors, Jeansonne targeted 18 MSN TV users in an online squabble. The boxes connected to the Internet through a local dial-up number. Additionally, the malicious script posted victims' browser histories to a particular website and emailed their hardware serial number to the free Web mail account timmy@postmark.net. Investigators at Microsoft's MSN unit searched email logs and found messages between Jeansonne and an online friend that suggested Jeansonne was responsible for the hack. The FBI raided his home and seized his computers. According to court records the hack resulted in police responding 10 times to false alarms at subscribers' homes, either in person or by phoning them back. It's unclear what happened to the other calls to 911. Jeansonne appeared in federal court in New Orleans and was released on $25,000 bail.[5]

- **Russian Gas Monopoly.** According to Russia's Interior Minister, the state-run gas monopoly, Gazprom, was hit by hackers who collaborated with a Gazprom insider. Gazprom is the world's largest natural gas producer and the largest gas supplier to Western Europe. The hackers were said to have used a Trojan horse to gain control of the central switchboard, which controls gas flows in pipelines. Fearing a Trojan horse of their own, the U.S. State Department sent an urgent cable to about 170 embassies asking them to remove software which it had discovered was written by citizens of the former Soviet Union.[1]

- **Planned Columbine-like Attack.** Lukasz Lagucik, a 17-year-old student at Forest Hills High School in Queens, New York, was arrested and charged with making a terrorist threat over the Internet to use bombs and guns in a shooting spree at his high school. New York state police learned from the principal of a high school in Wynne, Arkansas that he had obtained a copy of a note which said that youths had been chatting on the Internet about buying firearms and making bombs to engage in a "Columbine" type of killing spree at a New York high school. Arkansas police determined that one of the chat room participants was a 17-year-old female student at a local high school. When contacted, she gave Arkansas police the screen name of the student she had been chatting with. The information was passed on to the New York state police, who used it to obtain information about the defendant's Internet service provider, EarthLink. State Police obtained and executed a search warrant, and then arrested Lagucik, who faced up to seven years in prison if convicted.[6]

- **Planned Holy War.** Two Atlanta-area men were arrested on terrorism charges for planning to wage a holy war in the United States, including a possible attack on Dobbins Air Reserve Base in Marietta. Syed Haris Ahmed, 21, and Ehsanul Islam Sadequee, 19, were said to have traveled to Toronto a year before and met with others to identify locations suitable for terrorist attacks, which included oil storage facilities, refineries, and the U.S. Capitol. The indictment claimed Ahmed and Sadequee had videotaped targets and provided clips to Younis Tsouli, a co-conspirator in the United Kingdom. Tsouli allegedly ran an online information network where terrorists could obtain instructions on such things as building car bombs. The indictment also alleged Ahmed, who was born in Pakistan, traveled back to his homeland the previous summer with the intention of getting religious education and paramilitary training. Sadequee had traveled to Bangladesh the same summer to get married and further pursue his violent jihad support activity, the indictment said.[7]

- **Terrorism Fundraising Websites.** A British man, Syed Talha Ahsan, 26, was arrested on charges of conspiracy to support terrorists and conspiracy to kill or injure people abroad. It was said that he helped run terrorism fundraising websites, set up terrorists with temporary housing in England, and possessed a classified U.S. Navy document that revealed troop movements. Officials believed they disrupted a network that recruited and financed terrorists, outfitted them with equipment, and dispatched them to fight in countries such as Afghanistan. A co-conspirator, Babar Ahmad, a British computer specialist, was also charged. Both men were accused of running several websites, including www.Azzam.com, which investigators said was used to recruit members for the al Qaeda network, Afghanistan's ousted Taliban regime, and Chechen rebels.[8]

TIPS TO PROTECT YOURSELF

For individual computer users the news is good. Terrorists are not interested in you. Their focus is on targets where they can do the most damage, such as military and industrial complexes. That said, you should still keep your computer operating system up to date, maintain up-to-date antivirus and anti-spyware programs, and regularly back up your data.

References

1. Denning, Dorothy E., Cyberterrorism, Testimony before the Special Oversight Panel on Terrorism Committee on Armed Services, U.S. House of Representatives, www.cs.georgetown.edu/~-denning/infosec/cyberterror.html, May 23, 2000.
2. Weimann, Gabriel, Terror and the Internet, Potomic Books, Dulles, 2006.
3. Denial of Service Attack, Answer.com, www.answers.com/topic/denial-of-service-attack.
4. Michigan Man Arrested for Using New Jersey Juvenile to Launch Destructive "DDOS for Hire" Computer Attacks on Competitors, U.S. Department of Justice, ww.usdoj.gov/usao/nj/publicaffairs/ NJ_Press/ files/arab0318_r.htm, March 18, 2005.
5. Poulsen, Kevin, Alleged WebTV 911 hacker charged with cyberterrorism, Security Focus, www.securityfocus.com/news/8136, February 26, 2004.
6. Queens student charged with making internet terror threat, New York State Governor's Press Releases, www.state.ny.us/ governor/press/03/jan24_3_03.htm, January 23, 2004.
7. Scott, Jeffrey, Georgia terror suspects accused of Dobbins plot, Atlanta Journal-Constitution, www.ajc.com/metro/content/metro/atlanta/stories/0720metterror.htm l?cxntnid=amn072006e, July 20, 2006.
8. U.K. man faces terrorism charge in Conn., CBS News, www.cbsnews.com/stories/2006/07/19/terror/main1818342.shtml?so urce=RSS&attr=U.S._1818342, July 19, 2006.

Chapter 16

Dating, Marriage, and Divorce Scams

DATING SCAMS

Online dating is big business. In the United States alone consumers spent $245.2 million on online personals and dating services in the first half of 2005. It's not surprising then that scam artists have gotten involved. An online dating scam occurs when a male or female makes contact with another person through an online dating agency and pretends to be looking for romance or marriage, but the only thing really wanted is money.[1,2]

Scammers can sign up to online dating agencies or chat rooms just like anyone else. They take advantage of the anonymity of the Internet to determine profiles of people who seem suitable for ripping off. They first flatter their potential victim as they attempt to establish a relationship, and then they move on to the scam.

The most common "reasons" dating scammers give for needing your money include: (1) Don't have enough money to travel to meet you, (2) have financial problems and need help, (3) have had some illness or accident, (4) have been robbed, and (5) need money for a visa. If you agree to send money, they then ask you to send it via a money transfer agent, such as Western Union, so it can't be traced.[1,2,3]

And of course there's always the possibility that the online dating service itself may pull a scam.

Examples of Dating Scams

Consumer Fraud

- **Lost More than $3000.** In his first venture into the world of online dating, Dale Brown of West Allis, Wisconsin lost thousands of dollars because of a dating trap that originated halfway around the world. One site found him "the girl of his dreams." Her name was Oladee. She sent pictures to him along with several months of romantic emails. Then she said she only needed $700 for a plane ticket, so Bell sent her the money. Then she emailed him and said the airport told her she needed a basic traveling allowance of $450, so he sent that too. She kept asking for money, and he kept sending it on the promise that she was coming to Wisconsin to be with him. Soon, Bell had sent more than $3,000 to a woman he had never met, and there was still no sign of her. WISN 12 News discovered the photos she had sent him were actually of a Hawaiian model named Nicole. Her modeling agency said photos of many of its models had been stolen from the company's website and were being used by con artists to lure victims into scams through online dating websites.[4]

- **Lost More Than Money.** Raymond Merrill, a 56-year-old divorced carpenter, met Regina Filomena Rachid through an online dating service. Merrill and Rachid exchanged dozens of emails, calls, and photographs. He gave her $10,000 to start a skin care clinic and bought her a $20,000 sport utility vehicle. He visited Rachid twice in Sao Jose dos Campos, an industrial city about 60 miles from Sao Paulo. On the third trip, he overstayed his return date, but didn't call to inform anyone of his intentions. Sometime after he arrived, Rachid and her real boyfriend, Nelson Siqueira Neves, drugged Merrill, kept him in a room in Rachid's house, and drained his bank accounts, stealing about $200,000, according to Brazilian authorities. Then they reportedly hired Evandro Celso Augusto Ribeiro for $5,600 to help kill Merrill. Then Rachid was said to have driven the victim to a vacant lot where they strangled him with copper wire, doused his body with fuel, and set it on fire. Rachid and Ribeiro were arrested and charged with armed robbery followed by death.[5]

- **Date Rape.** Jeffrey J. Marsalis, a tall, clean-cut man with a taste for upscale bars and restaurants, faced trial on nine rape counts involving eight women, while a 10th charge was pending. Marsalis, 33, met most of the victims through the popular online dating site, match.com, authorities said. At various times he reportedly said he was a doctor, an astronaut, and a spy. In reality he was really an on-and-off nursing student. With woman after woman he was said to have slipped something, thought to be a date-rape drug, into their drinks, and then raped them. The women told strikingly similar stories of meeting Marsalis, then feeling unusually intoxicated after returning from the bathroom or letting him buy a round from the bar. They said they woke up hours later, back at his apartment — groggy and sometimes undressed — after an apparent sexual encounter or even in the middle of intercourse. His lawyer claimed the sex was consensual.[6]

Dating Service Fraud

- **Company Employee.** Frustrated online daters said they were victims of fraud by two top Internet matchmaking services and took their complaints to court. Match.com was accused in a federal lawsuit of goading members into renewing their subscriptions through bogus romantic emails sent out by company employees. In some instances, the suit contended, people on the Match.com payroll even went on sham dates with subscribers as a marketing ploy. Matthew Evans contended he went out with a woman he met through the website who turned out to work for the company. Evans said Match.com set up the date for him because it didn't want him to cancel his subscription and was hoping he'd tell other potential members about the attractive woman he met through the service. Evans found out about the alleged scam after the woman confessed she was employed by Match.com. Match.com denied all the charges.[1]

- **Fictitious Dating Partners.** Yahoo's personals service was accused of posting profiles of fictitious potential dating partners on its website to make it look as though many more singles subscribe to the service than actually do. The Yahoo suit, filed by Robert Anthony of Broward County, Florida, accused the company of breach of contract, fraud, and unfair trade practices.[1]

MARRIAGE SCAMS

Online marriage fraud is booming among the young ladies of the Russian city of Barnaul, situated in southern Siberia. The women give painful descriptions of their hardships and then ask kind-hearted, marriage-minded men, primarily in the United States, for money. American men are said to be especially sensitive to bogus stories such as: "My parents are unemployed, and we are starving," "I am a victim of domestic violence," "My mother is a drunkard," "My house burned down," and "Chechens kidnapped my brother and demand a ransom."

The girls are said to conduct meetings once a week and compete with one another in terms of the amount of money raised from men. The girls read each other the most touching passages from their correspondence, and together brainstorm new tales for future letters. The girls involve their friends in this scheme by showing them how to write letters that will touch foreigners deeply and not raise suspicions. When newcomers begin receiving money from abroad, they are required to share 20 percent of their online "earnings" with the girls who got them in the business.[7]

Examples of Marriage Scams

Scams by Women

- **Doing Them a Favor.** Twenty-five-year-old Svetlana said that at one point of her life she realized she could profit from the myths foreigners have about Russia—that Russia is all about criminals and beggars. She makes the men she emails feel sorry for the beautiful girl living under such "gloomy" circumstances. This feeling of pity is transformed into remittances of money to Svetlana. She is not conscience stricken about this. On the contrary, she claims she is doing a good thing for foreign men by teaching them to be kind, considerate, and humane. She believes that the women make the men feel confident by telling them that they are the best. In this way, the men get rid of their inferiority complexes. She feels that she should charge them more for doing the job she does.[7]

More Like a Business letter. The following is one of the emails received by a suitor of a Russian woman. It sounds more like a business letter than a love letter.

- "Dear Himanshu, Write to me the phone number and I shall call you tomorrow in 5 p.m. Moscow time. I hope itt will be convenient for you. As I can send you a copy of my passport that your doubts have ended. I looked the approximate prices for air tickets for the current month. On the average cost — 1050 $. Inform me if this sum is a problem. ... Write to me soon and I shall call to you tomorrow. I love you. Your ELENA."[7]

Scams by Men

Some Russian men run marriage scams too.

- **Men Do It Too.** A man from Chelyabinsk, an engineer by profession, posed as a girl for dozens of foreign men with whom he had correspondence for five years. When their correspondence turned into "friendship," the "girl" said she wanted to visit the foreigner, but was short of money. The foreign man sent the money, and then the correspondence stopped.[7]

DIVORCE SCAMS

Some websites offer those who want a quick divorce an opportunity to obtain one in the Dominican Republic, or other foreign countries, for $1,000 or more, without even leaving the United States. However, to be legal, at least one of the couple must come to the country, and the divorce must be by mutual consent. These sites often contain false, misleading, or legally inaccurate information about the process for obtaining such divorces; that is, that neither spouse has to visit the country in which the divorce is being sought or mutual consent is not necessary.

Typically, people who send money to one of these schemes eventually receive false assurances that they are legally divorced, when, in fact, they have been victims of the scheme. They have neither received legitimate legal services nor obtained valid divorces.[8]

Another divorce scam occurs when a person pretends to be a lawyer and charges money to file divorce papers. And of course the person can advertise his or her "services" on the Internet.

Example of a Divorce Scam

- **Disbarred Lawyer**. In Phoenix, Arizona, Gary Jay Karpin, 54, was indicted for posing as a divorce lawyer. Prosecutors said there were are at least 150 victims that they knew of, many of whom learned they were not divorced or did not have custody of their children because Karpin had filed paperwork improperly. Karpin was a disbarred lawyer from Vermont and had allegedly been practicing law illegally since at least 1993, according to prosecutors. He was indicted on 16 counts of theft and fraud.[9]

TIPS TO PROTECT YOURSELF

Dating/Marriage

Be Skeptical. Be skeptical if a person who is not your usual dating type offline is showing you particular attention online; for example, if you are over 60 years of age and you are being frequently contacted by a person in his or her early 20s.[10]

Dating Service. Stay alert for online dating services that might not have the people available to date they say they do.[1]

Home Address. Be wary of a person who gives you a post office address and a telephone number, which he or she never answers and which does not have voicemail. Test your "date" by asking lots of questions, trying to phone the person, or suggesting meeting him or her. If all attempts fail, you are probably dealing with a scammer.[3,10]

Money. The person asks for money to be sent by a money transfer agent such as Western Union. This is a tipoff that you are dealing with a fraud. Never send money to someone you don't know and whom you met online, no matter how valid the reason seems.[1,10]

Personal Data. Don't give out personal details, such as your personal or work telephone number, email address, home address, or place of work.[10]

Report. If you are scammed, report it to the dating service or chat room site where you met the person.[3]

Russia. Be especially leary of getting involved with a young woman from Russia. If you do and she asks for money, don't be a sucker. Run as fast as you can.[7]

Self Focus. The person talks a lot about himself or herself and doesn't answer your questions, probably because he or she, if it's actually a person of the claimed gender, is sending the same emails to hundreds of people.[10]

Travel. Be careful if you are asked to travel to another location to meet your "loved one," especially if that location is a foreign country. It could be dangerous.

Young and Beautiful. She is young and exceptually beautiful. This could be because the scammer has used a stolen picture from a modeling agency or other such source.[10]

Offshore Divorce

Know the Rules. If you are going to get an offshore divorce, be sure you know what the rules are and go by them to the letter.[9]

References

1. Online dating scam, www.2beinlove.com/dating-agency-scam.htm.
2. Online daters sue matchmaking websites for fraud, Reuters, http://today.reuters.com/business/newsarticle.aspx?type=media&stor yID=nN18708924&pageNumber=1&imageid=&cap=&sz=13&WT ModLoc=BizArt-C1-ArticlePage1, November 18, 2005.
3. Warning issued for online dating scams, OnlineDatingMagazine. com, www.onlinedatingmagazine.com/news2006/onlinedatings

cams.html, February 16, 2005.
4. Man looking for companionship falls victim to dating scam, WSIN, www.themilwaukeechannel.com/news/7542359, February 29, 2006.
5. Curtis, Kim and Stan Lehman, Dating scam ends in murder, The Associated Press, http://articles.news.aol.com/news/_a/dating-scam-ends-in-murder/20061031133109990001?, October 31, 2006.
6. Man accused of drugging, raping online daters, Associated Press, http://www.msnbc.msn.com/id/15549172, November 23, 2006.
7. Nesterov, Andrei, Russian online marriage fraud is booming, WorldPress.org, www.worldpress.org/Europe/2111.cfm, July 5, 2005.
8. Internet Fraud, United States Department of Justice, www.usdoj.gov/criminal/fraud/text/Internet.htm, May 8, 2000.
9. Ruark, Katie, Divorce scam sends dozens of victims to prosecutors Arizona Republic, www.azcentral.com/arizonarepublic/local/articles/1007phxattorney07.html, October 7 2005.
10. OFT says beware of scams when looking for love online, Office of Fair Trading, www.oft.gov.uk/News/Press+releases/Consumer+alerts/ dating.htm, February 14, 2006.

Chapter 17

Education Scams

If you or your children are looking for an easy college degree or easy scholarship money, be careful. Two of the most common education scams on the Internet are (1) diploma mills and (2) scholarship scams.

DIPLOMA MILLS

Diploma or *degree mills* are unaccredited online "colleges" or "universities" which offer fraudulent or virtually worthless degrees in exchange for payment alone or for payment and very minimal work—often a resume or single "research paper." These diploma mills often claim accreditation from accrediting agencies to mislead prospective students and employers. In fact, some of the bogus accrediting agencies are owned and operated by the same people who own and run the diploma mills.[1]

The legitimate-looking websites offer college degrees in a short period of time and for a set price, usually several thousand dollars. The diplomas from these "schools" look very real, and often the schools' names are chosen so that they will be confused with legitimate institutions. The "schools" provide fake transcripts, and some have telephone operators who verify graduations to employers who call. Some will also send "transcripts" directly to employers who request them. A few even offer class rings and laminated student ID cards, even though they have no physical buildings or campuses.[2]

Buyers who utilize these degrees fall into two categories: (1) Uninformed people who think the degrees come from legitimate sources and (2) people who knowingly purchase fraudulent degrees. People in this second group may do so for more recognition, pay increases, job promotions, or personal gain. Those who are uninformed and later discover the degrees are fraudulent are usually too embarrassed at their mistake to go public.

Many degree mills claim to have libraries, classrooms, and other essential educational tools and facilities, but most mills operate only at a desk with an Internet-connected computer. They may use photographs in advertisements of buildings not belonging to them. Most have P.O. Boxes or Suite mailing addresses.[2]

Diploma mill "registrars" deliver some or all of the following sales pitches:

Additional Fee. With an additional payment of $75 (or some such amount) in tuition, you will earn summa cum laude.[3]

Advanced Degrees. Bachelor's, masters, MBA, and Ph.D. diplomas are available in the field of your choice. No mention of prerequisite classes.[3]

Combined Degrees. You are told the school can get you a full scholarship for a masters degree, and that you will receive both a bachelor's degree and a master's degree, both for $1,200 (or some such amount) if you register that week.[3]

Everyone Welcome. No one is ever turned down (except those who don't have the money).

It's Quick. You will receive your diploma within days, weeks, or months. If you enroll today, we will send you your diploma, a laminated, wallet-sized replica of your diploma, honors of your choice, transcripts, and letters of recommendation.[3]

Life Experience. You can receive a diploma from our university based on your present knowledge and life experience.[3]

Low Cost. $825 (or some such amount) will certify you for a bachelor's degree from Cyberspace University.[3]

No Dreary Classes. Do you want a diploma without the dreary classes, droning professors, and annoying exams? If so, then Cyberspace University is for you.[3]

No Tests. There will be no required tests, classes, books, or interviews.[3]

Prosperous Future. You will obtain a prosperous future, money earning power, and the admiration of all.[3]

Unlimited Support. You will receive unlimited support from us, including verification of your credentials to prospective employers.[3]

Unfortunately, many of these schools are allowed to operate because it is almost impossible to write a law that will discriminate clearly between legitimate schools and degree mills. And many of these schools operate from other countries where their governments don't care that they are selling worthless degrees to foreigners. Employees armed with academic credentials from degree mills have held jobs as sex-abuse counselors, college vice presidents, child psychologists, athletic coaches, engineers, and physicians.[4]

Examples of Diploma Mills

- **Gaming Control Agent.** Michael Ray Rosenberry, an agent with the Pennsylvania Gaming Control Board's Investigations and Enforcement Bureau, was arrested after officials learned his college degree came from an online diploma mill. Rosenberry, 41, was charged with two counts of false swearing and three counts of unsworn falsification, all misdemeanors. He reportedly said during a background check that he had a Bachelor of Science degree in criminal justice administration from Stanton University, according to court records. However, he never attended one class, never purchased one book, never met with any instructors, and never prepared one paper. Rosenberry told police the diploma cost him $700. The degree and transcript did not contain an address for Stanton University, and its phone numbers were no longer in service. Rosenberry was suspended without pay by the Gaming Control Board. His annual salary was $64,000.[5]

- **Fake Doctor.** After Marion Kolitwenzew learned her eight-year-old daughter was diabetic, she took her to a naturopathic specialist in North Carolina for care. He seemed impressive, with an office full of medical supplies and a slew of medical "degrees" from universities. When the mother followed his advice and took her daughter off insulin, the girl began vomiting and died. It turned out those diplomas came from degree mills. Laurence Perry was found guilty of practicing medicine without a license and involuntary manslaughter, and was sentenced to up to 15 months in jail.[6]

- **MBA for a 6-year-old Cat.** A cat formed the basis of a $100,000 lawsuit filed against Trinity Southern University, which was run by two Texas brothers who subsequently were accused of selling fake degrees. Operators of the "school," which offered no classes, were found guilty of awarding a master of business administration degree to a deputy attorney general's six-year-old cat for $299.[7]

- **Diploma Mill Shut Down.** In 1999, Louisiana shut down Columbia State University, a notorious degree mill that advertised in prestigious publications, such as "The Economist," that students could earn legal, accredited degrees in 27 days. It also had a professional looking website and brochure, which showed pictures of a beautiful campus and stately buildings. Columbia State's real "administrative office" was P.O. Box 231 at Mailboxes Etc. in Metairie, Louisiana. When the two to three thousand dollar tuition fee was received, orders were forwarded to a California office where "admissions officers" fielded calls and mailed out thousands of Columbia State diplomas. Buyers of these bogus degrees included people from the highest levels, including two staffers in the Clinton White House. By the time of the shutdown, Louisiana officials estimated the school was taking in as much as $1 million a month. In the early 1990s, Columbia State's owner, Ronald Pellar, also know as Dr. Dante and the seventh ex-husband of film star Lana Turner, had been convicted of running a fake cosmetology school in California. He fled before being sentenced and was believed to be in Mexico.[8]

SCHOLARSHIP SCAMS

Every year, several hundred thousand students and parents are defrauded of millions of dollars by scholarship scams. The fraudulent programs look real. Their names often imitate legitimate government agencies, grant-giving foundations, education lenders, and scholarship matching services. And they use official-sounding names containing words like National, Federal, Foundation, or Administration. Usually victims write off the expense rather than report the scam because they think they simply didn't win the scholarship. There are a number of types of scholarship scams. They include:

Advance Fee Scholarship. This scam tells you that you've won a college scholarship worth thousands of dollars, but requires that you pay a "disbursement" or "redemption" fee or the "taxes" before they can release your prize. If someone says you've won a scholarship and you don't remember entering the contest or submitting an application, be suspicious.[10]

For Profit. This scam looks just like a real scholarship program, but requires an application fee. The typical scam receives 5,000 to 10,000 applications and charges fees of $5 to $35. They can afford to pay out a $1,000 scholarship or two and still pocket a hefty profit, if they happen to award any scholarships at all. Your odds of winning a scholarship from such scams are less than your chances of striking it rich in the lottery.[10]

Free Seminar. You may receive an email advertising a free financial aid seminar or "interviews" for financial assistance. Sometimes the seminars do provide some useful information, but often they are cleverly disguised sales pitches for financial aid consulting services, scholarship matching services, and overpriced student loans.[10]

Guaranteed Scholarship. Beware of scholarship matching services that guarantee you'll win a scholarship or they'll refund your money. They may simply pocket your money and disappear, or if you don't get a scholarship you'll find it extremely difficult to get that refund.[10]

Investment Required. Insurance companies and brokerage firms sometimes offer free financial aid seminars that are actually sales pitches for insurance, annuity, and investment products. When a sales pitch implies that purchasing such a product is a prerequisite to receiving a federal scholarship, it violates federal regulations and state insurance laws.[10]

Example of a Scholarship Scam

- **Music Education.** Wesley Watkins IV, a 23-year-old Stanford University graduate from Oakland, California, was accepted to a doctoral program in music education at Reading University in England, but was unable to afford the $17,000 annual fees. He searched the World Wide Web for scholarship possibilities and chanced upon World Education Access based in Dayton, Ohio, which vowed a "scholarship for everyone." He joined the organization for $1,289. In exchange he was told that his tuition would be covered. He flew to England and waited. The money never came. While a few individuals did receive money from World Education Access, others received invalid checks or no checks at all.[11]

TIPS TO PROTECT YOURSELF

Degree Mills

If you are considering pursuing an online degree there are some questions you should get answered. If the answer to any of them is yes, be careful.

Accreditation. Is there a claim of accreditation when there is no evidence of this status? Is there a claim of accreditation from a questionable accrediting organization?[12]

Campus Information. Does the operation fail to provide any information about a campus or business location or address and rely only on a post office box? [12]

Claims. Does the operation make claims in its publications for which there is no evidence?

Degree Requirements. Are degrees available based solely on life experience or a resume' or writing a "research paper?"[12]

Faculty. Does the operation fail to provide a list of its faculty and their qualifications?[12]

Licensure. Does the operation lack state or federal licensure or authority to operate?[12]

Name. Does the operation have a name similar to another

146

well-known college or university?[12]

Time. Is a very short period of time required to earn a degree?[12]

Work. Are you required to do a surprisingly small amount of work to obtain the degree, which amounts simply to purchasing the "degree?"[12]

Scholarship Scams

Advance Fee. Don't pay anyone who claims to be holding a scholarship for you if they want money upfront.[9]

Guaranteed. The scholarship is stated to be guaranteed or your money back. No one can guarantee that they can get you a scholarship. Refund guarantees often have conditions or strings attached.[9]

Check It Out. Before you apply for a scholarship, check it out. Make sure the foundation or program is legitimate.[9]

Emails. Be cautious about emails offering scholarship assistance. Many, if not most, unsolicited emails are fraudulent.[13]

No Work. "We'll do all the work." Don't be fooled. There's no way around it. You must apply for scholarships yourself.[9]

Only Source. You can't get this information anywhere else. This is not true. There are many free lists of available scholarships.[9]

Personal Information. If you are asked for your credit card or bank account number to hold a scholarship for you, it's an identity theft scam. Legitimate scholarship agencies won't ask for these. Decline to give the numbers.[9]

Selected. You've been selected by a national foundation to receive a scholarship or you're a finalist in a contest you never entered. Now you have to know this is a scam.[9]

References

1. Watch out for Diploma Mills, Online degrees, financial aid, and scholarships, www.online-degrees-and-scholarships.com/degreemills.htm.
2. Diploma mills - fraud in higher education, DegreeInfo.com, www.degreeinfo.com/article24_1.html.
3. Butler, David, Ivory Tower Rip Offs - How Online Degree Mills

Work, Learners.com, www.elearners.com/resources/diploma-mills.asp.

4. Karp, Jack, Counterfeit credentials, TechTV, www.techtv.com/cybercrime/internetfraud/story/0,23008,3327045,00.html, July 12, 2002.

5. Pa. gambling agent charged for citing degree from 'diploma mill', www.phillyburbs.com/pb-dyn/news/103-04252006-646966.html, April 25, 2006.

6. Armour, Stephanie. Diploma mills insert degree of fraud into job market, USA Today, September 9, 2003.

7. Sly cat: How to avoid education scams, Online Degrees, MSN Encarta, http://encarta.msn.com/encnet/Departments/elearning/?article=slycat.

8. Butler, David, Ivory tower rip offs - how online degree mills work, eLearners.com, www.elearners.com/resources/diploma-mills.asp.

9. Can you spot a college scholarship scam?, CollegeBoard.com, www.collegeboard.com/student/pay/scholarships-and-aid/408.html.

10. Bronner, Ethan, As College Costs Increase, Scholarship Fraud Follows New York Times, November 15, 1988.

11. Common Scholarship Scams, FinAid, www.finaid.org/scholarships/common.phtml.

12. Important questions about accreditation, degree mills and accreditation mills, Council for Higher Education Accreditation, www.chea.org/degreemills/main.asp.

13. Scholarship scams, National Consumer League' Internet Fraud Watch, Internet Fraud Tips, www.fraud.org/tips/internet/scholarship.htm.

Chapter 18

Gambling Fraud

ONLINE CASINO SCAMS

Poker, blackjack, slots, and even bingo can be played online for money. You can even place sports bets online. By logging onto a website with a credit card or online bank account you can gamble yourself deeply into debt, right from your own home. Some credit card companies ban the use of their cards for online gambling; others do not.[1,2]

Online gambling scams are fairly common. The most common one is the refusal of a "casino" to give you your winnings when you've finished gambling. Some gambling scams may make it almost impossible for you win due to absurdly low probabilities, and when you decide to quit they may refuse to let you cash out the money you have left in your account. Yet another fraud that has been perpetrated is selling shares in fraudulent online casinos.[3]

Unlike the past in which 90 percent of the people looking for help with gambling addictions were men, women now make up 40 percent of their ranks.[2] The following story illustrates the kind of problem an online gambler can get into:

- Online gambling led one woman to breaking the law by tapping into her boss's bank account. The courts convicted the

31-year-old of embezzling $65,000 from work, throwing a small company into the verge of bankruptcy. Initially, promising popup ads drew her to play poker online with a credit card and an online bank account. She said she lost track once it progressed into using other people's money. She gambled at home and at work at all hours of the day. She blew her $30,000 saving account. Then she proceeded to max out her credit cards. She decided to break into her boss's bank account to get more money. She also spent her salary into online gambling sites.[2]

Examples of Online Casino Fraud

Bonus Scam

Since online casinos are always in need of a continuous stream of deposits from proven gamblers, this bonus scam works by drawing in players who have played and since moved on to other sites. These players receive an email offering them a bonus if they deposit money into their existing account. However, after the player has deposited the money, no bonus is forthcoming. Casinos simply state that the player is not eligible to receive a bonus. Gamblers tend to play their deposit anyway, which is exactly what the casinos expect to happen.

Some casinos have been known to offer bonuses to get players to deposit money in their account, give them the bonus, and then refuse to pay anything, even their initial deposit, if the player wins. Some casinos then cite "Bonus Abuse" as the reason for denying the cash out, and simply refuse to respond to any requests for explanations by the player, knowing full well that there is no governing body who can act against them.[4]

Email Scam

After depositing $250 and playing for an hour or two, you take the steps to cash out what's left of your bankroll ($50). A few days later, when you still haven't received your cash, you query the "support" staff only to speak to someone who only speaks Spanish and broken English. Eventually you give up and kiss the $50 goodbye, knowing you've been scammed. A few months later you start getting emails from a new site. Unknown to you it's also a scam site, possibly even the sister site to the one that ripped you off in the first place. They got your email address from the registration form from the first site. The new site emails you compelling offers and sends you snail mail rewards packages and CD's with their software—anything to get you in their clutches again.

While it may not always be possible to avoid the first scam, there is a very easy way to get around the second—separate email accounts. Each time you register at a site, be sure to use a free email account, such as MSN Hotmail, Yahoo Mail, or AOL Mail, that you use only with that site. By doing this, if you get scammed, you'll know that any future correspondence to that email address is probably coming from another scammer.[4]

Investment Fraud

As you might imagine, investment fraud rears its ugly heard when it comes to gambling as with any other investment opportunity.

- **Online Gaming Companies.** In Northern California, Robert Robb, the owner of a pair of online gambling websites, was indicted for allegedly defrauding Silicon Valley investors of more than $4 million in an intricate scheme to garner investment for his online gaming companies, Millennium Networks and Junglegames.com. Robb, 23, was said to have forged signatures to make it look as though Las Vegas' top casinos were interested in his online gaming technology and claimed that Microsoft President Steven Ballmer had agreed to purchase his gaming patents for $50 million in cash. He also claimed he had backing from magician David Copperfield. Robb apparently spent a majority of the funds he raised gambling in Las Vegas. If convicted he faced up to five years in jail and fines of up to $250,000.[1]

Knock-Off Websites

Legitimate online gambling sites know they have to overcome the player's instinctive mistrust of both the Internet and gambling. To do this they have to look safe, and to achieve this they spend thousands of dollars on graphics, logos, banners, and general design. For very little money the cybercrooks simply copy what they like from these expensive sites and open fraudulent websites. Some sites even go as far as making exact copies of the testimonial pages of legitimate sites, thus making themselves appear to be great sites loaded with thousands of satisfied players.[3,4]

ONLINE SPORTS BETTING

Offshore sports-betting is illegal. Operators who use the telephones, Internet, or other forms of wire communications to solicit bettors from the United States are in violation of federal law.[5]

Example of Online Sports-Betting Fraud

- **Conspiracy to Transmit Bets and Wagers.** Owners, managers, and employees of five Internet sports-betting companies headquartered in the Caribbean were charged in Manhattan federal court with conspiracy to transmit bets and wagers on sporting events via the Internet and telephones. The defendants all were United States citizens. Worlds Sports Exchange and Galaxy Sports continued to operate sports-betting operations after the arrests of the owners and managers of those companies. In addition, owners or employees of three other sports betting operations—Global Sports Network (Dominican Republic), Grand Holiday Casino (Curacao) and World Wide Tele-sports (Antigua)—were charged. Laurence R. Stofan, the owner of Global Sports Network, operated his business out of Cliffside Park, New Jersey.[5]

TIPS TO PROTECT YOURSELF

Banking Systems. If you are the victim of an online casino fraud and used one of the Internet banking systems, such as Neteller or Firepay, remove any funds from the account.[6,7]
Cash Out. If you can cash out, do so immediately.[6,7]
Credit or Debit Cards. If credit or debit cards were used to deposit funds, contact the bank to inform them that you might

have been a victim of Internet fraud so that, if necessary, they can cancel your credit card and issue you another one with a different number.[6,7]

Customer Care. Contact the site's customer care if your cash out attempt fails. They should respond within forty eight hours to your inquiry. If not, contact them again.[6,7]

Forums. If you don't get satisfaction from other steps, report the incident to various player forums and web portals to help prevent the same thing from happening to other players.[6,7]

Players Association. Contact the Online Players Association, a mediating service designed to help settle disputes.[6,7]

References

1. Online gambling leads one woman to prison, WNDU, South Bend, Indiana, www.wndu.com/news/internetgambling/112003/internet gambling_33816.php, November 20, 2003.
2. Online Gambling Promoter Craps Out - Industry Trend or Event, Newsbytes, www.findarticles.com/p/articles/mi_m0NEW/is_2001
3. _June_4/ai_75278265, June 4, 2001.
4. Blackwood, Ace, Avoiding online gambling scams before they happen, www.hotlib.com/articles/show.php?t=Avoiding_Online_ Gambling_Scams_Before_They_Happen.
5. Vogel, Phillip, Avoiding online casino gambling scams, GoodCasinos.net, www.goodcasinos.net/avoiding-online-gambling-scams.htm, July 13, 2006.
6. Press release, U.S. Attorney Southern District of New York, http://permanent.access.gpo.gov/lps9890/lps9890/www.usdoj.gov/cr iminal/cybercrime/nypr.htm, March 26, 1998.
7. Betting sports legal, Legal.com, www.betting-sports-legal.com.
8. Ways to deal with online gambling scams, Gambling Lair, http://gamblinglair.com/ways-to-deal-with-online-gambling-scams, May 25, 2006.

Chapter 19

Hacking

A *hacker* is a person who is intensely interested in how complex systems, in particular computer systems, work. A *cracker* is said to extend this interest to unauthorized entry and modification of these systems. Nowadays, the term hacker and cracker usually are used interchangeably, much to the dismay of hackers who are sometimes called on to detect, repair, and prevent future damage by crackers. Hackers who do good work are sometimes known as *white hat hackers*, while crackers are known as *black hat hackers*.[1]

BRIEF HISTORY OF HACKING

In the 1960s, MIT geeks had an insatiable curiosity about how computers worked. The smarter programmers created what they called hacks (programming shortcuts) to complete computing tasks more quickly—hence the term "hacking." In 1981, IBM announced a stand-alone machine, the Personal Computer (PC). With the advent of the Internet, young computer enthusiasts began to apply their skills to breaking into other people's computers. The term hacking soon began to be applied to this activity.[2,3]

In the 1970s, phone hackers, known as *phreakers*, broke into regional and international phone networks to make free calls. One phreaker, John Draper, discovered that a toy whistle given away inside Cap'n Crunch cereal generated a 2600-hertz signal, the same high-pitched tone that accessed AT&T's long-distance switching system. Draper built a "blue box" that, when used in conjunction with the whistle and sounded into a phone receiver, allowed phreakers to make free calls. Steve Wozniak and Steve Jobs, future founders of Apple Computer, launched a home industry making and selling blue boxes. A *phracker* has been defined as one who combines phone phreaking with computer hacking.

In the 1980s, the precursor to Usenet newsgroups and email, electronic bulletin board systems (BBSs), sprang up and became the venue of choice for phreakers and hackers to gossip, trade tips, and share stolen computer passwords and credit card numbers. Hacking groups, such as one named Legion of Doom Chaos Computer Club, began to form.[4]

In Milwaukee in 1984 a group of hackers calling themselves the 414s (their area code) broke into systems at institutions ranging from the Los Alamos Laboratories to Manhattan's Memorial Sloan-Kettering Cancer Center. Other hackers soon followed. Internet users became fearful of hackers using tools like password sniffers to ferret out private information or spoofing, which tricked a computer into giving a hacker access. Hackers were no longer considered just kooky eccentrics.

Since a burgeoning online economy with the promise of conducting the world's business over the Internet needed protection, in 1986 Congress passed the Federal Computer Fraud and Abuse Act. The crime of felony hacking carried a sentence of up to five years in prison. Suddenly hackers were criminals. In 1988 Robert Morris, with his Internet worm, crashed 6,000 computers. This act earned him the distinction of being the first person convicted under the new Act's computer-crime provision. He received a $10,000 fine and many hours of community services.[2,3]

In 1989, the first cyber espionage case made international headlines. Hackers in West Germany, loosely affiliated with the Chaos Computer Club, were arrested for breaking into U.S. government and corporate computers and selling operating-system source code to the Soviet KGB. In 1990, after a prolonged sting investigation, Secret Service agents swooped down on hackers in 14 U.S. cities, conducting early-morning raids and arrests. In 1994, as information and easy-to-use tools become available to anyone with Internet access, the face of hacking began to change.[4]

In 1995, long-term hacker Kevin Mitnick was captured by federal agents and charged with stealing 20,000 credit card numbers. He was kept in prison for four years without a trial and became a celebrity in the hacking underground. In 1999 he pleaded guilty to seven charges and was sentenced to little more than time he had already served. He was released from prison in 2000 after serving a five-year sentence for costing companies millions of dollars by stealing software and altering computer information. His supporters, who, during his time behind bars, plastered the phrase "Free Kevin" on hundreds of websites and maintained that his crimes were vastly exaggerated.[4,5]

Also in 1999 Russian hackers siphoned $10 million from Citibank and transferred the money to bank accounts around the world. Vladimir Levin, the 30-year-old ringleader, used his work laptop after hours to transfer the funds to accounts in Finland and Israel. Levin stood trial in the United States and was sentenced to three years in prison. Authorities recovered all but $400,000 of the stolen money.[4]

In 2001, Microsoft became the victim of a new type of hack that attacks the domain name server. In these denial-of-service (DoS) attacks, the DNS (Domain Name System) paths that take users to Microsoft's websites were corrupted. The hack was detected within a few hours, but prevented millions of users from reaching Microsoft webpages for two days.[4]

EXAMPLES OF HACKING

- **Modified Army Computer Contents.** In 1999, one of the founders of a hacker group called Global Hell was arrested and, in a federal complaint, it was alleged he hacked into a protected U.S. Army computer at the Pentagon and maliciously interfered with the communications system. The defendant, Chad Davis, 19, of Green Bay, Wisconsin, was alleged to have gained illegal access to an Army webpage and modified its contents and to have gained access to an unclassified Army network, removing and modifying its computer files to prevent detection. It was said that interference with government computer systems was not just electronic vandalism but ran the risk of compromising critical information infrastructure systems.[6]

- **To Improve Internet Security.** In 2000, two 18-year-old British men were arrested in connection with the theft of more than 26,000 credit card accounts over the Internet. One of the men, who referred to himself as Curador, claimed the break-ins were aimed at exposing common insecurities in commercial websites and that he was on a crusade to eradicate computer security weaknesses in online shopping services. The losses connected with the intrusions were thought to exceed $3 million. As part of his campaign, Curador said he had begun posting thousands of stolen credit card numbers, addresses, and expiration dates on public websites. The two young men had written a simple program that systematically searched tens of thousands of websites looking for a specific vulnerability in a Microsoft Internet Web server. When notified that the illegal credit cards were posted on the Web hosting services, several of the Internet service providers contacted law-enforcement agencies. Curador said he believed that unless he continued to demonstrate the vulnerability of many websites, computer security would not be improved.[7]

- **Trying to Be Helpful.** In 2003, Adrian Lamo, 22, was charged for unauthorized access to a protected computer and illegal possession of stolen access devices—a term that includes passwords and credit card numbers. Lamo had become famous for publicly exposing gaping security holes at large corporations, and then voluntarily helping the companies fix the problems. He had been praised by the then communications giant, WorldCom, after he discovered security holes in their computer system that threatened to expose the private networks of Bank of America, CitiCorp, JP Morgan, and others. He then helped WorldCom fix the problems. Then he penetrated the New York Times and discovered seven misconfigured proxy servers that acted as doorways between the Internet and the Time's private computer system, making the latter accessible to hackers. Once inside he browsed such information as the names and

Social Security numbers of the paper's employees, logs of home delivery customers' stop and start orders, instructions and computer dial-ups for file stories, lists of contacts used by the Metro and Business desks, and the "WireWatch" keywords particular reporters had selected for monitoring wire services. He also accessed a database of 3,000 contributors to the Times op-ed page, containing such information as the Social Security numbers for former U.N. weapons inspector Richard Butler, Democratic operative James Carville, former Secretary of State James Baker, and actor Robert Redford. He also accessed the home telephone numbers of a number of people, including William F. Buckley Jr., Jeanne Kirkpatrick, Rush Limbaugh, Warren Beatty, and former president Jimmy Carter. In 2004, Lamo pleaded guilty to the Times break-in. Under sentencing guidelines, he faced six to 12 months of jail time. In addition, he was ordered to pay a fine of $2,000 to $20,000 and to reimburse the money that his offenses had cost, which amounted to $30,000 to $70,000.[8,9]

- **Famous Hacker Hacked.** In 2003, the world's best-known computer hacker, Kevin Mitnick, suffered the indignity of having someone break into his new security consulting company's website. Mitnick, whose federal probation on hacking charges had ended a few weeks earlier, acknowledged that the electronic break-in at Defensive Thinking, Inc. of Los Angeles was actually the second time in weeks that hackers had found a way into the computer running the firm's website. A hacker calling himself "BugBear" added a message to Mitnick's corporate website which said "Welcome back to freedom, Mr. Kevin," and added that "It was fun and easy to break into your box." The hacker included a photograph of a polar bear with two cubs. The previous break-in was by a hacker in Texas who asked Mitnick to hire him as the company's security officer. In neither instance did hackers vandalize the company's webpages, and one said in an email that he didn't do damage out of respect for Mitnick. Mitnick thought it all was amusing. "All the hackers out there figure if they can hack Kevin Mitnick's site, they're the king of the hill."[5]

- **To Change His Grades.** In California in 2005, Alexander Ochoa was accused of breaking into the Laguna High School's computer. The honor student and football captain was arraigned on three counts of commercial burglary and 86 counts of gaining unauthorized access to the school computer. Ochoa was a juvenile when the alleged crimes occurred. Authorities accused the then-senior of changing his grades and those of other students. Officials believed Ochoa learned a teacher's password, which allowed him to gain access to school computers. He was not allowed to participate in graduation ceremonies.[10]

- **To Get Membership Information.** In 2006 William Bailey, Jr. of Charlotte, North Carolina was charged with 11 counts of unauthorized access to the membership database of the American College of Physicians in Philadelphia and downloading information regarding more than 80,000 members. Bailey ran a business in North Carolina that marketed databases to people interested in marketing to physicians, dentists, lawyers, and other professionals. The American College of Physicians called the FBI immediately. If convicted, Bailey faced a maximum possible sentence of 55 years imprisonment, $2,750,000 in fines, and a special assessment of $1,100.[11]

To Sell Internet Phone Services. Voice over Internet Protocol (VoIP) is a technology for making telephone calls over the Internet. Several companies, including Vonage, Packet8, and Verizon, offer this service at a cost that is less than traditional telephone service. You are required to buy a special adapter into which you plug your telephone and your broadband Internet line. To date there have not been any widespread attempts to exploit this technology, but this will undoubtedly change in the future.[12]

- In 2006, Federal authorities arrested Edwin Andres Pena in Miami and Robert Moore in Spokane in connection with what they said was a hacking scheme involving the resale of Internet telephone service that netted them more than $1 million. Pena used two companies he created to offer wholesale phone connections at discounted rates to small Internet phone companies. Instead of buying access to other networks to connect his clients' calls, he paid about $20,000 to Moore to create what amounted to free routes by hacking into the computer networks of unwitting Internet phone providers, and then routing his customers' calls over those providers' systems. In one three-week period the victimized Internet phone providers received about 500,000 rerouted calls. In all, more than 15 Internet phone companies were left having to pay as much as $300,000 each in connection fees for routing the phone traffic to other carriers, without receiving any revenue for them.[13]

TIPS TO PROTECT YOURSELF

To protect your self from being hacked it is very important that you create virtual security for you computer as discussed in Chapter 1.

References

1. Hacker, cracker, phracker, spy: What's in a name, On Computer and Network Security, Netsurfer Focus, www.netsurf.com/nsf/v01/ 01/nsf.01.01.html#s14, Volume 1/Issue 1, April 26, 1995.
2. Greatest hackers in the whole world, Hackers Hall of Fame, www.geocities.com/vienna/4 3 45/zero .htm.
3. Slatalla, Michelle. A Brief History of Hacking, TLC Discovery, http://tlc.discovery.com/convergence/hackers/articles.
4. Timeline: A 40-year year history of hacking, CNN.com, http://archives.cnn.com/2001/TECH/internet/11/19/hack.history.idg, November 19, 2001.
5. Famous hacker Kevin Mitnick gets hacked, CNN.Com., www.cnn.eom/2003/TECH/internet/02/1 1/hacker.hacked.ap/, February 11, 2003.
6. Wisconsin hacker charged with military break-in, U.S. Department of Justice, www.usdoj.gov/opa/pr/1999/August/387crm.htm, August 10, 1999.
7. Markoff, John, 2 British Youths Held in Theft of Credit Card Accounts on Internet, http://partners.nytimes.com/library/tech/ 00/03/biztech/ articles/25hack.html, March 25, 2000.
8. Poulsen, Kevin, Adrian Lamo charged with computer crimes, Security Focus, http://www.securityfocus.com/news/6888,

September 5,2003.

9. Poulsen, Kevin, Lamo Pleads Guilty to Times Hack, Security Focus, http://www.securityfocus.com/news/7771, January 8, 2004.

10. Bishop, Elizabeth, Accused student hacker faces 89 charges, News10.net, www.news10.net/storyfull2.aspx?storyid=13532, October 7, 2005.

11. North Carolina Man Charged with Illegally Accessing American College of Physicians Database, U.S. Department of Justice, www.cybercrime.gov/baileyCharge.htm, June 15, 2006.

12. Conry-Murray, Andrew and Vincent Weafer, The Symantec Guide to Home Internet Security, Addison-Wesley, Boston, 2006.

13. Belson, Ken and Tom Zeller, Hacker said to resell Internet phone service, Technology, The New York Times, www.nytimes.com/2006/06/07/technology/07cnd-voice.html?, June 7, 2006.

Chapter 20

Identity Theft

Identity theft is stealing the identity of others by using their credit card, driver's license, Social Security, or other personal identification numbers. *With true-name identity theft*, the criminal uses the information to open new accounts. With *account-takeover identity theft*, the criminal uses the information to access existing accounts.

The crooks use the information to purchase items, take out bank loans, or withdraw money in your name. They also may sell your information to other criminals. Not only can the criminals run up big bills for you, but they can ruin your credit and even commit financial crimes pretending to be you, and you may have difficulty proving otherwise.

According to the FBI, identity theft is the nation's fastest growing crime. Approximately 10 million people a year fall victim to identity theft in one form or another.[1]

Identity theft using the Internet is classified as phishing, vishing, or pharming.

PHISHING

Phishing schemes are usually delivered online through spam email purported to be from banks, credit card companies, e-commerce sites, and other institutions in which money normally changes hands. A link in the email leads to a fraudulent webpage, which is a replica of an existing webpage and has a log-on area for you to submit personal data, such as username, account number, and password. Many spoof sites get greedy and ask for additional information, like your Social Security number, credit card number, or bank account number.

Modern browsers, like Internet Explorer 7.0, come equipped with an anti-phishing function that warns you when you access a phishing website.

Phishing is a play on words. It is derived from the word "fishing." The cybercrook puts out the bait and waits to see if you will take it.[2]

Examples of Phishing

FDIC

- **A Message from Tom Ridge.** An email, purported to be from the Federal Deposit Insurance Corporation (FDIC), said that the Department of Homeland Security Director, Tom Ridge, advised the agency to suspend all deposit insurance on the email recipient's bank account because of suspected violations of the USA Patriot Act. The title of the email was "Important News about Your Bank Account." The fraudulent email, which included a link to a website set up to look like the FDIC's site, said that deposit insurance would be suspended until the consumer provide personal data, including bank account information. The FDIC said the emails had been tracked down to servers in Pakistan, Taiwan, China, and Russia.[3]

EBay

An identity theft scam gaining in popularity comes from scammers claiming to be from the potential victim's credit card company, eBay, or PayPal. The con artist sends an email message that states the company needs to verify the potential victim's account information to make sure it's protected. The scammers then use the information they obtain to make fraudulent charges to the account.[4] The following is a sample email purported to be from eBay:

- "Dear eBay User,
  During our regular update and verification of the accounts, we couldn't verify your current information. Either your information has changed or it is incomplete. As a result, your access to bid or buy on eBay has been restricted. To start using your eBay account fully, please update and verify your information by clicking below:
  https://scgi.ebay.com/saw-gi/eBayISAPI.dll?VerifyInformation
  Regards,
  eBay"[4]

Clicking on the link in the above email led to a fraudulent eBay knock-off website.

- **Your Account is Expiring.** The email looked like the real thing—full of eBay logos and links. It stated that Nikki Rizzi's account was expiring, and requested that he fill out a form or risk losing his current auctions. So Rizzi, 25, typed in everything from his driver's license number to his credit card PIN. Then later, during one 15-minute span, someone made seven separate $200 cash-advance withdrawals from his credit card. He became aware there was a problem when he was coming home from the gym and tried to use his credit card. The card was invalid. He changed banks, canceled all credit cards, and moved, making most of the stolen data useless. Unfortunately, he couldn't change his Social Security number.[5]

AOL

- **Update Your Billing Information.** Jeffrey Brett Goodin, 45, of Azusa, California was arrested on federal charges that he sent thousands of emails to America Online users that appeared to be from AOL's Billing Department. The emails urged the subscribers to update their AOL billing information or lose service, and referred them to one of several fraudulent

Internet websites where they could input personal information, including name, address, AOL account information, and credit or debit card data. Goodin later used the information to make unauthorized credit and debit card purchases. If convicted he faced a maximum possible penalty of 30 years in federal prison.[6]

Online Pharmacy

*   **Strange-looking Package.** A customer ordered medication from an on-line pharmacy. After entering all requested information, including credit card number, the site went on to say that he would see the payment on his credit card under a name that had nothing to do with the site. He didn't give it much thought at the time. Two months later he received a strange-looking package in the mail. The return address was some place in India, and the "medication" wasn't in a pill bottle but in sandwich bag and appeared suspicious. Six months later the victim's credit card was charged for over $500 for a phone card. He called his credit card company and obtained the number to call about the charges. Not only was it a call center in India, but the person answering the phone refused to give him any information about the order or the company.[7]

A Nightmare

*   **Really Ripped Off.** In Connecticut, John Harrison spent over 2,000 hours trying to reclaim his life after 20-year-old Jerry Phillips stole his identity and went on a shopping spree—items from Lowes, Home Depot, Sears, and JC Penny, and two cars from Ford, a Harley, and a Kawasaki motorcycle. All told, Phillips made about $265,000 in charges in four months. Police arrested and prosecuted Phillips for the crime and he went to prison for three years. Despite letters from the Justice Department confirming that Harrison was a victim, he continued to be harassed by creditors. What angered Harrison was that he had followed all the rules and still found himself in debt because of a thief.[8]

VISHING

Whereas phishing criminals send you an email and try to get you to go to a website where you can be tricked into giving up sensitive financial and personal information, *vishing* occurs when a scammer sends you an email hoping to get you to telephone a voice mail box to disclose the information. Vishing is also known as *voice phishing.*

Many of the emails are faked to look like they were sent from companies like American Express, Bank of America, and other major companies. They inform customers that they need to update their records. New tools, including software that helps locate phony websites, have made phishing more difficult to pull off, but the vishing scam gets around computer safeguards by using the telephone.[9]

A variant of vishing is for the email to ask that your personal information be faxed, rather than phoned, to bogus security investigators. The email warning appears to come from PayPal. It says that someone tried to reset your password and asks you to participate in an investigation. The email directs you to a Microsoft Word document hosted on a Web site and urges you to download the form, fill it out, and fax it to a toll-free number. The form asks for credit card information. The new tactic comes as people are becoming more suspicious of emails asking them to fill out sensitive information online or call it in to a stated phone number. The scammers are hoping people will feel it's safer to fax back a form.[10]

Con artists use personal data collected through vishing to access online bank accounts and transfer money or make fraudulent online purchases with the stolen credit card numbers.[11]

Example of Vishing

- **Dial a Phone Number.** Customers of Santa Barbara Bank & Trust received emails telling them their accounts with the company's online banking system had been disabled after the bank detected unauthorized access. They were told to dial a telephone number with a local Southern California area code where an automated voice prompted them to enter their account numbers, personal access codes, and other details. It's not clear who was on the other end of the phone line, but it wasn't Santa Barbara Bank & Trust. The FBI said it had traced the Santa Barbara scheme to computers inside and outside the United States, but by that time the phone number had been deactivated.[11]

PHARMING

Pharming (pronounced farming) is very similar to phishing; however, with pharming cybercrooks obtain a legitimate website's IP (Internet Protocol) address and hijack Internet users as they attempt to go to the desired website, redirecting them to an identical-looking fraudulent website. Whereas phishers drop a line in the water and wait to see who will take the bait, pharmers plant the software to steal the Web addresses of legitimate websites and harvest the results. The legitimate website might be that of a bank, eBay, or any other institution that makes financial transactions.

Pharming scams are more difficult to detect because they are not reliant upon you accepting a "bait" to click on an enticing link in an email message or making a phone call. Even if you correctly enter a URL (web address) into a browser's address bar, the attacker can still redirect you to a malicious website.

The key to recognizing an attempt to redirect you to a pharming website is a certificate mismatch. Legitimate secure websites file a certificate of authenticity with Microsoft. If the fraudulent website does not match the domain name of the legitimate website, your browser displays a Security Alert Window. If you click yes in response the question "Do you want to proceed?" there's a good chance you will end up on a pharming website.[12]

Examples of Pharming

- **Duped ISP.** One of the first known pharming attacks was conducted in early 2005. Instead of taking advantage of a software flaw, the attacker duped the personnel at an Internet service provider into entering the "Transfer of Location" from one place to another. Once the original address was moved to the new address, the attacker had effectively hijacked the website and made the genuine site impossible to reach.[12]

- **American Express Popup.** A popup message appeared when customers tried to access the website of American Express by keying in the legitimate and highly secure website address. The message read "We are currently performing regular maintenance of our security measures. Please fill in the correct information for the following category to verify your identity." In the form given below the message, users were told to enter their Social Security number, mother's maiden name, and date of birth. The culprit was Win32.Qhost.v, which is a Trojan that redirected browsers to the malicious website.[13]

Trojans are discussed in Chapter 35.

TIPS TO PROTECT YOURSELF

Attachments. Open email attachments only if you know the person the email is from.[13]

Concern. If you are concerned that there may actually be a problem with your account, pick up the phone and call customer service. Or close the email and type the URL of the company into your browser. Do not copy and past the URL from the email.[14]

Credit Card Statements. Check your bank and credit card statements carefully every month, more often if you can do so online. You also may want to check your credit report annually, since to do so is free.[15]

Emails. The most common form of phishing is emails pretending to be from a legitimate retailer, bank, organization, or government agency. The sender asks you to confirm your personal information for some made-up reason—your account is about to be closed, an order for something has been placed in your name, or your information has been lost because of a computer problem. Never give personal information that is requested as the result of an email.[14]

If Hooked. Act immediately if you've provided account numbers, PINS, or passwords to a phisher. Notify the companies with whom you have the accounts right away, and put a fraud alert on your files at the credit reporting bureaus.[14]

Job Seekers. Job seekers also should be careful. Some

phishers target people who list themselves on job search sites. Pretending to be potential employers, they ask for your Social Security number and other personal information. Verify the person's identity before providing any personal information.[14]

Links. Don't click on links within spam emails. Fraudsters use these links to lure people to phony websites that looks just like the real sites of the company, organization, or agency they're impersonating. If you feel the need to check whether the message is really from the source it claims, call the company, organization, or agency directly.[14]

Pharming. In this latest version of online ID theft, a virus or malicious program is secretly planted in your computer and hijacks your Web browser. When you type in the address of a legitimate website you are taken to a fake copy of the site without realizing it. Any personal information you provide at the phony site can be stolen and fraudulently used.[14]

Popup Window. Sometimes a phisher will direct you to a real company's, organization's, or agency's website, but then an unauthorized popup screen created by the scammer appears, with blanks in which to provide your personal information. Legitimate companies, agencies, and organizations don't ask for personal information via popup screens. Close the window with Alt-F4.[14]

Security. Protect your computer with spam filters, antivirus and anti-spyware software, and a firewall, and keep the programs up to date. Also keep your operating system up to date.[13]

Spelling and Grammar. Legitimate companies take great care to avoid spelling and grammar mistakes in their communications with customers. Be wary of messages with spelling or grammar mistakes.[15]

Vishing. If you receive an email requesting that you call or fax someone about an account, more than likely it is an attempt to get you to reveal your personal information. Be careful.[11,12]

References

1. Identity theft, Technology, Answers.com, www.answers.com/ identity %20theft.
2. Milhorn, H. Thomas, Cybercrime, In Crime: Computer Viruses to Twin Towers, Universal Publishers, Boca Raton, 2005, Pp 46-70.
3. Sullivan, Bob. Who falls for e-mail scams?, MSNBC.com,

http://msnbc.msn.com/id/3404534/,November 4,2003.

4. EBay email scam—phishing, ZinkWeb, www.zincweb.co.uk/ scams_news_ebay.htm.

5. Hampton, Peter, 1RS warns taxpayers about identity theft e-mails, InterGov International, www.intergov.org/, April 30, 2004.

6. Azusa 'Phisher' Arrested for Posing as America Online Billing Representative and Obtaining Personal Information from Subscribers, U.S. Department of Justice, Central District of California, www.cybercrime.gov/goodinArrest.htm, January 26, 2006.

7. Ordering Medication from Online Pharmacy Lead to Identity Theft, Privacy Rights Clearing House, www.privacyrights.org/cases/victim33.htm.

8. An identity theft nightmare, CBSNews.com, www.cbsnews.com/stories/2005/02/25/eveningnews/consumer/ main676597.shtml, February 25, 2005.

9. Beware of vishing email scam, NewsMax.com, www.newsmax. com/ archives/ic/2006/7/17/134937.shtml?s=te, July 17, 2006.

10. Kawamoto, Dawn, New scam asks people to fax away data, CnetNews.com, http://news.com.com/New+scam+asks+ people+ to+fax+away+data/2100-7349_3-5828551.html?tag= nefd.top, August 11, 2005.

11. Lavallee, Andrew, Email Scammers Try New Bait in 'Vishing' For Fresh Victims, The Wall Street Journal Online, http://online.wsj.com/public/article/SB1153092 44673308174-dWwztRkdlWIvH6bL_mhk7RlSW7I_ 20070717.html?mod=blogs, January 17, 2006.

12. Online Fraud: Pharming, Symantec, http://sarc.com/avcenter/ cybercrime/pharming.html.

13. ID theft pop-ups target American Express web site, NetSecurity.org, www.net-security.org/secworld.php?id=3997, May 11, 2006.

14. Phishing, National Consumer League's Internet Fraud Watch, Internet Fraud Tips, www.fraud.org/tips/internet/phishing.htm.

15. Conry-Murray, Andrew and Vincent Weafer, The Symantec Guide to Home Internet Security, Addison-Wesley, Boston, 2006.

Chapter 21

Immigration Fraud

Immigration fraud involves any attempt to get around the immigration laws of the United States. Information about immigration and immigration laws can be found on the website of the U.S. Citizenship and Immigration Services (www.uscis.gov). *Illegal alien fraud* involves promising immigration assistance for a fee, usually a very significant fee, and then failing to provide the promised help.[1]

Many non-governmental websites provide legitimate and useful immigration and visa related information and services. Regardless of the content of these other sites, the federal government does not endorse, recommend, or sponsor any information or material shown at these other sites.

The fraudulent government website problem occurs when non-governmental sites try to mislead members of the public into thinking they are official websites. These sites may attempt to require potential victims to pay for services, such as forms and information about immigration procedures, which are otherwise free on the Department of State visa services website or overseas through the Embassy Consular Section websites. Additionally, these other websites may require you to pay for services you will not receive. These web sites may contact you by email to lure you to their offer. Also, be wary of sending any personal information that might be used for identity theft to these sites.[2]

EXAMPLES OF IMMIGRATION FRAUD

- **Illegal Immigrant Assistance.** In Los Angeles, a man ran a scam in which he claimed to provide immigration assistance to aliens seeking to become residents or citizens of the United States. Using websites (also newspaper advertisements, recruiters, and word of mouth) to offer their services, the scheme typically charged more than $10,000 per client, and promised that the client would receive immigration documents. In some cases, however, the scheme provided clients with counterfeit or false immigration documents. In other cases, it provided no documents at all, and blamed the government and the legal system for the delay in providing the promised documents. The man was sentenced to 87 months imprisonment.[3]

- **Guest Worker Program.** Scammers targeted Hispanic immigrants, claiming to be able to help them apply for benefits under a guest worker program. No such program existed, but because news reports had been covering Congressional debate over immigration legislation, some immigrants were easily persuaded that they were entitled to benefits. Scammers were extracting fees from the immigrants for as much as $1,000.[4]

TIPS TO PROTECT YOURSELF

Third-Party Help. If you are a non-citizen of the United States and wish to immigrate here, be aware that you don't need third party help to do so. See the U.S. Citizenship and Immigration website (www.uscis.gov) for this information.

Upfront Money. Never pay anyone upfront money to assist you in an effort to immigrate to the United States. This is most likely a scam and you will lose your money.

References

1. Milhorn, H. Thomas, Cybercrime, In Crime: Computer Viruses to Twin Towers, Universal Publishers, Boca Raton, 2005, Pp 46-70.

2. Website fraud warning, U.S. Department of State, http://travel.state.gov/visa/immigrants/types/types_1749.html.
3. Internet Fraud, United States Department of Justice, www.internetfraudusdoj.gov, May 15, 2001.
4. Scammers cash in on immigration debate, ConsumerAffairs.com, www.consumeraffairs.com/news04/2006/04/scammers_immigration. html, April 12, 2006.

Chapter 22

Investment Fraud

The Internet serves as an excellent tool for investors, allowing them to easily and inexpensively research investment opportunities. But the Internet is also an excellent tool for fraudsters. Anyone can reach tens of thousands of people by building an Internet website, posting a message on an online bulletin board, entering a discussion in a live "chat" room, or sending mass emails. Fraudulent messages often look real and credible.[1]

Investment fraud includes market manipulation, non-existent companies and products, and Ponzi schemes.[2]

EXAMPLES OF INVESTMENT FRAUD

Market Manipulation

Criminals use two basic methods to manipulate securities markets for their personal profit—pump and dump and short-selling.

Pump and Dump

Criminals disseminate false information in chat rooms, on financial news bulletin boards, on websites, and by mass emails to cause dramatic price increases in stocks (the *pump*), then immediately sell off their holdings of those stocks (the *dump*) to realize substantial profits before the stock price falls back to its usual lower level. Another way to make money on this scam is to place a bet that a company's stock will rise in value.[2]

- **Spread False Information.** Two Southern California men, Hootan Melamed and Arash Aziz-Golshani, bought large blocks of NEI Web World, Inc. stock during a three day period when the company's common stock was trading for pennies a share. Using computers at their college library, the men spread false information on the Internet that NEI was about to be acquired by another company. They then were said to have sold their stock in the rising market, making a profit of about $364,000. Both men were arrested and pleaded guilty. Aziz-Golshani, an Iranian national, was sentenced to 15 months in U.S. prison, while Melamed received a 10-month sentence. The two were also ordered to pay an undetermined amount of penalties.[3]

Short Selling

In this scheme, false information is dissimulated in an effort to cause price decreases in a particular company's stock. Stock is purchased after the fall in value, and then sold when the stock returns to its normal value. Another way to make money on this scam is to place a bet that a company's stock will fall in value.[2]

- **Bogus Press Release.** Mark Jokob allegedly carried out a financial fraud which caused shares in data networking equipment maker, Emulex, to plunge 60 percent following the issue of a false news release on the Internet. Emulex is one of the world's largest suppliers of data networking equipment. The press release claimed that the company's chief executive had resigned and that it had inflated its previous earnings. Jokob, 23, had worked at Internet Wire, which distributed the fake press release. Once it became clear the information was false, the shares recovered nearly all of their losses. Jokob was said to have made nearly $250,000 from the fraud by placing a bet that the company's stock would decrease in value.[4]

Non-existent Companies or Products

This is a very simple scheme, and one that is almost all profit. One or more individuals offer stock in a non-existent company or fraudulently claim a company has a new product, usually through email spam. Then they take their ill-gotten funds and skip town.

Companies

- **Internet Bank.** In Charlotte, North Carolina, David Allen Bear, 49; James Lee Skeen, 33; and Paula Rae Skeen, 28, were indicted on 31 charges by a federal grand jury on fraud and money laundering charges stemming from their operation of an Internet bank. The three were said to have operated Netware International and Netware International Bank from an office in Mooresville, North Carolina. Banking services offered through Netware included a guaranteed 20 percent return on savings, low-interest credit cards, and loans at two percentage points above prime. The bank wasn't recognized by any state or federal regulator and hadn't applied for a license. Defendants used the money they received from the scam to buy a boat, an airplane, and a Jeep for their own use.[5]

Products

- **TV Streaming Video.** Matthew Brown, 41, the head of the Charlotte, North Carolina based company, Future Network Broadcasting, was arrested and accused of attracting $562,000 in investments that he was said to have used for things other than company business. He reportedly told potential investors his company had developed a unique technology that allowed television-quality video to be streamed over the Internet, but no such technology existed. He was charged with securities fraud, wire fraud, money laundering, bank fraud, possession of counterfeit checks, and interstate transportation of stolen property. He also was accused of lying about his college degree, working with the U.S. Marshals Service, and his computer credentials. If convicted he faced a maximum sentence of 450 years in prison.[6]

Ponzi Scheme

A *Ponzi scheme* is a pyramid scheme that involves investment fraud. It is a swindle where investors are enticed with the promise of extremely high returns or dividends over a very short period of time. The scheme is named after Carl Ponzi, an Italian immigrant who in 1920 collected $9.8 million from 10,550 people, including three-fourths of the Boston police force, in an investment fraud. He then paid out $7.8 million in just 8 months, keeping $2 million for himself. He offered profits of 50 percent every 45 days. This short period between payouts and high rate of return is required to create the impetus for the investing frenzy that is to follow as word leaks out.

In the true sense of borrowing from Peter to pay Paul, Ponzi schemes are a simple fraud whereby initial "investors" are paid dividends as interest checks from the deposits of a growing number of new "investors." Profits to investors are not created by the success of the underlying business venture, but instead are derived fraudulently from the contributions of these other "investors." Usually there is no actual investment involved, just money being shipped in from new "investors" to pay the earlier ones. Like every pyramid scheme, Ponzi schemes eventually collapse because the underlying asset upon which the investment was based either never existed, or was grossly overvalued.[7]

- **Autosurf Program.** In Los Angeles the Securities and Exchange Commission filed charges against Charis Johnson of operating a Ponzi scam. The complaint claimed that she ran 12dailypro.com, which was a paid autosurf program. An autosurf program is a type of online advertising that claims to generate advertising revenue by automatically rotating advertised websites into a viewer's Internet browser. Johnson's company was, in fact, said to be a massive Ponzi scheme. She allegedly raised more than $50 million from over 300,000 "investors" worldwide by offering a 44 percent return on their investments in just 12 days. She falsely represented that earlier members' earnings were financed not only by incoming member fees, but also by multiple income streams, including advertising and off-site investments. In fact, at least 95 percent of 12dailyPro.com's revenues came from new investments in the form of membership fees from new or existing members. Of the $50 million her scheme raked in, Johnson transferred $1.9 million to her personal bank account.[8]

TIPS TO PROTECT YOURSELF

Appearance. Don't invest in anything based on appearances. Just because an individual or company has a flashy website doesn't mean it is legitimate. Websites can be created in just a few days, and after a short period of collecting money a site can vanish without a trace.[9]

Big Profits. Beware of promises that you'll make big profits fast. No one can accurately predict how an investment will do. It stands to reason that the investments that promise the biggest pay-off are also the most risky. If someone offers to share "inside" information that is bound to lead to a big profit on your investment, not only is it illegal but most likely a fraud.[10]

Check Offers. Take the time to check out investment offers. A good place to start is with your state securities regulator. The federal Securities and Exchange Commission is another resource for information to help you make wise investment decisions.[10]

Commodities. Be especially wary of investments in commodities. Crooks often promise that the value of investments in coins, precious metals, artwork, oil leases, gemstones, and other commodities will rise. The truth is that the value of these types of investments can go up or down significantly.[10]

Details. Before you invest get the details in writing. Legitimate companies will be happy to give you all the information you need.[10]

Emails. Be cautious about emails for investments. Many unsolicited emails are fraudulent. My advice is that if you get an email about an investment, don't even read it. Delete it.

Greed. Don't be greedy. Remember, if it sounds too good to be true it probably is.[10]

Offshore Investments. Steer clear of offshore investments and investment opportunities in other countries. These are often promoted as a way to avoid taxes. Actually, you are still liable for taxes, and the investments themselves are usually very risky or fraudulent. When you send money abroad and something goes wrong, it's more difficult, if not impossible, to get your money back.[10]

Pressure. Don't agree to anything on the spot. Pressure to act immediately is a warning sign of possible fraud.[10]

Risk. Don't believe claims that there is no risk. There is always risk in investments, and no one but a con artist will tell you otherwise. Words like "guarantee," "high return," "limited offer," or "as safe as a certificate of deposit" may be a red flag.[10]

Testimonials. Don't put much stock in testimonials from strangers. Testimonials are a dime a dozen.[10]

Understand. Understand your investments. If you don't know the difference between stocks and bonds, margin accounts and cash accounts, options and futures, mutual funds and certificates of deposit you've got a lot of work to do before you invest.[10]

References

1. Internet Fraud, U.S. Department of Justice, www.internet fraudusdoj.gov, May 15, 2001.
2. Milhorn, H. Thomas, Cybercrime, In Crime: Computer Viruses to Twin Towers, Universal Publishers, Boca Raton, 2005, Pp 46-70.
3. Micek, John L., Internet stock jammers jailed, News Factor Network, www.newsfactor.com/perl/story/6951.html, January 24, 2001.
4. FBI arrests man in shares hoax, BBC News, http://news.bbc. co.uk/ 2/hi/business/905315.stm, September 1, 2000.
5. Three charged with fraud in Internet bank, The Augusta Chronicle, September 22, 1998.
6. Man arrested for Internet fraud, KGET.com, www.kget.com/ news/ local/story.aspx?content_id=3BBCE7A2-85D4-4BBA-81DD-B9DA3D4441C0, March 8, 2005.
7. Bubble and Ponzi Schemes used in Investment Fraud Scams, Ponzi, Schemes, Scams, Fraud, Crimes of Persuasion, www.crimes -of-persuasion.com/Crimes/InPerson/MajorPerson/ ponzi.htm.
8. McCandless, Jen, SEC puts a stop to online Ponzi scheme, Spotlight News, Wolters Kluwer, CCH Wall Street, www1.cchwallstreet.com/ws-portal/content/news/container.jsp? fn=03-03-06Financial Services, March 3, 2006.
9. Online investment fraud, Columbia Bank, www.columbiabank. com/Page.aspx?hid=254.
10. Investment fraud, Internet fraud tips, National Consumers

League's Internet Fraud Watch, www.fraud.org/tips/
internet/investment.htm.

Chapter 23

Laptop Theft

Laptop computers are made for traveling; consequently they make tempting targets for thieves. They attract everyone from common thieves and dishonest housekeeping employees to sophisticated con men, hi-tech crime rings, and industrial spies. Having a laptop stolen is doubly bad, since not only have you have lost your computer, but you also have to deal with the possibility of data theft.[1,2]

Laptops have been stolen from automobiles, cafes', work places, homes, airports, hotels, and about any other place you can name. Business travelers are at particular risk of having their laptops stolen.

EXAMPLES OF LAPTOP THEFT

Automobile

- **Aetna.** Health insurer company, Aetna, reported that a laptop computer containing personal information on about 38,000 of its members was stolen from an employee's car. The data included names, addresses, and Social Security numbers, but no personal banking information or health claim data. The car, with locked doors, was broken into while it was in an outdoor public parking lot. The company notified all affected members by letter and offered to pay for credit monitoring services to help prevent potential consequences of misuse of the information. Aetna said the employee did not follow their corporate policies about laptop security.[3]

Café

- **Outside Table.** Raul Saucedo was sitting at an outside table at Hudson Bay Café in Oakland, California browsing online when a man suddenly grabbed his laptop and ran down the street. Saucedo ran after the thief yelling at him. He caught up with him, but the man threw the laptop at Saucedo, hitting him in the chest and shoulders. The computer fell to the ground and was damaged as the thief ran to a getaway car. Saucedo, was a graduate student at Cornell University in New York who was on a fellowship at the University of California, Berkeley.[4]

Work

- **University of California.** The University of California, Berkeley warned more than 98,000 people that the theft of a laptop from its graduate school admissions office had exposed their personal information. It contained the names, dates of birth, addresses, and Social Security numbers of graduate students and graduate school applicants. The files went back three decades in some cases. The school urged affected individuals to consider putting a fraud alert out at credit reporting agencies. It also said it since had taken extra measures to prevent similar data losses, such as putting encryption software on computers that store Social Security numbers and increasing security throughout its facilities.[5]

Home

- **Department of Veterans Affairs.** Sensitive information on 26.5 million veterans discharged since 1975 was stolen from the home of a Department of Veterans Affairs employee who had brought the material home to work on. The theft, which was one of the largest breaches of identity security ever, occurred even though the VA had been on notice for years from its inspector general that its information security was lax. Privacy advocates were astonished that the data wasn't encrypted, which would have rendered it useless to all but the most sophisticated computer hackers.[6] Two teenagers eventually were arrested for the theft after the laptop and hard drive were turned into the FBI by an unidentified person in response to a $50,000 reward offer.[7]

Airport

You place your laptop on the conveyor belt for X-ray scanning and move into the line for the metal detector. Then the scam begins. There are at least two people involved in the theft, both just ahead of you. The first person passes through the metal detector without difficulty. The second person carries metal objects, such as a heavy set of keys, which guarantee the metal detector will be set off. As the person's search delays your passage through to the other side, the person who has already passed through security takes your laptop as it comes out of the X-ray scanner and disappears.[8]

Another common airport scam is for a beautiful young woman to walk up behind you, smear mustard or some other condiment on your back without you knowing it, and then stop you and offer to help you clean it up. While you are occupied with the shirt or coat stain (and the beautiful woman), her accomplice, who is standing a few feet behind you, waits for you to set your laptop down. You do, and it's gone.

Another scam is as follows: You're sitting in a chair at an airport. Your laptop is in the chair next to you. A person "accidentally" drops a semi-valuable item in front of you in the hopes that you will chase him or her to return it. Being the nice person that you are, you do just that. While your back is turned, an accomplice picks up your laptop and calmly walks away with it.[2]

- **Ahold Supermarket Chain.** A laptop computer containing the pension data of former employees of Ahold supermarket chains disappeared during a commercial flight between Philadelphia and Boston. It contained information for determining pension benefits of retirees and other former employees of Ahold subsidiaries, and included names, Social Security numbers, birth dates, benefit amounts, and related administrative information. Ahold owns four chains in the Eastern United States—Stop and Stop & Shop Supermarket Co., Giant Food Stores, Giant Food LLC, and Tops Markets. The four chains have a combined current work force of about 139,000. The employee who "lost" the laptop reportedly violated his company's policy by checking the computer with baggage rather that taking the computer as carry-on luggage.[9]

Hotel

• Connecticut-based General Electric Co. reported that a company laptop containing the names and Social Security numbers of 50,000 current and former employees had been stolen from a locked hotel room. The laptop had been issued to a GE official who was authorized to have the data. Afterward, the company mailed letters to the people whose personal information was on the laptop to notify them of the breach and to offer a year's free access to a credit-monitoring service. A GE spokesman declined to give details about where the theft took place. He said evidence suggested the thief was after the stolen computer rather than the data on it, and said there was no sign that the information had been used improperly.[10]

TIPS TO PROTECT YOURSELF

The following suggestions for protecting your laptop and sensitive data are pretty much all inclusive. They cover a range from the basic computer user to computer professionals who deal with sensitive or even classified information. Since all computer users are different, you will have to decide for yourself which suggestions best apply to you and your laptop.

Protect Your Laptop

Air Travel. There are a number of sophisticated professional crime rings that prey on business travelers carrying laptops. They look for brand new, high-end laptops and often shadow the airport curb-side check in, airline and rental car check-in counters, airport shops, and security checkpoints. So be extra careful in these areas.[2]

Asset Tag. Use an asset tag or engrave the laptop. Permanently marking the outer case of the laptop with your name, address, and phone number may greatly increase your odds of getting it returned if it is stolen. Also, marking your laptop may deter casual thieves and may prevent it from being resold over the Internet via an online auction. Alternately, there are a number of metal, tamper-resistant commercial asset tags available that you can use.[2]

Automobile Travel. If renting a car, always rent one with a locking trunk (not a hatchback, minivan, or SUV), and never leave your laptop in a vehicle where a passing thief can see it through the window. Consider using a cable lock to secure it to the trunk lid so that it will be difficult to steal even if the thief manages to open the trunk. Thieves target popular lunch spots with crowded parking lots and often look for rental cars.[2]

Cable Lock or Alarm. Most laptops are equipped with a Universal Security Slot (USS) that allows them to be attached to a cable lock or laptop alarm. If you are going to leave your laptop in a hotel room or other such place, tether it to a strong immovable object. While this may not stop determined thieves with bolt cutters, it will effectively deter casual thieves.[1,2]

Carrying Case. Use a non-descript carrying case. Walking around a public place with a laptop case that has the computer manufacturer's name stamped on it is an invitation for theft. Consider buying a form-fitting padded sleeve for your laptop and carrying the computer in a nondescript carrying case.[2]

Conventions and Conferences. Laptop thieves target business conferences and conventions because they know you'll feel more relaxed around your peers. They look for events that use the same facilities for a few days because they're counting on you becoming careless as you become use to the surroundings and start to feel safe that it's okay to leave your laptop alone when you go on breaks or to lunch.[2]

Docking Station. In the office, use a docking station because the office is a major site of laptop theft. Housekeeping staff, contractors, and disgruntled employees are the usual suspects. A docking station, which permanently affixes your laptop to the desktop, can help prevent it from being stolen. If you are leaving it overnight or for the weekend, lock your laptop in a secure filing cabinet in your office and lock your office door.[2]

Payphones. Beware of payphones. Business travelers sometimes have to use the payphones in airports, restaurants, and hotel lobbies. As you dial the keypad, a thief may be waiting to see if you set your laptop down.[2]

PCMCIA Cards. Lock up your PCMCIA or similar cards. While locking your laptop to a desk with a cable lock may keep someone from walking away with it, it won't keep them from stealing the PCMCIA card or modem that is sticking out of the side of your computer. When not in use, eject these cards from the laptop bay and lock them in a safe place.[2]

Registration. Registering your laptop with the manufacturer will flag it if a thief ever sends it in for maintenance, and thus increases your odds of getting it back.

Safety. Never assume your laptop will be safe just sitting around. Prime target areas for laptop thieves are hotels, bars, airports, and convention centers. If possible, try to stay in physical contact with your laptop at all times.[2]

Serial Number. Write down your laptop's serial number and store it in a safe place. In the event it is stolen, it will be impossible for the police to return it if they can't trace it back to you.[2]

Tracking Software. There are a number of vendors that offer software that enables your laptop periodically to check in to a tracking center using a traceable signal. If your laptop is stolen, you report the theft to the maker of the software. If the new "owner" connects to the Internet, the company will know, and they will provide tracking information to the police.[1,2]

User Name. Prevent the last logged-in user name from being displayed. When you press Ctrl-Alt-Del, a login dialog box appears which displays the name of the last user who logged in to the computer. This user name can later be used in a password-guessing attack. This feature usually can be disabled using the security templates provided on the installation CD.[2]

When Traveling with a Companion. If you are traveling with a trusted friend or business associate use the buddy system to watch each other's laptops.[2]

While Staying in a Hotel. If you leave your laptop in your hotel room, anchor it securely to a metal post or fixed object. Consider locking your laptop up in the hotel's safe, and make sure you get a receipt.[2]

Protect Your Data

Administrator Account. Consider creating a dummy administrator account. Name this account "Administrator," and then give it no privileges and a difficult to guess 10-or-more digit password. Also, rename the actual administrator account something else. These steps will stop some amateur hackers and will slow the more determined ones.[2]

BIOS Password. Enable a strong BIOS (Basic Input/Output System) password. Most modern computers can be password protected by setting a password in the BIOS built into the motherboard of the computer. Find out from your laptop manufacturer if you can reset the BIOS password and if so what the procedure is. Also find out if the BIOS password locks the hard drive so it can't be removed and reinstalled into a similar laptop.[1,2]

Data. Always backup you laptop data before you do any traveling. There are several vendors that offer inexpensive external storage solutions that can hold a large amount of data on a disk small enough to fit easily into your pocket. By having a backup of the files you need, you can work from another PC in the event your laptop is stolen. For additional security you could encrypt the files and have them sent by FedEx or UPS to your destination hotel or office.[2]

Guest Account. Windows 2000 disables the guest account by default, but always check to make sure it is not enabled. For additional security, assign a complex password to the account.[2]

Encryption. Enable encrypting of both folders and files. Windows 2000 comes with an encryption system that adds an extra layer of security for drives, folders, and files. This helps prevent a hacker from accessing your files by physically mounting the hard drive in another computer.[2]

File System. If your operating system is Windows NT, 2000, or XP, use the NTFS file system to protect your data from laptop thieves. FAT and FAT32 file systems don't support file level security.[2]

Firewall. Use a personal firewall on your laptop. Personal firewalls are an effective and inexpensive layer of security that take only a few minutes to install.[2]

Infrared Port. It is possible to use the infrared port of a laptop to browse someone else's files from across a conference room table without them knowing it. Disable the infrared port via the BIOS, or simply cover it up with a small piece of black electrical tape.[2]

Operating System. Choose a secure operating system. Windows 2000 Professional and Windows XP Professional both offer secure logon, file level security, and the ability to encrypt data. If you are running an earlier version of Windows, anyone who picks up your laptop can access your data.[2]

Password. Choose a really good password. After stealing your laptop, the thief has all the time he needs in which to crack the password for your administrator account and get full access to your data. The more numbers, uppercase letters, lowercase letters, and symbols the harder it is to discover. Use no less than 6-digit passwords, preferably more. Make sure all user accounts have been assigned passwords.[1]

Wi-Fi Access. Be careful about using Wi-Fi (wireless) access. With unencrypted Wi-Fi, every password, email message, and webpage can be read by any other person who can gain access to that Wi-Fi network. That means you should only use encrypted email and should never enter a password or confidential information on a webpage over Wi-Fi unless it is a secure connection.[11]

References

1. Beginners Guides: Preventing Data Theft From a Stolen Laptop, PC Stats, www.pcstats.com/articleview.cfm?articleID=1508
2. Laptop Security Guidelines, Labmice.net, Types and Schemes of White Collar Crime, http://labmice.techtarget.com/articles/laptop security. htm, December 10, 2003.
3. MacMillan, Robert and Megan Davies, Aetna says laptop stolen with data on 38,000 members, Computer World Security, www.computerworld. com/securitytopics/security/story/ 0,10801,110987,00.html, April 28, 2006.
4. Higgins, Robin, Laptop theft runs rampant at cafes,

InsideBayArea.com, www.insidebayarea.com/oaklandtribune/ci_
4111498, July 29, 2006.

5. Hines, Matt, Laptop theft puts data of 98,000 at risk,
    CNETNews.com,
    http://news.com.com/Laptop+theft+puts+data+of+98,000+at+risk/21
    00-1029_3-5645362.html, March 29, 2005.

6. I.D. theft made easy, Editorial/Opinion, USA Today,
    www.usatoday.com/news/opinion/editorials/2006-05-23-id-theft-
    edit_x.htm?csp=34, May 23, 2006.

7. 2 teens arrested in theft of VA laptop, MSNBC, www.msnbc.
    msn.com/id/14206137, August 5, 2006.

8. Theft of laptops, Counterintelligence Awareness Guide,
    www.ntc.doe.gov/cita/CI_Awareness_Guide/V1comput/Laptops.htm

9. Personal information of supermarket chains' former workers stolen,
    SiliconValley.com, www.siliconvalley.com/mld/siliconvalley/news/
    editorial/14727604.htm, June2, 2006.

10. GE says laptop with data on 50,000 staffers stolen, Reuters,
    www.msnbc.msn.com/id/15018007/, September 26, 2006.

11. Laptop security tips, ScamBusters.org, www.scambusters.org/
    laptop.html.

Chapter 24

Loan and Grant Scams

LOAN SCAMS

You receive an offer in the mail for an unsecured personal loan with no questions asked. All you have to do to receive a $50,000 (or some similar figure) loan check is to mail the lender a small deposit, say $250.00. The email sounds legitimate and the loan company has an impressive name. Sound like a good deal? If so, you had better keep reading.[1]

Scam artists often impersonate legitimate lenders to entice consumers into falling for their bogus offers. Emails and website promotions guarantee that a loan will be approved regardless of your credit history. But to take advantage of the offer you have to pay an upfront fee. The scam artist takes off with your fee, and the loan never materializes.

Legitimate loan offers don't require an upfront payment. Although legitimate lenders may charge application, appraisal, or credit report fees, the fees are usually paid to the lender after the loan is approved and are generally taken from the amount borrowed. Legitimate lenders don't guarantee a loan, and especially don't do so regardless of your credit history.

Often, advance fee loan sharks claim their fees will go to a third party for credit insurance or a related service. Sometimes, they even fax materials using stolen or forged logos and letterheads from legitimate companies. And that may not be the worst. The loan application you filled out, listing your Social Security number, credit card number, and driver license number, can be used to commit identity theft.

Often, advance fee loan scammers direct applicants to send the fees via Western Union money transfers, payable to an individual rather than a business. They may ask you to use a password code with their Western Union payment, which allows the scammer to hide his or her identity. The company stays in operation only long enough to collect hundreds of upfront fees and then disappears before the authorities can catch up with the perpetrators.[2]

Sometimes the loan scam takes the form of the overpayment scam, which is discussed in Chapter 28. The "loan company" sends you a check for the loan, asks you to deposit it in your bank account, and requests that you mail a part of it back to them or someone else. The scam—the check is no good and you are out the money you sent back.

Examples of Loan Scams

Advance Fee/Fake Check Loans

- In West Virginia, a Canadian loan scam operating under the name Global Capital Solutions was shut down. Consumers said they were contacted by Global after submitting online loan applications, which included Social Security numbers, bank account numbers, and photocopies of driver's licenses. By sending in the application the consumers became candidates for identity theft. Global told consumers they were approved for loans through private individuals willing to invest their money by making small loans to other private individuals. Global also told consumers that before they could receive loans they must wire advance payments by Western Union to private lenders, all of whom were located in Canada. Global told the consumers that their loans would be direct deposited into their bank accounts after their deposits were received. However, consumers never received the loans, and Global stopped responding to telephone calls and emails.

Global allegedly sent some consumers fake certified checks that appeared to be drawn on a Bank of America account. The consumers were instructed to deposit the checks into their personal accounts, and then withdraw a portion of the money and wire it to the private lender in Canada. At least one consumer deposited the fake check, wired the money, and incurred a debt to his bank for $3,500.[3]

Cheap Mortgage Loan

• In the Southern District of Florida, the FTC charged a mortgage spamming operation, 30 Minute Mortgages, with using an array of deceptions to con consumers into sharing their personal financial data. The company reportedly sent spam and maintained websites where it advertised "3.95% 30 year mortgages." The applications required consumers to supply sensitive personal information, such as their names, addresses, phone numbers, Social Security numbers, employment information, income, first and second mortgage payments, and asset/account types and balances. The FTC said 30 Minute Mortgage was not a national mortgage lender and did not actually offer 3.95% 30 year loans. Instead, the company and its principals sold or offered to sell thousands of completed applications to nonaffiliated third parties without consumers' consent. The company's assets were frozen, and the defendants, Gregory P. Roth and Peter W. Stolz, agreed to halt the deceptive practices.[4]

We Now Own Your Loan

If you have a mortgage, auto loan, or student loan, be leery if an email arrives stating that your loan has been transferred to another company and that you should send all future payments to that company. It is not unusual for a loan to be sold to another company; however, the company currently servicing your loan should be the one that notifies you that your loan has been sold— not the company buying the loan. If your current creditor didn't notify you that your loan was transferred, check with them before mailing your checks to a new company.[1]

Mortgage Aid

The mortgage aid scam targets people whose home mortgages are in trouble. In emails the scammers promise to take care of problems with mortgage lenders or to obtain refinancing for the you the potential victim. Sometimes they ask you to make mortgage payments directly to them. They may even ask you to hand over your property deed. The scammers pocket all the money you pay and files for bankruptcy in your name, usually without your knowledge. You lose your money and your home and are left with a bankruptcy listed on your credit records.[5] The following is a typical spam email targeting debtors:

- "Be debt free in 12 months! Eliminate debt fast! Make one low monthly payment! Save 30%-50% and be debt free in 12 months! Would you like to be debt free in 12-30 months? Would you like to pay off your debt at 60 cents on the dollar? Debt mediation can help you accomplish this goal and get you back on your feet to financial freedom without bankruptcy, counseling program, or a loan."[5]

GRANT SCAMS

You receive an email in which the federal government offers to help you start or revitalize your business or pay off your household bills. The email subject might read "RE: The government has a grant for you."[6]

Example of a Grant Scam

Some people have received the following email:

- "Qualifying For A FREE Grant Is Easy!
  $10,000 to over $100,000 in FREE Grant Money is Available NOW!
  ~ Never Repay ~
  ~ No Credit Checks ~
  ~ No Interest Charges ~
  See if YOU meet the requirements

Click Here Now!"[7]

The "*Click Here Now!*" link leads to a webpage that touts a "Free Grant Give Away Program" funded by the U.S. Government and private foundations, and which allows only certain people that meet unusual requirements to get a free grant. The "service" being offered costs $28.00. This is to learn whether or not you qualify for one of the free grants. Furthermore, payment of the $28 can be made only online using a credit card or an online checking account transfer from your bank. Be aware that if you fall for this scam you are not only losing your $28 you are handing your credit card or bank account over to a stranger.[7]

As wonderful as it would be to have the government give money to lucky email recipients, it just doesn't happen. Governments and other organizations that provide grants do not give money away to people for personal needs, such as paying bills. Anyone who tells you differently is trying to steal your money.[6]

TIPS TO PROTECT YOURSELF

Advance Fee. Don't pay upfront. Legitimate lenders or grant donors don't ask for a fee upfront. If there is an application or processing fee, it should be very small, not the hundreds or even thousands of dollars that con artists request. And it should come out of the loan or grant, not be paid upfront.[8]

Costs and Details. Get all the costs and other details before you to apply for a loan or grant. Shop around for the best loan rates and fees.[8]

Credit Problems. Don't fall for promises that you'll get a loan regardless of your credit problems. If you have poor credit or haven't established a good credit record yet, it's unlikely that anyone will lend you money. Your credit history is one of the main things that legitimate lenders use to decide if you are a good credit risk.[8]

Emails. Be cautious about emails offering to help you get a loan or grant. Many unsolicited emails are fraudulent. It's best just to delete them.[8]

Government Grant. The government simply doesn't give away money to help you pay your bills. And it certainly doesn't send you emails telling you that it does.

Licensed Companies. Do business only with licensed companies. Ask your state banking or finance department about the licensing requirements for lenders and loan brokers, and find out if the company is licensed.[8]

Proof. Have proof of what you were promised. Get the agreement in writing or in an electronic form that you can use to document the deal.[8]

References

1. Credit & Loan Scams, BCSAlliance.com, www.bcsalliance.com/ scams~ns4.html.
2. The truth about advanced-fee loan scams, Facts for Consumers, Federal Trade Commission, www.ftc.gov/bcp/conline/pubs/tmarkg/loans.htm, May 2005.
3. West Virginia Shuts Down Advanced Fee Loan Scheme, ConsumerAffairs.com, www.consumeraffairs.com/news04/ 2006/ 03/wv_global_capital.html, March 24, 2006.
4. Deceptive mortgage scam halted, Federal Trade Commission, www.ftc.gov/opa/2003/03/thirty6.htm, March 20, 2003.
5. Fleitas, Amy C., Internet spam spawns scam, Bankrate.com, www. bankrate.com/brm/news/advice/20021025b.asp, March 26, 2003.
6. Government grant scams, Consumer Jungle, www.consumer jungle. org/junglemambo/ index.php?, March 2005.
7. Advanced fee loans, Internet Fraud Tips, National Consumer League's Internet Fraud Watch, www.fraud.org/tips/internet/ advance.htm.
8. Grants email scam alert, Ask.com, http://usgovinfo.about.com/ blscamalert.htm.

Chapter 25

Lottery Scams

A *lottery* is a contest in which tokens or tickets are sold, the winning number (or numbers) being secretly predetermined or ultimately selected in a random drawing. A *sweepstakes* is a lottery in which the participants contribute money to a fund which ultimately is awarded as a prize to one or several winners.[1,2]

Scam operators, often based in Canada, entice U.S. consumers to buy chances in high-stakes foreign lotteries from as far away as Australia and Europe. These lottery solicitations violate U.S. law, which prohibits the cross-border sale or purchase of lottery tickets.[3,4]

In the lottery scam you receive an unsolicited email which states that you have won a major prize in an international lottery. The winning numbers are quoted in the email and, although the lottery company to which the fraudster claims to belong may exist and the numbers may be actual winning numbers as published by the real company, this is nevertheless a scam. Lottery companies don't notify winners by email.

To claim your prize you are instructed to contact the official "agent" in charge of your case. You are also advised to keep the win confidential for security reasons. If you respond to the email, the scammer sends further messages or even contacts you by phone asking you to provide personal information, including banking details and copies of your driver's license and passport to facilitate the transfer of your winnings. And in addition to the identity theft, sooner or later the scammer requests an advance fee, supposedly to cover administration, legal, or delivery costs. Requests for additional money continue until you realize that you are involved in a scam or you run out of money.

In some cases the scammer gives victims the option of opening an account at a particular online bank as an alternative to paying an upfront fee. When contacted, the "bank" insists on an initial deposit of a sum of money, say $3,000, as a requirement for opening the account. The fake bank has a legitimate looking website to reinforce the scam. You may be asked to deposit the winning check (a fake) in your bank account and then send the scammer a cashier's check from your winnings to cover expenses. If you do this you lose the amount of the cashier's check.[5]

Scammers try to add a degree of legitimacy to their claims by mentioning real financial institutions, government departments, or well-known companies. They also may provide a link to a slick looking but fraudulent website. If the scammer is successful in establishing a dialogue with you, he or she may provide "proof," such as a scanned image of a government official's seal and even photographs of the "winnings" in cash.

If you buy one foreign lottery ticket, expect bogus offers for lottery or investment opportunities. Your name will be placed on sucker list that scammers buy and sell.[6]

EXAMPLES OF LOTTERY SCAMS

A Half Million Dollars. In the following scam email you are informed that you have won a half millions dollars. But don't spend it just yet.

- "Dear Winner,
  We are pleased to inform you of the result of the Lottery Winners International programs held on the 26/04/2004. Your e-mail address attached to ticket number 883734657492-5319 with serial number 7263-267, batch number 8254297137, lottery ref number 7336065782 and drew lucky numbers 14-22-28-37-40-44 which consequently won in the 1st category, You have therefore been approved for a lump sum pay out of

US$ 500,000.00 (Five Hundred Thousand United States Dollars). CONGRATULATIONS!!! Due to mix up of some numbers and names, we ask that you keep your winning information confidential until your claims has been processed and your money remitted to you. This is part of our security protocol to avoid double claiming and unwarranted abuse of this program by some participants. All participants were selected through a computer ballot system drawn from over 92,000 companies and 68,000,000 individual email addresses and names from all over the world. This promotional program takes place every year. This lottery was promoted and sponsored by Association of software producers. We hope with part of your winning, you will take part in our next year US$3 Million international lottery. To file for your claim, please contact our fiducial agent MR. VICTOR GRAHAMS of the, ROYAL TRUST AGENCY. TEL: 0031 629 435 359 Email: vgrahamsrta@netscape.net. Remember, all winnings must be claimed not later than 30th of May 2004. After this date all unclaimed funds will be included in the next stake. Please note in order to avoid unnecessary delays and complications, please remember to quote your reference number and batch numbers in all correspondence. Congratulations once more from our members of staff and thank you for being part of our promotional program. Note: Anybody under the age of 18 is automatically disqualified. Yours Sincerely,
Mrs. Hilda Gaspar, Lottery Co-ordinator"[7]

- **El Gordo.** One fake foreign lottery scam adopts the name of Spain's largest lottery prize, "El Gordo," to cheat consumers out of money. According to the Spanish government, people in the United States receive phony emails, letters, and forged materials purporting to be from Spanish banks and claim that the individuals have been the "lucky winners" of a large cash prize. To claim the prize, you are told to pay a sum of money that goes toward the taxes, bank costs, and processing fees necessary to deliver the prize money. The fraudsters use the actual addresses of official Spanish organizations to make their scam appear legitimate.[4]

- **Green Card.** A green card lottery scam operated by a husband and wife team, John Romano and Hoda Nofal, was shut down by the FTC, which filed criminal and civil law suites. The civil action against the couple and their company alleged that the defendants, through eight websites, misled consumers into believing the sites were affiliated with the U.S. government and that for a fee they could help consumers register for a lottery for a chance to apply for a permanent resident visa (green card). Romano pled guilty and was sentenced to 37 months in prison. Nofal was sentenced to six months in prison.[8]

- **Good Try but no Brass Ring.** In Pennsylvania, James A. Koons Jr., 37, was charged in an unsuccessful lottery scam in which a pool of 18 Roadway Express workers almost split $850,492 in winnings. He was accused of creating a bogus ticket for the drawing by scanning losing tickets into his home computer and altering their numbers. When a coworker, Brian Scott Miller, 34, attempted to cash the forged tickets they failed the first of several validation tests. Lottery officials asked Miller to return at a later date to claim his winnings. When he returned, an undercover agent gave him a fake check and then arrested him when he attempted to leave. Authorities said that Miller hadn't participated in the forgery so they only charged him with making a falsification to authorities. If convicted, Koons faced up to 10 years in prison and Miller could see up to two years. The other 16 members of the pool were not implicated in any criminal activity.[9]

TIPS TO PROTECT YOURSELF

Advance on Winnings. It's illegal for a company to require you to buy something or pay a fee to win or claim a prize. Be wary of offers to send you an advance on your "winnings." They send you a check for part of your "winnings" and instruct you to deposit it and then wire payment to them for taxes, bonding, or some other phony purpose. The check for the advance is of course fraudulent.[3]

Credit Card and Bank Account Numbers. Never give your credit card or bank account number to someone who claims you have won a lottery. There is no reason for a legitimate lottery to need these numbers.[3]

Details. Get all the details. Legitimate lottery companies will tell you exactly how the contest works, including the odds of winning, the value of the prize, the date that the contest ends, and how you can find out who won.[3]

Emails. Be cautious of emails telling you that you have won a lottery. Legitimate lottery companies don't inform winners by email.[13]

Foreign Companies. Be especially cautious about foreign lottery companies. Many fraudulent lottery companies targeting U.S. consumers are located in Canada or other countries, which makes it much more difficult for law enforcement agencies to pursue them.[10]

Imposters. Be on guard for imposters. Some con artists use company names that are identical or very similar to well-known, legitimate lottery operators. If you become suspicious contact the real company to ask if there is any connection.[3]

Improved Chances. Buying something doesn't improve your chances of winning. It's illegal for a company to even suggest that your chances will be better if you make a purchase.[10]

Legality. Although there are many legal lotteries in the United States it is illegal for a U.S. citizen to participate in a foreign lottery. So don't.[3]

Social Security Number. Never give your Social Security number to a lottery operator unless you have carefully checked out the lottery with the Better Business Bureau or your state or local consumer protection agency.[3]

References

1. Lottery, Answers.com, www.answers.com/topic/lottery.
2. Sweepstakes, Answers.com, www.answers.com/sweepstakes.
3. International lottery scams, FTC Consumer Alert, Federal Trade Commission, www.ftc.gov/bcp/conline/pubs/alerts/intlalrt.htm, January 2006.
4. FTC Urges Consumers to Be Wary of "El Gordo" Spanish Lottery Scam, Federal Trade Commission, www.ftc.gov/opa/2003/12/elgordo.htm, December 1, 2003.
5. 419 advance fee fraud scams and lottery scams, South African Government Services, and lottery scams www.services.gov.za/419 advancefeefraudand lotteryscam.aspx.

6. Email Lottery Scams - International Lottery Scam Information, HoaxSlayer.com, www.hoax-slayer.com/email-lottery-scams.html#email-lottery-scams.
7. World Wide International Stake Lottery - Email Lottery Scam Example, www.hoax-slayer.com, www.hoax-slayer.com/stake-lottery.html.
8. Green card lottery shut down, ConsumerAffairs.com, www.consumer affairs.com/news04/green_card.html, July 27, 2004.
9. Harkreader, Eric, Man charged in lottery scam, The Sentinel, www.cumberlink.com/articles/2006/03/18/news/news20.txt, March 18, 2006.
10. Prizes and Sweepstakes, Internet Fraud Tips, National Consumer League's Internet Fraud Watch, www.fraud.org /tips/internet/sweepstakes.htm.

Chapter 26

Nigerian Fraud

Defrauding Americans of nearly $200 million annually, *Nigerian* or *419 fraud* is the best know of the advance fee frauds. It gets its name from the Nigerian legal code for fraud, which is the number 419. It is a scheme to extract money from "investors" living in rich countries in Europe, Australia, or North America.

The Nigerian fraud is a subtype of the confidence game commonly referred to as "The Spanish Prisoner," which dates back to 1588. In its original form, the confidence artist told his potential victim that he was in correspondence with a wealthy person who had been imprisoned in Spain, originally by King Philip II, under a false identity. The alleged prisoner was not able to reveal his identity without serious repercussions, and was said to rely on the confidence artist to raise money to secure his release. The confidence artist offered to let the potential victim supply some of the money, with a promise that when the prisoner was released the potential victim would be rewarded generously, both financially and by being allowed to marry the prisoner's beautiful daughter. Props included a treasure map and a provocative picture of the "daughter." However, once the victim turned over his money he learned that further difficulties had arisen, requiring more money, until the mark was cleaned out financially.[1]

Nowadays, as a potential victim of the Nigerian fraud, you typically receive an unsolicited email, often from a "Nigerian" claiming to be a senior civil servant, an oil company executive, a bank officer, someone with a large inheritance, or someone with a high rank in any organization. In the email the person informs you that he is seeking a reputable individual into whose bank account he can deposit funds, typically ranging from $10 to $60 million. He is willing to pay you a healthy percentage of the money (20 to 30 percent) for the temporary use of your bank account. There is always a seemingly logical reason why he has to have the participation of someone outside his country.[2,3,4]

The money is stated to have come from the Nigerian government which overpaid on some procurement, a disbursement, a will, purchase of real estate, conversion of hard currency, sale of crude oil, an award, paper currency conversion, and any number of other sources. Once you've agreed to the arrangement you are requested to pay upfront fees, which may consist of lawyers' fees, taxes, transaction fees, insurance processing fees, or bribes. The fees add up to several thousand dollars, and each must be sent quickly or it will be too late.[2,4]

By requesting personal information, advance fee scammers also are able to steal your identity to obtain credit cards and forge travel documents. If you stop sending money, scammers use the personal information to drain your bank accounts and max out your credit cards until all assets are depleted.[5]

The reason this type of scam is referred to as a Nigerian fraud is because it is thought to have originated in Nigeria in the 1970s. Criminals from other countries have picked up on the scam, so the emails may not come from Nigeria at all, and in fact may come from within the United States.[2]

TACTICS

The Nigerian fraud frequently uses the following tactics:

Email Received. You receive an email from an alleged "official" representing a foreign government, bank, agency, or other important entity.[4]

Offer Made. An offer is made to transfer millions of dollars in funds into your personal bank account for which you get a significant percentage.[4]

You Agree. You agree to have the "fortune" deposited in your bank account.

Request Made. You are requested to provide bank account information, telephone/fax numbers, and so forth.[4]

Documents Received. You receive numerous documents with official looking stamps, seals, and logos testifying to the authenticity of the proposal.[4]

Provide Advance Fee. You are asked to provide upfront fees for various taxes, attorney fees, transaction fees, or bribes. No sooner do you pay one fee than another is requested.[4]

Travel. You may be asked to travel to a foreign country to complete the transaction.

EXAMPLES OF NIGERIAN FRAUD

Effect on People's Lives

The following cases illustrate people who have fallen for Nigerian fraud emails. Because the scam usually involves a large sum of money, the effect on victims' lives can be devastating.

- **Lost His Home.** A Singapore family man named Eric faced selling his home after falling for a multimillion dollar Nigerian email scam. Eric said he had lost almost $190,750 in payments he made to a Nigerian fraudster. He received an email from a man claiming to be the manager of the Diamond Bank of Nigeria offering him a 30 percent share of a $25 million inheritance. In return, Eric had to transfer first $17,000 to a lawyer to handle the transaction and then another $18,000 for the attorney's travel expenses. He was then asked to come up with more money, including $129,000 dollars to facilitate the deal. As instructed, he flew to London where he was shown a large amount of what turned out to be counterfeit money. After seeing the "money," Eric was determined not to give up, so he complied with the man's request. Eric then owed money to the bank and to his friends, and had to put his house up for sale.[6]

- **Murdered Her Husband.** In Selmer, Tennessee, Pastor Matthew Winker was found dead by church members after the family failed to show for church. His wife Mary, age 32, and their three young girls, ranging in age from one to eight years, turned up missing. All four were subsequently located in Georgia. Mary told police she shot her husband after they argued about family financial troubles. Defense attorneys said she was a victim of an overseas check scam thought to be a Nigerian Fraud. She was indicted for premeditated murder of her husband.[7]

Email Examples

Russian Email. The following email is said to be from the personal treasurer to the richest man in Russia. Notice the typical misspelled words, poor grammar, and incorrect punctuation.

- "Date: Sat, 4 Jun 2005 05:22:11 +0200
From: RUIKVASSILY [ruikvassily1@ny.com]
Subject: DEAR FREIND I NEED YOUR ASSISTANCE
Dear Friend,
I am a personal treasurer to Mikhail Khodorkovsky the Richest man in Russia and owner of the following companies: Chairman CEO:YUKOS OIL (Russian Largest Oil Company) Chairman CEO:Menatep SBP Bank (A well reputable financial institution with its Branches all over the world) SOURCE OF FUNDS: I have a profiling amount in an excess of US$100.5M, which I seek your Partnership in accommodating for me. You will be rewarded with 4% of The total sum for your partnership. Can you be my partner on this? INTRODUCTION OF MY SELF As a personal consultant to him, authority Was handed over to me in transfer of money of an American oil merchant For his last oil deal with my boss Mikhail Khodorkovsky. Already the funds have left the shore of Russia to an European private Bank where the final crediting is expected to be carried out.While I was on the process, My Boss got arrested for hisInvolvement in politics by financing the leading And opposing political parties (the Union of Right Forces,Led by Boris Nemtsov, and Yabloko, a liberal/social democratic party Led by Gregor Yavlinsky)

which poses treat to President Vladimir Putin Second Tenure as Russian president. You can catch more of the story on This website: http://newsfromrussia.com/main/2003/11/13/51215. Html. YOUR ROLE: All I need from you is to stand as the beneficiary of the Above quoted Sum and I will re-profile the funds with your name, which will enable The European bank transfer the sum to you. I have decided to use this Sum to relocate to American continent and never to be connected to any Of Mikhail Khodorkovsky conglomerates. The transaction has to be Concluded In 2 weeks before Mikhail Khodorkovsky is out on bail. As Soon as I confirm your readiness to conclude the transaction with me, I Will provide you with the details. Please reach me through my alternative email box: (ruikvassily2@yahoo.com)
Thank your very much.
Regards, Ruik Vassily"[3]

Trapped Funds. The following email is said to be from Federal Government Contract Review Panel in Nigeria.

- "From: "Matthew Ogburu" <ogburum@ngbusiness.s5.com> Subject: REQUEST FOR URGENT BUSINESS RELATIONSHIP
First, I must solicit your strictest confidence in this transaction. This is by virtue of its nature as being utterly confidential and "top secret". We are top officials of the Federal Government Contract Review Panel who are interested in importation of goods into our country with funds that are presently trapped in Nigeria. In order to commence this business, we solicit your assistance to enable us transfer into your account the said-trapped fund. The source of the fund is as follows: During the regime of the last Military transitional government of Gen. Abdulsalami Abubakar, government officials set up companies and awarded themselves contracts which were grossly over invoiced in various ministries. The present democratic government of President Olusegun Obasanjo set up the Contract Review Panel and we have identified a lot of inflated contract funds that are presently floating in the Central Bank of Nigeria ready for payment. However, by virtue of our position as civil servants and members of this panel, we cannot acquire

this money in our names. I have therefore been delegated as a matter of trust by my colleagues in the panel, to look for an oversea partner into whose account we would transfer the sum of US$31,320,000.00 (Thirty-One Million, Three Hundred and Twenty thousand United States Dollars) in which we hope to use in purchasing Agro Allied equipment, and to enable us to own properties and invest in the stable economy of your country. Hence, we are sending you this email message. We have agreed to share the money thus:

1. 20% for the account owner (you)
2. 70% for us (the officials of the CRP)
3. 10% to be used in settling taxation and all local and foreign expenses.

Due to our poor Telecommunication system and for purpose of strict confidentiality you are to respond via Fax No: 1516977909 or e-mail: ogburum@ngbusiness.s5.com. Please acknowledge receipt of this message for proper briefing on the safe modality for the execution.
Yours faithfully"
Dr. Matthew Ogburu"[8]

Saddam's Daughter Email. The following email would come as a surprise to Saddam's actual daughters, Raghad and Ranaho, who were last seen in Jordan.

• "Dear friend,
Please I need urgent assistance and advice. My name is Jume Hasa Hussein. I am daughter of Sadam Hussein, former ruler of Iraq Islamic Republic now in captivity. I was a student of Environmetal Microbiology at Islamic University Al-Athmia before the United Nations weapons inspectors arrived Iraq and subsequent outbreak of hostilities between my father and the Coalition forces. Eventually, my father was arrested at Ad-Dawr, Tikrit on the 13th day of december 2003. To my understanding, the american soldiers have narcotized my father. There is a saying in Iraq "a lion in a cage is still a lion." All my father's known assets have been confiscated by the united nation's coalition group as illegally acquired at the expense of our country. Three of my brothers where tortured to death by the US soldiers for withholding information of my

father's whereabout. Other members of our family have fled our country for fear of persecution. I am presently broke and trapped in a hidden location in our country pending when I secure help from a good samaritan who will assist me to claim a sum of US$30million which my father deposited in my name in a secured vault in Victoria Island in 1995 during my twenty first birthday out of foresight should we his children ever find ourselves in this kind of situation. Most importantly, apart from helping me claim this funds into your custody you will also help me relocate from iraq, to a place where I will conclude my studies with relative peace of mind. For your assistance I am willing to offer you a generous compensation, if you help me.Send your response to my secure email address: deepsolar@123.com to enable me further this relationship.

sincerely

Ms. J. Hasana Hussein"[9]

TIPS TO PROTECT YOURSELF

A Nigerian fraud email has a number of characteristics which you should become familiar with. Avoid responding to any email with these characteristics.

Banking Information. The email requests your banking information. The purpose is for transferring the large sum of "money" to the account. You are promised a cut of the cash for use of your bank account. Never provide your bank account number or other financial information in response to an email. This information can be used to withdraw money from your account.[5,10]

Basic Rule. The basic rule is "Never respond to any email that looks suspicious or sounds too good to be true." If it sounds too good to be true, it most likely is. Just delete the email.

Capital Letters. For emphasis, emails are frequently written partly, if not entirely, in capital letters.[5]

Commission. Scammers promise victims millions of dollars in commission in exchange for access to their banking information and paying upfront fees.[5]

Confidentiality. Scammers emphasize the need for keeping all transactions confidential.[5]

Email Services. Most correspondence is handled by email because it is efficient and easy to distribute as spam. Scammers rely on a variety of free email services, such as Yahoo, MSN, and AOL, to deliver their messages.[5]

Grammar. English usually is not the first language of most Nigerian fraud scammers. Many emails are filled with grammar mistakes and spelling and punctuation errors.[5]

Immediate Action. In every instance of advance fee fraud, scammers phrase emails as a call to immediate action, prompting you to respond urgently, expecting you to do so without thinking carefully.[5]

Important Person. Senders almost always impersonate someone in power or with authority, such as a government official, a bank official, or an oil company executive. They believe this adds credibility to the scam.[5]

Letter Head. The letter head is usually that of a bank, an oil company, a government agency, or some other important entity.[5]

Photographs. Don't believe photographs of the "treasure." One common ploy is to tape money around a block of wood or bundles of paper to make it look like a large amount of currency.[10]

Travel. In some cases scammers may ask you to travel to a foreign country to claim the money. Don't agree to travel anywhere to meet these people. They avoid coming to the United States because they fear arrest. Victims who have traveled to foreign countries have been robbed and even murdered.[5,10]

References

1. Spanish Prisoner Game (AKA: The Nigerian Letter Scam), Scams that Keep Being Used on People, The Unclaimed Funds Scams http://home.austin.rr.com/tsote/scams/various.html.
2. Milhorn, H. Thomas, Cybercrime, In Crime: Computer Viruses to Twin Towers, Universal Publishers, Boca Raton, 2005, Pp 46-70.
3. Nigerian Fraud Email Gallery, www.potifos.com/fraud/
4. Public awareness advisory regarding "4-1-9" or "advance fee fraud" schemes, United States Secret Service, www.secretservice.gov/alert419.shtml.
5. Exposing email-borne fraud: Advanced fee fraud, email security fraud detection: whitepaper provided by Planetmagpie partner Vircom, www.planetmagpie.com/support/advanced-fee-fraud.aspx.

6. Singaporean to lose home after falling for Nigerian Internet scam, Singapore Window, Novembers 2003.
7. Turner, Dennis, Pastor's Wife Allegedly Caught Up in Nigerian Scam Before Murder, Channel 3 News, www.wreg.com/Global/story.asp?S=5101901, July2, 2006.
8. Scams that keep being used on people, Scams, Nigerian trapped funds email, http://home.austin.rr.com/tsote/scams/index.html.
9. Haines, Lestor, 419ers enlist Saddam's daughter, The Register, www.theregister.co.uk/2004/01/30/419ers_enlist_saddams_daughter, January 30, 2004.
10. Nigerian Money Offers, National Consumer League's Internet Fraud Watch, www.fraud.org/tips/internet/nigerian.htm.

Chapter 27

Organized Crime

Organized crime is crime carried out systematically by formal criminal organizations. Crime is now organized on the Internet, giving rise to the term *geekfathers.* Cyberspace mobs operate under names such as Carderplanet, Stealthdivision, Darkprofits, and Shadowcrew.[1]

Organized crime syndicates operate extortion rackets, child-pornography rings, and elaborate financial scams, and in the process they collect millions of dollars a year. The most vulnerable target is the computer user.

Organized crime rings are based in every corner of the globe, particularly in Eastern European countries, including Ukraine, Russia, and Latvia. The crime rings recruit technically savvy programmers to concoct fraud schemes against individuals, banks, and businesses. An increasingly common scam hitting financial institutions is known as *website spoofing* in which a fraudster sets up a bogus online business that closely resembles a bank or business website. The aim is to lure unsuspecting Internet users to the phony site in an effort to get them to submit their credit card and bank details.

Hacking attacks, once considered the domain of bored computer geeks, have become an increasingly common weapon in organized crime's arsenal. Some criminals have launched denial of service attacks, which consist of a crippling barrage of data capable of shutting down Internet companies, such as Internet service providers and online casinos. And they have been known to threaten to unleash the attacks on businesses unless they pay a ransom.[2]

Examples of Organized Crime

- **Shadowcrew.** According to the U.S. Secret Service, in a two year period Shadowcrew's 4,000 members ran a worldwide scam in which 1.5 million credit card numbers, 18 million email accounts, and scores of identification documents—everything from passports to driver's licenses to student IDs—were offered on websites to the highest bidder. Many of the credit card numbers sold on the sites were subsequently used by Shadowcrew's "customers." As a result, more than $4 million in losses were suffered by card issuers and banks. Officials said that Shadowcrew was a Web mob, a highly organized group of criminals. Members know each other by computer aliases, interact with each other through the Internet, and commit their crimes in the privacy of cyberspace. The electronic marketplaces they establish to trade their illicit wares can be set up and then disbanded with little more than a few keystrokes.[1]

- **Telephone Cramming.** Two members of the Gambino crime family in New York, along with several associates, were charged with defrauding users of telephone services amounting to $200 million over a five-year period. Callers responding to advertisements for free samples of services, such as psychic telephone advice, dating services, and telephone chat rooms, were unknowingly charged up to $40 per month on their telephone bills for services they never requested or used. The defendants were charged with using a company that consolidated billings and collections for service providers (through local telephone companies) with innocuous sounding titles like "voice mail services" that were hidden deep within the telephone bills.[3]

- **Romanian Hacker.** A federal grand jury indicted a Romanian computer hacker, Calin Mateias, and five U.S. citizens on charges of a widespread conspiracy to steal more than $10 million in computer equipment from the world's largest technology distributor. The indictment alleged Mateias, 24, hacked into the online ordering system of Ingram Micro in Santa Ana, California and placed fraudulent orders for computers and computer equipment. Mateias, who used the online nickname of Dr. Mengele, directed the equipment be sent to dozens of addresses scattered throughout the United States as part of an Internet fraud ring. The defendants in the United States either sold the equipment and sent the proceeds to Mateias or repackaged the equipment and sent it to Romania.[4]

- **Adult Businesses.** Thousands of Web surfers who thought they were taking a free peek at sexually explicit material were charged $59.99 a month by a company allegedly founded by members of the Gambino family. Officials of the company, Lexitrans Inc., were indicted on federal charges. The company's Kansas offices contained 7,000 square feet of data center space with redundant power and huge fiber-optic pipes for Internet access, and it paid $100,000 a day for placement on search engines such as AltaVista. Lexitrans programmers hatched the idea of inundating users with popup ads for related pornographic sites. The idea worked. The adult websites that Lexitrans ran flourished. Each of the shell companies was controlled by the Mafia and used to defraud consumers through Internet and telephone schemes.[5]

- **Bank Robbery.** In 2000, organized criminals were believed to have carried out the first Internet "bank robbery." Hackers who were part of an organized crime syndicate were thought to have removed several hundreds of thousands of pounds from Egg, which is owned by Prudential and has 1.2 million customers. The suspected fraud came to light after officers from the National Crime Squad carried out a series of early morning raids at seven homes. Three men in their 30s were arrested and questioned by police. The seven A.M. raids, codenamed Operation Skoda, followed a six month inquiry by the National Crime Squad into Internet banking fraud. They were assisted by computer experts from a civilian consultancy company.[6]

- **Prescription Drugs.** The Drug Enforcement Administration's Operation "Cyber Chase" targeted major pharmaceutical drug traffickers who allegedly shipped Schedule II through V pharmaceutical controlled substances, including narcotics, amphetamines, and anabolic steroids, directly to buyers of all ages without the medical examination by a physician required by U.S. law. These e-traffickers used more than 200 websites to illicitly distribute the pharmaceutical substances. An international Internet drug trafficking organization based in Philadelphia was said to be headed by Indian nationals Brij Bansal and Akhil Bansal. The Organization distributed approximately 2.5 million dosage units of controlled substances, including Vicodin (hydrocodone plus acetaminophen), anabolic steroids, and amphetamines, per month. The drugs were manufactured overseas in unregulated facilities (primarily in India), smuggled into the United States in an uncontrolled environment, repackaged, and distributed without oversight of a licensed physician or pharmacist. The indictment sought forfeiture of 41 bank accounts, 26 in the U.S. and the remaining in Cyprus, India, Singapore, the Channel Islands, Isle of Man, West Indies, Antigua, and Ireland.[7]

TIPS TO PROTECT YOURSELF

The rules for protecting yourself from organized crime include the things discussed in Chapter 1: (1) Create a virtual shield, (2) beware of imposters, (3) don't take the bait, (4) stay away from high-risk websites, (5) download with caution, (6) physically protect your laptop, and (7) keep an eye on your children.

References

1. McCormick, Johan and Deborah Gage, Shadowcrew: Web Mobs, Basline: The Project Manager Center, www.baselinemag.com/article2/0,1540,1774393,00.asp, March 7, 2005.

2. Mobs turn net into money machine, Wired News, http://wired.com/ news/ technology/0,1282,60735,00.html, October 7, 2003.
3. FTC exposes top 10 Web scams, CNN .Com, Mob accused of $200 million phone fraud, New York Times, February 11, 2004.
4. Romanian hacker hits high-tech distributor, Organized Crime Digest, www.findarticles.com/p/articles/mi_qa4441/is_200408/ai_n16058948, August 10, 2004.
5. McCafferty, Dennis, Organized cybercrime, Whir News, www. thewhir. com/features/organized-cybercrime.cfm, September 1, 2004.
6. Bennetto, Jason, Three arrested in first Internet bank robbery, The Independent, www.landfield.com/isn/mail-archive/2000/Aug/ 0129.html, August 23, 2000.
7. 20 arrested in Internet prescription drug scheme, Science Blog, www.scienceblog.com/cms/node/7637, April 21, 2005.

Chapter 28

Overpayment Scams

Overpayment scams usually target consumers selling cars, boats, or other valuable items online. However, there are many variations on the scam. It may start with someone offering to pay you to work at home, give you an advance on a lottery you supposedly won but didn't enter, or pay the first installment on the millions that you'll receive for agreeing to have money in a foreign country transferred to your bank account. Whatever the set-up, the bottom line is "If someone you don't know wants to pay you by check, but wants you to wire some of the money back, it's a scam." Don't do it.

The crooks often claim to be in other countries and say it's too hard to make payment directly, so they'll have someone in the U.S. who owes them money, send you a check. Though the checks are counterfeit, they may look good enough to fool bank tellers. The amount of the check is more than you are owed for an online purchase or whatever. You are instructed to deposit the check in your bank account and wire the excess back. Or scammers may tell you to wire some of the money back as fees to collect your "winnings." By the time the checks bounce you have already wired the money to the crooks. Because you are responsible for the checks you deposit, you are left to repay the bank the money you withdrew to send the crooks.[1,2]

HOW IT WORKS

Typically, an overpayment scam works as follows:

Advertisement. You place an Internet advertisement for a car, boat, or other expensive item. Let's say the selling price is $10,000.[3]

Offer Made. You receive an email from someone who wishes to buy the item and agrees to the asking price.[3]

Check Arrives. The scammer then sends a check, or more often a money order, for the item. However, the payment sent is for more than the specified amount, say $13,000.[3]

Overpayment. The scammer provides some legitimate-sounding reason for this overpayment and asks that the balance ($3,000) be electronically transferred to a specified bank account. For example, he might claim that the extra funds are to pay the fees of an agent who will pick up the goods or to cover shipping costs.[3]

Transfer. You take the amount ($3,000) out of your own funds and send the "buyer" the money.[3]

Discovery. Later, you discover that your bank has dishonored the check or money order sent by the scammer. Thus you have been bilked out of a substantial amount of money ($3,000), with little or no chance of recovering it. Furthermore, the item remains unsold and you may have rejected legitimate offers in the meantime—that is if you are lucky. If you ship the item after the bank mistakenly clears the bogus check you are out the item as well as the money.[3]

The supposed buyers usually originate from West Africa, notably Nigeria, but might be based in Holland, the UK, Canada, or even the United States.[3]

EXAMPLES OF OVERPAYMENT SCAMS

- **Car for Sale.** When Michelle Brown offered her car for sale online, a foreign buyer sent a cashier's check for nearly $6,000 more than her asking price. He told her to keep the portion for her car and send the rest (the $6,000) to his shipper. She deposited the cashier's check with no problems and sent the money. Ten days later the bank notified her that the check was bad. CBS tried to track the scam artist, but the London address

217

turned out to be fake. The scammer had used untraceable Nigerian cell phones and vanished after picking up the money the victim had wired to a Western Union. Despite being out $6,000, Brown said she felt like she was being treated like a criminal—like she had done it on purpose.[4]

- **Nigerian Scam.** In Meridian, Mississippi, a man was scammed after responding to an email that he received from someone in Nigeria. In the email, the sender said he had $10,000 "locked" in an account in Nigeria and he needed help getting it. The sender told the victim that he would send him a money order for $10,000 and that the Meridian man was to cash it, keep $4,000 of it, and send the remaining $6,000 back to Nigeria. The Meridian man did just that. However, although the money order looked real, is was counterfeit. The victim had to pay the $6,000 back to the bank.[5]

- **Not Everyone Becomes a Victim.** Rob de Lint knew something was up the minute he received an email asking about accommodations at his Over the Hill Bed-and-Breakfast. The sender, Dr. Kathleen Clinton, claimed to be a consultant employed by the World Health Organization and living in London. She was looking for a place to stay while on assignment in Canada and his place seemed to be the right spot. De Lint spotted glaring errors and odd sentence structure in the email and immediately suspected someone was trying to pull a scam. He decided to play along. It turned out to be the classic overpayment scam. Clinton booked two weeks' accommodations. However, her Dad, suffering from throat cancer, she said, fell into a coma and had to be rushed to surgery. That meant her departure to Canada was delayed. However, her office had already sent Mr. de Lint four $700 international postal money orders by mistake; some of the money was supposed to have covered her air fare. Lacking funds to pay for her flight she suggested that de Lint keep what was owed him and return the balance ($2,100) to her by Western Union so she could pay for her ticket and clear her father's hospital's bills. She even sent a picture of herself—a busty blonde wearing a low-cut black top—so he would recognize her when he went to pick her up at the airport. Had he done what he was told to do, he would have had to cover the bank's loss once it realized weeks later that a fraud had been committed.[6]

TIPS TO PROTECT YOURSELF

Bank's Phone Number. If a bank is involved on the other end, get the bank's phone number from directory assistance or an Internet site that you know and trust, not from the person who sent you the check. Give the bank a call to check out the legitimacy of the check.[1,8]

Know Buyer. Know who you're dealing with. In any transaction, independently confirm the buyer's name, street address, and telephone number.[1,8]

Money Back. Don't accept a check for more than your selling price, no matter how tempting the deal is. Ask the buyer to write the check for the correct amount or forget it. And if the buyer does send a check for more than the asking price, send it back.[7]

Payment Method. Consider an alternative method of payment. As a seller, you can suggest an escrow service or online payment service. If the buyer insists on using a particular escrow or online payment service you've never heard of, check it out. Visit its website and read its terms of agreement and privacy policy. Call the customer service line. If there isn't one or if you call and can't get answers about the service's reliability, don't use the service.[1,8]

Payment by Check. If you accept payment by check, ask for a check drawn on a bank with a local branch. That way you can make a personal visit to make sure the check is valid. If that's not possible, call the bank where the check originated and ask if the check is valid.[1,8]

Pressure. Resist any pressure to act now. If the buyer's offer is good now, it should be good after the check clears the issuing bank.[1,8]

Wiring Money. If the buyer insists that you wire back funds, end the transaction immediately. Legitimate buyers don't ask you to send money by Western Union or a similar company. In addition, you have little recourse if there's a problem with a wire transaction.[1,8]

References

1. FTC Warns Consumers about "Check Overpayment" Scams, Federal Trade Commission, www.ftc.gov/opa/2004/12/checkoverpayment. htm, December 24, 2004.
2. Internet scams, Ammonet.com, www.ammonet.com/ammonet-com/ammonet-ecommerce-scams-eng.htm.
3. Growing Menace: Fake Check Scams, ComsumerAffairs.com, www.consumeraffairs.com/news04/fake_check_scams.html, August 12, 2004.
4. Cashier's checks used in web scams, CBSNews.com, www.cbsnews.com/stories/2003/12/05/eveningnews/consumer/main 587162.shtml, December 5, 2003.
5. Williams, Andrea, E-mail scam, ABC11 News Center, www.wtok.com/news/headlines/1322027.html.
6. Campbell, John, B and B operator warns of e-mail scam, The Independent, www.eastnorthumberland.com/article.php?id=221& from=archives&PHPSESSID=9edcb4f6eb505fe822b2698bf56369 d2, April 12, 2006.
7. Fake check scams, National Consumer Leagues' Internet Fraud Watch, www.fraud.org/tips/internet/fakecheck.htm.
8. Check Overpayment Scams: Seller Beware, FTC Consumer Alert, Federal Trade Commission, www.ftc.gov/bcp/conline/pubs/alerts/ overpayalrt.htm.

Chapter 29

Predatory Behavior

Online predators establish contact with children, adolescents, and teenagers through conversations in chat rooms, instant messaging, email, or discussion boards. They try to gradually seduce their targets through attention, affection, kindness, and even gifts. They devote considerable time, money, and energy to the effort. They are aware of the latest music and hobbies likely to interest young people. They listen to and sympathize with the problems of potential victims. Then they gradually introduce sexual content into the conversations or show sexually explicit material. And they may evaluate potential victims for future face-to-face encounters.

Because of the way the Internet works, young people don't always know with whom they are interacting. Someone who says he is another child in actuality might be an adult predator.[1]

Young adolescents are the most at risk of being approached by an online predator because individuals in this age group are exploring their sexuality, moving away from parental control, and looking for new relationships outside the family. They are more likely to take risks online without fully understanding the possible implications.[2]

Clues Your Child Might Be in Contact With a Predator

Computer Monitor. Your child turns the computer monitor

off or quickly changes the screen on the monitor when you come into the room. A child looking at pornographic images or having sexually explicit conversations does not want you to see it on the screen.[3]

Gifts. As part of the seduction process, offenders commonly send letters, photographs, and gifts to their potential victims. Computer sex offenders have even sent plane tickets for the child to travel across the country to meet him.[3]

Internet Access. Even if you don't subscribe to an Internet service, your child may meet an offender while on-line at a friend's house or the library. So keep this in mind.[3]

Time Online. Most children who fall victim to computer sex offenders spend large amounts of time on-line, particularly at night, and in chat rooms. They may go online after dinner and on the weekends. And they may be latchkey kids who must stay home unsupervised after school. And what better time to use the computer. However, most online predators work during the day and spend their evenings on line trying to locate and lure children.[3]

On-line Account. Be very suspicious if your child is using an online account belonging to someone else. Computer sex offenders will sometimes provide potential victims with a Internet account for communications with them.[3]

Pornography. Sex offenders often supply their potential victims with pornography as a means of opening sexual discussions and for seduction, so you might find pornography on your child's computer. Child pornography may be used to show the potential victim that sex between children and adults is okay. Parents should be conscious of the fact that a child may hide the pornographic files from them on diskettes or other storage devices. This may be especially true if the computer is used by other family members.[3]

Telephone. While talking to a child victim online is a thrill for a computer-sex offender, it can be very cumbersome. Most of them want to talk to the children on the telephone. So be suspicious if your child is receiving phone calls from adults you don't know, or is making calls, sometimes long distance, to numbers you don't recognize. Even if a child is unwilling to give out his or her phone number, with Caller ID computer sex offenders can readily find out the phone number. Some computer sex offenders have even obtained toll-free 800 numbers so that their potential victims can call them without their parents finding out. Others will tell the child to call collect.[3]

Withdrawn. Children who are the victims of online sex offenders often become withdrawn from the family. Computer sex offenders work very hard at driving a wedge between children and their parents. They will accentuate any minor problems at home your child might have.[3]

EXAMPLES OF PREDATORY BEHAVIOR

- **College Student.** Wayne State University graduate student, Mohammed Shaik, was arrested by the Wayne State Police on two counts of child sexual abuse for allegedly soliciting sex with a minor over the Internet. Shaik, 24, was said to have began logging onto an Internet chat room and speaking inappropriately at various times with two police officers who posed as two different girls, one 13 and the other 14 years old. It all came to a head when Shaik arranged a date with the "13-year-old girl" for sex. When he arrived at the meeting location, instead of being met by the teenager he was instead met by officers of the Internet Crimes Unit. Shaik was arraigned on six felony counts—two counts of illegal use of the Internet, two counts of child sexual abuse, and two counts of felonious assault for resisting and opposing police officers. A District Court issued a $500,000 bond for his release. Shaik, who had been in the United States for two years on a student visa, faced two maximum 20-year sentences on both the child sexual abuse charges and the illegal Internet use charges.[4]

- **Police Sting.** During a 10-day period in the Washington D.C. area, 13 undercover police officers witnessed sexual predators soliciting sex from computer screens in front of them. The officers had assumed the roles of children and used fictitious names and identities in chat rooms online. As a result, nine men were arrested as they arrived at prearranged meeting spots. The men ranged in age from 19 to 22 and were identified as a youth minister, a security guard, an auto painter, a teaching assistant, a volunteer firefighter, a student, a Navy employee, an engineer; and someone who was self employed. Each faced at least one count of the felony charges of attempting to take indecent liberties with a juvenile and using an electronic communications device to solicit a minor. The arrests came after the men allegedly drove from their homes to parking lots to meet what they thought were girls ages 11 to 14.[5]

- **Held Her Captive.** A 24-year-old Japanese man, Yasuyoshi Kobayashi, allegedly chained a teenaged girl with a dog collar for more than three months and repeatedly raped and beat her after meeting her in an Internet chat room. Police said the 19-year-old girl traveled from the western province of Hyogo to Tokyo to see Kobayashi after he threatened on the Internet to send gangsters to her home if she didn't obey him. He allegedly kept her in hotels and his apartment, demanding she address him as "master." Kobayashi pretended he had guards to dissuade the girl from leaving, and he periodically called her home in Hyogo to assure her family that everything was fine. The girl was rescued after she escaped and called for help from a shop. Kobayashi denied the accusation and said he could not remember his involvement with the girl and that he suffered from schizophrenia.[6]

- **Webcams.** In Dayton, Ohio, Mark Wayne Miller, age 45, developed sexual relationships with minor-aged females over the Internet, usually in online chat rooms. Using a fictitious name and a photo of an unknown young male, he persuaded the minors to engage in sexually explicit conduct in front of active webcams. Miller watched and recorded the girls, and distributed at least some of the recorded footage to others. His activities were exposed after one of the girls sent a love letter to the fictitious young male, addressed to Miller's former place of employment. Miller's former employer received the letter, found additional evidence relating to child pornography while cleaning out Miller's work area, and notified local law enforcement, which contacted the FBI. Miller was on probation with the State of Ohio and was a registered sex offender when he was arrested. He pled guilty to one count of sexual exploitation of children and one count of computer intrusion, and faced a minimum of 35 years, and up to life, in prison.[7]

- **It Works Both Ways.** A Jacksonville, Florida man said he was duped and robbed by two girls after attempting to meet a woman he met on the Internet. The victim said he chatted online with a woman, known on her MySpace.com profile as Natalia, for two weeks before deciding to meet with her. He said her profile showed sexy photos and a blurb which said "just lookin' for something fun." They decided to meet at what she called her home at the Bentley Green Apartments. He went to the door of the apartment where two girls, ages 14 and 15, approached him. One of the girls put a gun to his head and told him to empty his pockets, which he did. Then they let him go unharmed, and he called the police. Police did a search of the area and found the two teens with another male suspect. The so-called Natalia had told the victim that she was 18, so he was shocked to learn he had been talking to a 14-year-old. The teenagers were charged with armed robbery and carrying a concealed firearm.[8]

- **An Unusual Approach.** Gerald Krein Jr., 27, tried to organize a Valentine's Day mass suicide. For his effort he was charged with solicitation to commit murder and sentenced to up to 20 years in a state mental hospital. He was alleged to have formed a Yahoo chat room to organize "Suicide Party 2005," asking women to hang themselves naked on Valentine's Day. After his arrest a psychiatrist determined he was mentally ill. A woman concerned that children might be harmed alerted authorities to the suicide plot. Detectives found six women who expressed interest in his plan.[9]

TIPS TO PROTECT YOUR CHILDREN

Keeping an eye on your children was discussed in Chapter 1. You should review that material. In addition, if you suspect your child might be involved with an undesirable person online you should do the following:

Don't Underestimate. Never underestimate the persistence of an Internet predator. They are incredibly persistent and totally obsessed with luring victims.[7,10]

Evidence Eraser. Don't allow your child to access any type of evidence eraser, Internet washer, or any other type of hard drive scrubber. Evidence is impossible to discover once a computer's hard drive has been scrubbed.[7,10]

Internet History. Regularly search the Internet history on every computer with Internet access in your home. Be aware that every browser has a Clear History button. While clearing the history prevents you from seeing what sites your children have visited it also may indicate that they have been visiting websites they don't want you to know about. So have a family rule—no one clears the browser history.[7,10,11]

Out of Sight. For places outside your supervision—public library, school, or friends' homes—find out what computer safeguards are used. Don't be hesitant to question the parents of other children your child may visit.[2,7]

Pornography. Check your computer for pornographic files or any type of sexual communication. Be aware that your child may store such files on disks or other devices instead of the computer.[2]

Storage Expansion Devices. Do not allow your child to possess devices that can be used to store and exchange photos and video clips. These devices include zip drives, CD-ROM and DVD disks, additional hard drives, flash drives, video capture cards, and so forth.[7,10]

Talk to your children. Talk to your children about sexual predators and potential online dangers. Instruct them to (1) never arrange a face-to-face meeting with someone they met on-line unless a parent is present at the meting; (2) never upload pictures of themselves onto the Internet to people they do not personally know; (3) never give out identifying information, such as their name, age, home address, school name, or telephone number; (4) never download pictures from an unknown source, as there is a good chance there could be sexually explicit images; (5) never respond to messages or bulletin board postings that are suggestive, obscene, belligerent, or harassing; (6) choose a gender-neutral screen name that doesn't contain sexually suggestive words or reveal personal information; and (7) don't trust what is told to them online by strangers, including the strangers age and sex.[2,3]

Telephone. Monitor who your child calls on the phone and who calls them. Very often predators initiate phone contact after a few Internet chats. Predators frequently send children pre-paid phone cards to use so that the calls will not be detected on your phone bill.[7,10]

Unlimited Access. Don't allow your child unlimited access to the Internet; it may well be the most dangerous entertainment, toy, or babysitter, you could select.[7,10]

Video Devices. Don't allow your child to use a Web Cam, digital camera, or video camera without your close supervision. If you do, don't allow them to have it in their bedrooms.[7,10]

References

1. Hughes, Donna Rice, Sexual predators online, ProtectKids.com, www.protectkids.com/dangers/onlinepred.htm, 2001.
2. Online Predators, Web Aware, www.bewebaware.ca/english/Online Predators.aspx#a1.
3. A Parent's Guide to Internet Safety, Federal Bureau of Investigation, Cyber Division, www.fbi.gov/publications/pguide/pguidee.htm.
4. Kendrick, Kim, WSU student arrested for predatory online behavior, The South End: The student Voice of Wayne State University, www.southend.wayne.edu/modules/news/article.php?storyid=544 November 10, 2004..
5. Stockwell, Jamie, On-line child sex sting results in 9 arrests, WashingtonPost.com, www.washingtonpost.com/wp-dyn/articles/A19962-2005Apr1.html, April 2, 2005.
6. Internet date becomes a nightmare, News24.com, www.news24.com/News24/World/News/0,6119,2-10-1462_1703823,00.html, May 13, 2005.
7. Dayton Man Pleads Guilty to Sexual Exploitation Crimes Involving Minors, U.S. Department of Justice Southern District of Ohio, www.cybercrime.gov/millerPlea.htm, January 19, 2006.
8. Teenaged girls rob man they met on MySpace, WAOI.com, _id=7F710484-5201-42E7-934B-D86CF9E6B65F, June 28, 2006.
9. Man send to hospital in suicide party plan, Associated Press, www.breitbart.com/news/2006/06/21/D8ICPOQ80.html, June 21,2006.
10. Internet child sexual predators, Crisis Connection, www.crisis connectioninc.org/sexualassault/internet_child_sexual_predators.htm

Chapter 30

Pyramid Schemes and Email Chain Letters

PYRAMID SCHEMES

In the classic *pyramid scheme*, participants attempt to make money solely by recruiting new participants into the program. The hallmark of these schemes is the promise of large returns in a short period of time for doing nothing other than handing over your money and getting others to do the same. Over time, the hierarchy of participants resembles a pyramid as newer, larger layers of participants join the established structure. Although pyramid schemes have been declared illegal, they still persist in many forms.[1,2]

The distinguishing feature of a pyramid scheme is the fact that the "product" being sold has little to no intrinsic value. The "products" may be disguised as games, buying clubs, Internet malls, motivational companies, mail order operations, or investment organizations. In reality, the products may be only brochures and cassette tapes explaining to the purchaser how to enroll new members into the scheme. Therefore, your earning potential in such a scheme depends primarily on how many people you sign up, not how much merchandise you sell.[1]

The fraudsters behind a pyramid scheme may go to great

lengths to make the program look like a legitimate multi-level marketing program, such as Avon and Mary Kay Cosmetics. But despite their claims to have legitimate products or services to sell, these fraudsters usually use money coming in from new recruits to pay off earlier investors. But eventually the pyramid collapses. At some point the schemes get too big, the promoter cannot raise enough money from new investors to pay earlier investors, and many people lose their money.[1,3]

A pyramid scheme differs from a Ponzi scheme (discussed in Chapter 22) only in that a Ponzi scheme is the promotion of what starts out to be, or appears to be, a real financial investment opportunity to which investors may passively contribute. The pyramid scheme, on the other hand, doesn't make such a claim.[4]

Examples of Pyramid Schemes

- **Educational Software.** The U.S. government charged four Tulsa, Oklahoma companies with using the Internet to con consumers around the globe out of about $175 million in a massive pyramid scheme. Sky-Biz.com and three partner companies promoted a work-at-home business, charging $125 for an educational software package and the opportunity to earn money by receiving commissions for recruiting others to buy the packages. The FTC charged that the SkyBiz companies and their officers violated federal laws by making false claims that consumers would earn large incomes and failing to mention that most people in such schemes lose money. The government started investigating the company after receiving complaints from American consumers and from people in Australia, Thailand, India, South Africa, and other countries.[5]

- **Dietary Supplements.** The FTC brought suit against a fraudulent Internet operation posing as a legitimate multi-level marketing business, but which reportedly was an illegal pyramid scheme that used phony promises of easy income to scam consumers across the country. The operators of the scam used websites, radio, direct mail, and print advertisements to promote Streamline, a "business opportunity" whose members purportedly distributed a line of dietary supplements and health-care products. Marketing materials contained claims such as: "Yes, you can make $500-$2,000 per month forever!!!" and "No more working for the next 10, 20, 30 or 40 years. Work part-time this year and retire next year." But the majority of participants in the program achieved little or no financial success. The defendants required participants to make minimum monthly purchases in order to be eligible to earn recruitment-related commissions from the purchases of individuals beneath them in the organization. The FTC charged that the resale of these products by participants, which was neither encouraged nor required by defendants, was incidental to making money through the recruitment of new participants.[6]

EMAIL CHAIN LETTERS

An *email chain letter* is a text that advocates its own reproduction: "Please copy this message and send it to 10, 20, or 30 other people." Virtually all chain letters hold out some sort of reward for complying—blessings, good luck, a clear conscience, or money. On the flip side are threats of calamity for failing to circulate the requisite number of copies; for example, "One person did not pass this letter along and died a week later." Email chain letters that request money or other items of value and promise a substantial return to the participants are illegal.[7]

Example of an Email Chain Letter

- **Pentagono.** Known as the Pentagono scam, Future Strategies International claims to be registered with the Italian Chamber of Commerce and to be completely approved by the Italian authorities. In the scheme, investors have to purchase a membership certificate from "a friend" priced at $60. Seven people's names are printed on the certificate; the friend's name is on the bottom. Once the certificate has been purchased, you are asked to send $60 to the person who is shown in the top position. You are also asked to send an additional $60 to Future Strategies International to cover administrative costs. Once this has been paid, it states, you will receive three additional certificates with your name in the seventh position.

You must then sell each additional certificate at $60 each. By the time your name reaches the top of the list, the company claims you can earn a total of $131,220.[8]

TIPS TO PROTECT YOURSELF

Big Earnings. Be wary of big earnings claims. No one can guarantee how much you'll make in a multi-level marketing program. That depends on how hard you work and whether consumers like your products or services.[9]

Check It Out. Check the program out before you commit. Print out all the information and contact your state or local consumer protection agency for advice. In some states, multilevel marketing companies must register with the government and comply with other requirements.[9]

Collapse. Be aware that all pyramids schemes are doomed to collapse. That's because it's impossible to keep on getting fresh recruits who will pay to participate.[9]

Emails. Be cautious about emails for money-making opportunities. Many unsolicited emails are fraudulent. If email chain letters want you to send money, it's illegal.[9]

Gifting Clubs. Be aware that some pyramids are disguised as "gifting clubs." New recruits give money (gifts) to current members with the promise that they will receive money from future recruits.[9]

Inventory. Beware of plans that ask new distributors to purchase expensive inventory. These plans can collapse quickly, and also may be thinly-disguised pyramids.[10]

New Members. Plans that promise profits mainly for recruiting new members are illegal pyramid schemes. In legitimate multilevel marketing plans, profits come primarily from selling goods and services to consumers.[9,10]

Products or Services. Legitimate multilevel marketing plans only succeed if they offer products or services that customers want. All successful businesses depend on repeat sales. If there isn't constant demand for the products or services, the business will fail.[9]

Sales. Sales to other distributors don't count. Legitimate multilevel marketing plans aren't based on sales to distributors. Profits should come from sales that you and any distributors under you make to the end-users.[9]

References

1. Illegal pyramid selling schemes, Schemes, Scams, Frauds, www.crimes-of-persuasion.com/Crimes/Delivered/ pyramids.htm.
2. Milhorn, H. Thomas, Cybercrime, In Crime: Computer Viruses to Twin Towers, Universal Publishers, Boca Raton, 2005, Pp 46-70.
3. Pyramid Schemes, U.S. Securities and Exchange Commission, www.sec.gov/answers/pyramid.htm, September 9, 2004.
4. Bubble and Ponzi Schemes used in Investment Fraud Scams, Ponzi, Schemes, Scams, Fraud, Crimes of Persuasion, www.crimes-of-persuasion.com/Crimes/InPerson/MajorPerson/ ponzi.htm.
5. Skybiz Pyramid Settlement to Provide $20 Million for Consumers, Federal Trade Commission. www.ftc.gov/opa/2003/03/skybiz.htm, March24, 2003.
6. FTC sues nationwide Internet scam, Federal Trade Commission, www.ftc.gov/opa/2001/06/streamline.htm, June 20, 2001.
7. Emery, David, Q. What is a chain letter?, Urban Legends and Folklore, http://urbanlegends.about.com/od/internet/f/chain_ letter.htm.
8. Future Strategies SRL – Pentagono, Royal Canadian Mounted Police, www.rcmp-grc.gc.ca/scams/pentagono_e.htm, December 9, 1998.
9. Pyramids and multilevel marketing, Internet Fraud Tips, National Consumer League's Internet Fraud Watch, www.fraud.org/tips/internet/pyramid.htm.
10. Multilevel marketing plans, Federal Trade Commission, www.ftc.gov/bcp/conline/pubs/invest/mlm.htm, November 1996.

Chapter 31

Prostitution

It had to happen sooner or later—online prostitution has joined cyberspace and apparently is doing quite well. It exists in two forms—adult prostitution and child prostitution.

ADULT PROSTITUTION

Prostitution is the act of offering one's self for hire to engage in sexual relations. It is illegal in all states except Nevada, where it is strictly regulated. Most webpages that advertise prostitution don't blatantly advertise sex for money. Instead, they use obvious code words such as escort or full service. *Incalls* means that you come to her place, *outcalls* means she comes to your place.[1]

Examples of Adult Prostitution

- **Police Sting.** Lubbock Police used an Internet website to crack down on a local prostitution ring. A sting operation led to the arrests of seven people, including one high-profile attorney and one Texas Tech student. The operation began with an online advertisement soliciting sex. The police got 189 responses and continued to get more. Once a reply was confirmed as a truthful lead, police, acting as prostitutes, began a dialogue. When an agreement was made to purchase sex, they set up a meeting spot—either a hotel or a public place, like a park. In Texas prostitution is a Class B Misdemeanor punishable by a maximum fine of $2,000 and a maximum of six months in jail for the first offense. A second offense is a Class A Misdemeanor punishable by a maximum fine of $4,000 and one year in jail.[2]

- **Made the Circuit.** Eleven women, ages 18 to 42, arrested for alleged prostitution said they had thought advertising for sex on the Internet was simpler, safer, and more profitable than street walking, and less visible to the police. The women had all used Craigslist.com to post lewd photos of themselves, their body measurements, phone numbers, and promises of sexual activities for rates up to $500. Craigslist.com is used by millions searching for roommates, homes, and automobiles, and is free to people posting and browsing ads. The prostitutes posted ads under the "Erotic Services" category in multiple cities, working a track from Oregon to Las Vegas, through the San Francisco Bay Area and Reno. Many of the women arrested were from outside the Reno area and advertised they would be in town for the weekend only. The women made appointments through email, instant messaging, or cell phones, and usually met customers at hotels, a home, or some other designated location.[3]

- **To the Highest Bidder.** Something new has surfaced as a result of online auctions—prostitution. Tamika Jones and Melissa Justine, two prostitutes, elected to embrace the Internet and peddled themselves on eBay, as well as other auction sites. Jones said it just made financial sense. Justine concurred. Jones also cited safety and independence as well as other reasons for her going virtual—no pimps, no cops. Many of the online prostitutes put photos of themselves on the sites, often nude.[4]

- **Sex Worker Turned Educator.** In California, Veronica Monet, 42, had her own homepage. Visitors could view photographs of her and find out about her public appearances.

Internet users also could call or email her to set up an appointment to have sex with her. She said that the Internet was an ideal way to reach potential clients—that it might be the first time they had entertained the idea of paying for sex, and that they were a totally different class of people. She offered to create for potential customers "erotic splendors yet unknown." More recently, Monet launched a service providing advice on sex and dating to the public, based on her 13 years experience as a prostitute. This sex worker turned sex educator offers expert advice and opinions on topics pertaining to sex, gender, feminism, and sexual civil rights. She lectures at colleges and universities across the United States.[5]

- **Virginity for Sale.** In England, an 18-year-old student, Rosie Reid, was so hard up for money she decided to make the ultimate sacrifice—sell her virginity to the highest bidder on the Internet. And she was willing to sleep with a man despite being a lesbian. Three months into her Bachelor of Science work in social policy at the University of Bristol she was already 300 pounds in debt. She was working long hours in poorly paid, part-time jobs to pay her tuition fees. After she placed her advertisement on the eBay website she said that more than 400 men, many of them sickos, placed bids offering her up to 10,000 pounds for sex.[6] Later it was reported that Rosie slept with a 44-year-old divorced engineer and father of two in a hotel room in Euston after he paid her 8,400 pounds. Her lesbian partner, Jess Cameron, stayed in the same hotel while Rosie went through with the act. The police were investigating if Reid was guilty of soliciting (prostitution).[7]

CHILD PROSTITUTION

Child prostitution is the sexual exploitation of a child for remuneration in cash or kind. It is illegal in all states.

Examples of Child Prostitution

- **Young and Younger.** In Oakland, California a 14-year-old runaway girl was working as a prostitute, posting ads on

Craigslist.com. Police said a 20-year-old woman was pimping the girl. Both posted erotic photos of themselves. Police said it was obvious by the photos and some of the words that they were involved with sexual encounters. Undercover officers arrested the pair at a South San Francisco hotel. The manager said he had no idea there was prostitution going on. This was the second time in a week that Bay Area investigators connected Craigslist.com with online solicitation. The first case was a 22-year-old woman who was arrested for attempting to prostitute her 4-year-old daughter.[8]

- **Buy an 8-year-old Girl.** In Albany, New York, a man named Threasa Pasquale was arrested and accused of trying to buy an 8-year-old, African-American girl for $300 to have sex with her. An informant had notified police that there was a man who wanted to purchase a young child, and had sexual interests in the child. The police subsequently had a number of conversations over the Internet with Pasquale, as well as a number of telephone conversations with him. He wasn't aware that he was being snared by a sting operation. As instructed, he went to a Motel 6 in Albany fully expecting to acquire the girl. When he arrived at the hotel, officers made the arrest. Pasquale was charged with attempted kidnapping and attempted sodomy.[9]

TIPS TO PROTECT YOURSELF

The obvious way to protect yourself from online prostitution is to stay away from websites were such is offered. If you accidentally end up on one of these sites, click on the back arrow or the X in the upper right-hand corner of your browser. If you decide to get involved personally with the people who are advertised on these sites do so at your own risk.

References

1. Milhorn, H. Thomas, Cybercrime, In Crime: Computer Viruses to Twin Towers, Universal Publishers, Boca Raton, 2005, Pp 46-70.
2. Roberts, Paul, Prostitution sting leads to student arrest, The Daily Toreador, http://media.www.dailytoreador.com/media/storage/

paper870/news/2006/05/01/News/Prostitution.Sting.Leads.To.Stude
nt.Arrest-1896733.shtml?sourcedomain=www.dailytoreador.com
&MIIHost=media.collegepublisher.com, May 1, 2006.

3. O'Malley, Jaclyn, 11 women arrested in prostitution sting, Reno-Gazette Journal, http://news.rgj.com/apps/pbcs.dll/article?AID=/20060703/NEWS01/607030334/1002/NEW, July 23, 2006.
4. Lieberman, Jonny, Name your own price...for hookers?!? E-Bay and Priceline.com muscle in on the world's oldest business model, online hookers, www.sidewalkbubblegum.com/pctyrant.com/hookers.html.
5. The World's Oldest Profession Meets the New Economy, TechTV, http://wᵀw\v.techtv.com/cybercrime/viceonline/story/0,23008,3301846.₁0 0.html, December 30, 2003.
6. Student sells virginity on web, BBC News, http://news.bbc.co.Uk /l/hi/england/bristol/3429769jtti January 26, 2004.
7. Oates, John, Internet virgin faces police probe, The Register, www.theregister.co.uk/2004/03/22/internet_virgin_faces_police_ probe, March 22, 2004.
8. Kim, Lilian, Crackdown on prostitutes using website, 14-year-old runaway arrested, ABC7, http://abclocal.go.com/kgo/story?section= local&id=3627517, November 5, 2005.
9. O'Grady, Sean, Two arrested in child pornography ring, CapitalNews9, www.capitalnews9.com/content/your_news/capital_ region/default.asp?ArID=124522, March 31, 2005.

Chapter 32

Sales Fraud

Although many of the goods and services found online are the same as those sold in stores, the Internet offers a way to search worldwide to find an item that best suits your needs and for the best price. And many items that can't be found locally can be found online. All in all, the Internet is a safe place to shop; however, there are some things to look out for. These include (1) buyer's clubs, (2) faked testimonials, (3) false/deceptive advertising, (4) illegal/stolen items, (5) inflated shipping and handling charges, (6) magazine sales, and (7) nonexistent items.

EXAMPLES OF ONLINE SALES FRAUD

Buyer's Clubs

In emails and on websites fraudsters advertise products at incredibly cheap prices or free if you pay for shipping. These offers may be designed to lure you into a buyer's club membership. And if you join you may be charged automatically for a membership when the free time ends unless you contact the club to cancel, and actually canceling the membership may be extremely difficult.

Watch out for "welcome packages." What looks like an offer

to join a buyer's club may actually be a notice that you've already enrolled. Don't assume you won't be charged because you didn't give your bank account or credit card number. The club already may have obtained this information from another company with which you've done business. Read the information carefully, and contact the club immediately to cancel if you didn't agree to join or the deal was misrepresented, and challenge unauthorized charges or debits immediately. Contact your credit card issuer or bank to explain the problem and ask for your account to be credited. Follow up in writing, and keep a copy of your letter.

Despite the claims, the selection and prices that a buyers club offers may not be as good as you can find yourself. So, comparison shop for the best deal.[1]

Faked Testimonials

"Absolutely the best company I've ever dealt with," said the testimonial. "The best 'thingamabob' on the market," "Works fantastically for me every time," according to other testimonials. What they don't tell you is that the testimonials were written by the website owner or one of his friends.[2]

False/Deceptive Advertising

The advertising could be false, describing and even showing a picture of something that will not be delivered at all. Or it could be misleading, omitting important information or implying something that's not true, such as a computer for zero money down. The advertisement fails to tell you that there is a $295 fee for joining a buyer's club or some other catch to get the computer.[2]

- **Inkjet Printer Cartridge Refills.** The FTC alleged that on-line sellers of generic and remanufactured inkjet printer cartridge refills, E-Babylon, and its two principals, Michael Zaya and Aidin Yousif, deceptively represented that their replacement cartridges were brand-name items and then compared their prices for their products with the brand-name products available at office superstores. E-Babylon, based in Simi Valley, California, was said to operate over a dozen websites, including ProInkjets.com and 123inkjets.com, selling the products. The proposed decree also required the defendants to provide redress to consumers who were entitled to but did not receive a refund. In addition they were required to pay a $40,000 civil penalty.[3]

Illegal/Stolen Items

The item for sale, say a computer, may be adequately and realistically described by the advertisement. The only problem is that it's been stolen. So all the money the fraudster collects is profit. Furthermore, if an investigation leads authorities to you, they will confiscate the stolen computer. Then you will be out your money and the computer.[2]

- **Counterfeit Replicas.** The U.S. District Court in Columbia, South Carolina convicted Mark Dipadova and Theresa Gayle Ford of selling counterfeit versions of Rolex and Cartier watches and Montblanc pens through their website fakegifts.com. During their operation, they shipped over 10,000 packages to domestic and foreign destinations. Dipadova, who also went by Mark Voiers, James English, and Jack Norris, was sentenced to 24 months in federal prison, to be followed by three years of supervised release. In addition, he was ordered to pay a total of $138,264.85 in restitution. Ford was to be sentenced later.[4]

Inflated Shipping and Handling Charges

This is a very common deception and unfortunately one that is legal. The seller advertises a computer hard drive for $59—a real bargain. So you order the item, only to discover that the shipping and handling charge was $49—a total of $108. Now it's not such a good bargain. So never sign out on buying something online until you know what the shipping and handling charges will be.[2]

Magazine Sales

You either receive an email or visit a website advertising popular magazine subscriptions at great prices. So you pick out one and pay for a one year subscription with your credit card. You receive the magazine every month just as advertised and for the price advertised. The problem—other charges for things you didn't sign up for start appearing on your credit card statement. Either that or a year later a charge appears on your credit card for automatic renewal of the subscription despite the fact that you didn't authorize it. No problem, right. You just email, write, or call the company and tell them about the mistake. Don't bet on it. Finding out where the charge originated may be a problem. The magazine company itself tells you that the subscription wasn't ordered through them so there's nothing they can do. The best thing to do is get in touch with your credit card company and tell them you didn't order the renewal and find out who made the charge to your credit card. The company should have a phone number listed when the charge was made.[2]

- **Magazines and More.** Vicky Higgins, 68, signed up for a trial subscription to "Travel + Leisure" magazine, published by American Express. Soon after, she said she was billed $171 for merchandise she didn't order—golf and cooking club memberships and an appointment book. She said she was livid when those items turned up unauthorized on her credit card. Higgins' lawyer filed a lawsuit in a state court in Tennessee, accusing American Express of fraud and deceit. Responding to complaints, an American Express spokeswoman said it is not the company's policy to bill consumers for unwanted merchandise and that charges to consumers are refunded immediately in such billing disputes.[5]

Nonexistent Items

This is the simplest and most common online shopping fraud. The item you want is there on the webpage. It's perfect, and the price is just right. So you order it and sit back and wait—and wait and wait. It never comes. In fact, it never existed at all. You've been scammed. If this happens to you, report it to your credit card company and request that the charge be disallowed, and then watch your credit card statements carefully to make sure unordered items don't start appearing on it. If they do, report these as well, and you may have to request that your current card be cancelled and a new one with a different number issued.

And then there's the advance fee scam. You may be asked to send money in advance, such as a down payment, before the seller ships the item to you. You mail the down payment—end of story. The item never arrives.

And still more—the fake check scam in which the seller gets ripped off. You offer an item for sale online. You get an answer from someone who wants to buy your item. You agree on the price, say $10,000. The purchaser sends you a check for the agreed upon amount. You deposit the check in your bank account and ship the item. Then the bank contacts you; the check bounced. You're out the item.

- **Nonexistent Computer Stuff.** In Oxford, Mississippi, a woman used webpages and interactive computer locations on the Internet to falsely advertise the availability of various computer hardware and software and computer accessories that didn't exist. She was arrested for fraud and sentenced to 15 months' imprisonment and $9,432 restitution.[6]

- **Down Payment Required.** When an Internet site offered a BMW for a sale price of $20,000, a Pennsylvania man forwarded a $2,500 down payment to the seller, David M. Calabretta of Berkley. The problem was that Calabretta, 29, didn't have the BMW to sell. So the purchaser never received it. Calabretta had copied a picture of a BMW from another seller and posted it as his own. He was arrested and pleaded guilty to theft by deception. Calabretta was sentenced to three years in state prison and ordered to make full restitution to the BMW victim as well as other victims he had scammed.[7]

- **Fake Check Scam.** Stay-at-home mom, Isabel Negrete, tried to sell a vintage stove on-line. Someone in Nigeria wanted to buy it and sent her a cashier's check for the amount. She deposited the check in her account with Bank America and shipped the stove. Bank of America called the issuing bank, found out the check was counterfeit, and then called the police. The police promptly arrested, handcuffed, and took

Negrete to a county jail where she was booked, photographed, and stripped-searched. Eventually, the police decided not to charge her with passing a bad check.[8]

- **Land Scam.** The Internet is reviving the land scam. Thousands of lots in phantom subdivisions that were sold decades ago to people who hoped to build retirement homes in warm states are reappearing on online websites. In one case, an elderly woman from the East Coast, who had bought "land" on the Internet sight unseen, roamed the Arizona desert in search of her lot in a subdivision. Instead she found an arid wasteland in the middle of nowhere. She got lost, ran out of gas and water, and had to be rescued by a rancher.[9]

TIPS TO PROTECT YOURSELF

Magazines Sales

Cancellation Policy. Know the cancellation policy. Some magazine subscription services don't allow cancellations once they have placed the orders with the publishers. And when your one-year subscription is up you may have trouble canceling the subscription.[10]

Check the prices. It might be cheaper to buy the magazines directly from the publishers than through an online subscription service.[10]

Details. Get all the details before you decide to subscribe to a magazine. The cost may be described as "pennies a month." but you need to know the length of the subscription commitment and the actual cost. Legitimate companies give all the details upfront.[9]

Free Prizes. Be wary of "free prizes." They're not free if you have to buy magazines to get them.[10]

Imposters. Watch out for imposters. Crooks may pretend to be acting on behalf of well-known magazine publishers when they have absolutely no connection with them at all and will simply pocket your money.[10]

Buyer's Clubs

Cheap or Free. Beware of ads for products at incredibly

cheap prices, or free if you pay for shipping. The ads may be designed to lure you into a buyer's club membership.[1]

Trial Offer. Understand how a trial offer works. In many cases, you will automatically be charged for a membership in a buyer's club when the free time ends unless you contact the club to cancel.[1]

Welcome Packages. Watch out for "welcome packages." What looks like an offer to join a buyers club may actually be a notice that you've already enrolled. Read the information carefully, and contact the club immediately to cancel if you didn't agree to join or the deal was misrepresented.[1]

Comparison Shop. Comparison shop for the best deals. Despite the claims, the selection and prices that a buyer's club offers may not be as good as you can find yourself.[1]

Charge. Don't assume that you won't be charged because you didn't give your account number. The buyer's club may already have obtained your bank account or credit card number from another company with which you've done business.[1]

In Writing. Ask for the details in writing before you agree to join a buyer's club. The deal may not be as great as it sounds once you see exactly how the club works.[1]

General Guidelines

Complaints. Look for information about how complaints are handled by the online merchant. It can be difficult to resolve complaints, especially if the seller is located in another country. Be aware that "no complaints" is not a guarantee of a good online sales merchant. Fraudulent operators open and close quickly, so the fact that no one has made a complaint yet doesn't mean the seller is legitimate.[11]

Emails. Be cautious of unsolicited emails. They are often fraudulent. If you are familiar with the company that sent you the email and you don't want to receive further messages, send a reply asking to be removed from their email list. However, if you are unfamiliar with the company, the best approach may simply be to delete the email.[11]

Imposters. Beware of imposters. Someone might send you an email pretending to be connected with a business by using a website that looks just like that of a well-known company. If you're not sure that you're dealing with the real thing, find another way to contact the legitimate business and ask.[11]

Low Prices and Rebates. Be skeptical about incredibly low prices or rebates that promise to cover the entire cost of the product. The goods may not exist at all or the seller may be on the verge of going out of business and never deliver the promised rebate.[11]

Payment. Credit cards are the safest way to pay for online purchases because you can dispute the charges if you never get the goods or if the offer was misrepresented. Federal law limits your liability to $50 if someone makes unauthorized charges to your account, and most credit card issuers will remove them completely if you report the problem promptly, usually within 60 days.[11]

Personal Information. Guard your personal information. Don't provide your credit card or bank account number unless you are actually paying for something. Your Social Security number should never be necessary to purchase something online. Be especially suspicious if someone claiming to be from a company with whom you have an account asks for information that the business should already have.[11]

Pressure. Resist pressure. Legitimate companies will be happy to give you time to make a decision. It's probably a scam if they demand that you act immediately or won't take "No" for an answer.

Seller. Know who you're dealing with. If the seller is unfamiliar, check with your state or local consumer protection agency and the Better Business Bureau. Some websites have feedback forums which can provide useful information about other people's experiences with particular sellers. Get the physical address and phone number in case there is a problem later.[11]

The Offer. Understand the offer. A legitimate seller will give you all the details about the products, the total price, the delivery time, the refund and cancellation policies, and the terms of any warranty.[11]

References

1. Buyer's clubs, National Consumer League' Internet Fraud Watch, www.fraud.org/tips/internet/buyers.htm.

2. Thomes, James T., Dotcons: Con Games, Fraud, and Deceit on the Internet, Writers Club Press, New York, 2000.
3. On-line sellers of inkjet printer cartridge refills agree to pay $40,000 civil penalty to settle with the FTC, Federal Trade Commission, www.ftc.gov/opa/2002/08/ebabylon.htm, August 23, 2003.
4. Defendant who operated fakegifts.com sentenced, U.S. Department of Justice, District of South Carolina, www.cybercrime.gov/ DipadovaSent.htm, December 17, 2001.
5. Fleck, Carole, Deceptive magazine sales, Consumer Alert, AARP Bulletin, www.aarp.org/bulletin/consumer/a2004-08-26- mag_scam.html, September 2004.
6. Internet Fraud, White Collar Offenses, TheBestDefense.com, www.thebestdefense.com/Crimes/white_collar/internet_fraud.html.
7. Hopkins, Kathleen, Berkley man pleads guilty to Internet fraud, Toms River Bureau, Asbury Park Press, www.app.com/apps/ pbcs.dll/article?AID=/20060324/NEWS02/603240452/1070, March 24, 2006.
8. Cashier's checks used in web scams, Crime Stoopers, Winnebego County Wide, www.winnebagocrimestoppers.org/story3a.htm, December 5, 2005.
9. Nasser, Haya El, Old-fashioned land scams go high-tech, USA Today, www.usatoday.com/tech/news/2006-09-26-land- scams_x.htm, September 27, 2006.
10. Magazine sales scams, internet fraud tips, National Consumer League' Internet Fraud Watch, www.fraud.org/tips/internet/magazine.htm.
11. General Merchandise Sales, Internet Fraud Tips, National Consumer League' Internet Fraud Watch, www.fraud.org/tips/internet/ merchandise.htm.

Chapter 33

Spam

Spam is defined as unwanted email, usually as a form of commercial advertising sent out in bulk. However, the definition has to be altered to include those emails that have the intent of defrauding you of something or stealing your identity. *Spamming* is flooding the Internet with many copies of the same message to multiple addresses. A spammer sends millions of emails in hope that one or two percent will find their way into inboxes and that a further one to two percent will generate a response. Spam messages are almost always sent with false return address information. Spam is also known as *junk email*.

Federal legislation to ban spam and authorize the FTC to enforce a nationwide do-not-spam list passed Congress in December of 2003. The bill, which established fines and prison terms, marked the federal government's first move to control spam. There is some fear that spammers will be able to sidestep new laws by moving operations offshore. Indeed, spam continues to be a problem and spammers have gotten more and more sophisticated in preventing their emails being blocked by computer software known as spam filters.[1,2]

Spam proxies are computers that have been hijacked to send spam. Spam proxies are valuable to spammers because they mask the true origin of the spam emails. Once the spam proxy gets discovered by the legitimate user's Internet service provider and is blacklisted, the spammers simply abandon the blacklisted proxies and "recruit" new ones.

Fighting spam is difficult because spammers have a financial incentive to persist, innovate, and win out. As software gets better at identifying and blocking spam, spammers get smarter at outfoxing the software. A new strain of spam appearing in email boxes contains images touting everything from stock scams to generic Viagra. Spam filters have a harder time detecting image-based spam than the usual text-based spam, and consumers are more likely to read an email with a picture or graphic. The spam uses technology that varies the content of individual messages through colors, backgrounds, picture sizes, or font size. As a result, no two are alike.[3]

COMMON SPAM SCAMS

People respond to spam offers for two reasons: (1) Spam addresses three human desires—sex (Viagra, pornography), money (pyramid schemes, Nigerian fraud), and improved self image (weight loss, penis or breast enlargement), and (2) spam provides a measure of anonymity. A person too embarrassed to buy pornography or penis enlargement pills face to face in a store may find it a lot easier to do so through the Internet.[4]

The following are some of the common scams you are apt to get in your inbox:

Business Opportunity. Most of these scams promise a lot of income for a small investment of time and money. Some are actually old fashioned pyramid schemes camouflaged to look like multi-level marketing programs. And email messages offer the chance to earn money in the comfort of your own home. Three popular versions of the home employment scam pitch envelope stuffing, craft assembly, and medical billing. But nobody will really pay you for stuffing envelopes, craft assembly promoters usually refuse to buy the crafts claiming the work doesn't meet their quality standards, and you can't find any clients for your medical billing business. The bottom line is that you should be wary of money-making schemes that sound too good to be true, because they almost always are.[5]

Charity. After every natural disaster spam emails flood email inboxes requesting donations to bogus charities. Avoid "contributing" to these. Simply delete the emails.

Credit Repair. These scams target consumers with poor credit records. For an upfront fee they offer to clear up a bad credit record or give you a completely clean credit slate by showing you how to get an Employer Identification Number. No one can erase a bad credit record if it's accurate, and using an Employer Identification Number to set up a new credit identity is against the law.[5]

Dating and Marriage. Beware of emails for women seeking companionship. If you agree to correspond with the person named in the email you next will be asked for money. Be especially leery if the named individual is from Russia.

Easy Money. Offers such as "Learn how to make $4,000 in one week," or "Make unlimited profits exchanging money on world currency markets" are bogus. If making money was that easy, everyone would be a millionaire.[5]

Email Chain Letters. These electronic versions of the old fashioned chain letter usually arrive with claims like, "You are about to make $50,000 in less than 90 days!" But of course that's a scam. These electronic chain letters are every bit as illegal as the old fashioned paper versions.[5]

Get Something Free. The lure of valuable, free items, like computers or long-distance phone cards, gets you to pay membership fees to sign up with these scams. After you pay the fee, you learn that you don't qualify for the "free" gift until you recruit other "members." These scams are often pyramid schemes, which are illegal. Other scams in this category include the Nigerian Fraud in which you are asked for use of your bank account in return for a share of a large amount of money.[5]

Guaranteed Loans or Credit. Some emails offer home-equity loans, even if you don't have any equity in your home. Others offer guaranteed, unsecured credit cards, regardless of your credit history. The "loans" turn out to be lists of lending institutions and the credit cards never arrive.[5]

Health and Diet. These scams offer "scientific breakthroughs," "miraculous cures," "exclusive products," "secret formulas," and "ancient ingredients." Some come with testimonials from "cured" consumers or endorsements from "famous medical experts" no one's ever heard of. And some

Canadian pharmacies are flooding the Internet with ads for all sorts of real medicines (supposedly cheaper than if bought in the United States) and fraudsters pitch "generic Viagra" and pills to make your penis longer or your breasts larger.

Identity Theft. Phishing emails attempt to trick you into disclosing personal details, such as user names, passwords, PIN numbers, and credit card numbers. These details are then used to steal your money or buy goods or services in your name.

Investment Opportunities. These scams may tout very high rates of return with no risk. The promoters may suggest they have high-level financial connections, that they are privy to inside information, or that they guarantee the investment. However, they're just like all the other scams.[5]

Sending Bulk Emailings. These schemes claim that you can make money sending your own solicitations via bulk email. They offer to sell you lists of email addresses or software to allow you to make the mailings. What they don't mention is that the lists are of poor quality, sending bulk email violates the terms of service of most Internet service providers, virtually no legitimate businesses engage in bulk emailings, and sending bulk email is illegal.[5]

Vacation Prize Promotions. These email "prize Promotions" tell you that you've been selected to receive a "luxury" vacation at a bargain-basement price. But the accommodations aren't deluxe and upgrades are expensive. Airfare is not included and you are required to purchase it from a designated travel agency at an inflated price.[5]

HOW THEY GET YOUR EMAIL ADDRESS

How do they get my email address you might ask? One way to gather a list of addresses is to scan websites with automated tools which have this as their sole purpose. The email addresses they gather then get added to a database, which then may be used by a spammer and then sold to other spammers.

And then there are some websites that ask you to register before giving you access to certain aspects or enable you to order a product. Some of these may sell their mailing list to other parties or they simply may get hacked into with your email address being stolen.

The final method spammers use is to guess your email address.

From the last part of email addresses (@yourISP.com or @your ISP.net) they just add thousands of random "user" names. Because they are able to send out millions of spam messages each day, it doesn't matter to them that 90 percent or more of them don't get delivered.

Spammers often buy their lists of email addresses from people who use the above methods to collect them. A million emails may cost as little as $40.

If you have an email address then you will be a target of spam. Unfortunately, that is a fact of today's Internet. There is little you can do to avoid ending up on a list of targets for spammers except avoid giving your primary email address online. I recommend using a secondary email address when online.[4,6]

EXAMPLES OF SPAM

- **Pumping Spam.** Two North Carolina men, Jeremy Jaynes and Richard Rutowski, were charged in Virginia with running one of the word's biggest spam operations in the first felony indictments ever brought in the U.S. against junk email senders. The operation was a non-stop group of porn spammers with access to high-speed T1 lines using multiple machines to pump scam and porn spam around the clock. The operation reportedly sent more than 10,000 emails a day during one three day period and more than 100,000 in a 30-day period. AOL cooperated in the investigation, providing thousands of complaints by customers who used the ISP's "report spam" feature. Electronic fingerprints helped investigators track the spammers down by following domain names in the emails, the ISPs they used, and their Internet connections. Jaynes and Rutowski faced as much as five years in prison and $2,500 in fines on each of the four counts against them. [7]

- **AOL Employee.** Officials arrested an America Online (AOL) employee, Jason Smathers, for allegedly stealing 92 million members' screen names, which were later sold to spammers. Smathers, a 24-year-old AOL computer engineer, was said to have sold the screen names to Internet marketer, Sean Dunaway, who in turn sold the list to spammers for $52,000.

Dunaway, a 21-year-old Las Vegas resident, also was accused of using the screen names to illegally promote his Internet gambling operation. The spammers were said to have used the lists to market "herbal penile enlargement pills." Smathers and Dunaway faced conspiracy charges under the anti-spam law, which took effect on January 1, 2004. If convicted, the two men each faced up to five years in prison and a fine of $250,000, or twice the gross gain from the offense.[8]

- **Dialer Software.** Three defendants, Christopher Baith, Cosme Monarrez, Jr., and Sorabh Verma, were accused of sending spam which promised a free Sony Playstation 2. Consumers who received the emails were told to click a hyperlink to collect their prize. The emails often had subject headings that said "Yahoo Sweepstakes Winner" and "You have just won a gift from Yahoo." Once a consumer clicked on the hyperlink they were taken to a Yahoo look-alike website where they were instructed to press "YES" to download software needed to complete a form to claim their prize. Once the consumer clicked "YES" and completed the download, his computer was unknowingly disconnected from its Internet connection and reconnected through a 900-number with a per-minute charge of up to $3.99. The settlement shut down the scam and permanently bared the group from sending any email that misrepresented the identity of the sender or the subject of the email. The court also ordered Baith to pay $2,500 of a $10,000 fine. He was to pay the remaining sum if it was determined that he had misrepresented his financial situation.[9]

- **Get Rich Quick.** The FTC alleged that an operation spammed consumers with email that claimed they could make substantial income by signing up for a work-at-home business opportunity. The email contained claims like, "Do you think you would be interested in becoming a permanent home-based worker for our company and earning an extra guaranteed $30,000 to $100,000 A Year?" The emails stated that recipients could obtain a "home mailing kit" for a shipping and handling fee of $24.77; that the "company" would pay consumers $4 for each envelope they stuffed and mailed; and that the offer was backed by a 30-day money back guarantee.

However, the "kit" received by most consumers was a two-page letter and a CD-ROM showing consumers how to perpetuate the scam. Consumers who tried to get the defendants to honor the 30-day, money-back guarantee were ignored, falsely told that the returned material was damaged, or told they failed to act within the 30-day trial period.[10]

TIPS TO PROTECT YOURSELF

Blind Carbon Copy. When you send email messages to a large number of recipients use the blind carbon copy (BCC) field to conceal their email addresses. Sending email where all recipient addresses are exposed makes them vulnerable to harvesting by a spammer.[11]

Email. Be suspicious if (1) the email address is one you've never seen before; (2) the domain is a foreign country; (3) the text in the subject line has an odd spelling (such as Vigr@), uses vague but compelling language (such as "Urgent," or "Important Notification," or uses "Re:" and vague language (such as "Your Document" or "As we discussed;" (4) the email claims to be from a bank, credit card company, or e-commerce site that you don't do business with, or (5) the email demands immediate attention.[4]

Email Address. Think carefully before you provide your email address on websites, newsgroup lists, or other online public forums. Many spammers utilize web bots that automatically surf the Internet looking for email addresses.

Outlook Express Settings. Microsoft's Outlook Express comes with options that let you block email by simply checking on a menu that you don't want to receive email from a specific email address. When this doesn't work, because the spammer continually changes his email address, you can automatically delete those emails that contain a specific phrase (chosen by you) in the email. Some spam, at this time, is simply impossible to block.[1,2]

Preview Function. Avoid using the preview function of your email program. Many spammers use advertising techniques that can track when a message is viewed, even if you don't click on the message. Using the preview feature essentially opens an email and tells spammers you are a valid recipient, which can result in even more spam.[11]

Purchases. Never make a purchase from an unsolicited email. Not only can you fall prey to a potentially fraudulent sales scheme, but your email address can be added to the numerous email lists that are sold within the spamming community, further compounding the number of junk emails you receive.[11]

Response/Links. Never respond to any spam email message or click on any link in the message. Replying to any spam message, even to "unsubscribe" or be "removed" from the email list, only confirms to the spammer that you are a valid recipient and a perfect target for future spamming. It is best simply to delete the email unread.[11]

Secondary Address. Consider using one or two secondary email addresses. There are a number of email sites on the Internet that are free, such as Yahoo Mail, AOL Mail, and MSN Hotmail. If you need to fill out web registration forms or surveys at sites from which you don't want to receive further information, consider using the secondary addresses to protect your primary email account from spam abuse. Also, always look for a box that solicits future information/offers, and be sure to select or deselect as appropriate.[11]

Sender. If you don't know the sender of an unsolicited email message, don't read it; delete it. While most spam is usually just annoying text, a spam email message could actually contain a virus or other harmful program that could damage your computer.[11]

Spam Filter. If you are the victim of an excessive amount of spam on a daily basis you might want to invest in a spam filter.

Trust. Never give your primary email address to anyone or any site you don't trust. Share it only with your close friends and business colleagues.[11]

References

1. FTC Consumer Complaint Form, https://rn.ftc.gov/pls/dod/wsolcq$.startup?Z_ORG_CODE=PU01.
2. Milhorn, H. Thomas, Cybercrime, In Crime: Computer Viruses to Twin Towers, Universal Publishers, Boca Raton, 2005, Pp 46-70.
3. FTC Unveils "Dirty Dozen Spam Scams," Federal Trade Commission, www.ftc.gov/opa/1998/07/dozen.htm, July 14, 1998.
4. Conry-Murray, Andrew and Vincent Weafer, The Symantec Guide to Home Internet Security, Addison-Wesley, Boston, 2006.

5. Swartz, Jon, USA Today, www.usatoday.com/money/industries/technology/2006-07-23-sneaky-spam_x.htm, July 23, 2006.
6. Field, Dan, What is spam and how do the 'spammers' get your e-mail address, Academy, www.ecademy.com/node.php?id=66785&seen =1, April 25, 2006.
7. St.Onge, Jeff, Virginia brings first felony 'spam' charges in U.S., The Detroit News, December 12, 2003.
8. Haley, Colin C., AOL employ arrested in spam sting, InternetNews. com, www.internetnews.com/ec-news/article.php/3372711, June 23, 2004.
9. "Playstation 2 spammers" settle with FTC, Federal Trade Commission, www.ftc.gov/opa/2004/02/playstation2.htm, February 11, 2004.
10. FTC shuts down deceptive spam operation, Federal Trade Commission, www.ftc.gov/opa/2004/10/bryant.htm, October 5, 2004.
11. Simple steps to combat spam, Sophos, www.sophos.com/security/best-practice/spam.html.

Chapter 34

Travel Scams

For the relatively insignificant cost of a mass-mailing program and an Internet-access account, a travel-scam artist can reach thousands of people via their email addresses. If something does go wrong, a travel company on the Internet may be difficult to track down because it could be located literally anywhere in the world. And a travel website can disappear in a flash.[1]

EXAMPLES OF TRAVEL SCAMS

Free Trip

You may be told that you've won a free trip. These free, or incredibly cheap, trips often have hidden costs. Some cruises that are advertised as free don't include airfare to the departure point or hotel stays. The recipient of the "free trip" is required to make these extra reservations through a specific company—and the costs are much higher than market price. And you may be asked to pay taxes upfront on the stated value of the free trip.

Other free trips may require attending a long, high-pressure sales pitch for a time share or travel club membership as part of the trip. Still others are valid only if bringing a companion along at full fare, and this fair may be inflated.

And you may be told that the earliest departure date is two months away. This should sound an alarm, since the deadline for disputing a credit card charge is 60 days. You may be requested to dial a 900, 809, 758, or 664 area code. These numbers, and dozens more, are locations within the Caribbean that charge exorbitant per-minute rates.[1,2]

Advance Fee

Fraudulent "travel agents" sometimes offer tours for a relatively small upfront fee. Such offers are virtually always bogus.

- **Student Abroad Program.** Frank Abedi of the Student Summer Abroad Program, an unregistered seller of travel packages, faced a fine for falsely promising to high school students tours of two to six weeks in Europe, Africa, or Australia. The tours were offered via the Internet to students who sent in fees of $50 to $100 with an autobiographical essay. Abedi agreed to cease further operations and shut down the websites.[3]

Agent Kits

Travel mills sell fake travel-agent credentials under the premise that you can earn commissions on travel packages and take advantage of courtesy fares and hotel stays. Agent kits cost anywhere from a few hundred to several thousand dollars. Unfortunately, after you've paid the money you can't actually sell airline tickets or make travel arrangements unless you're affiliated with a formally accredited agency. And don't count on courtesy discounts.[1]

Cruise Vacations

This scam involves the auctioning off a "vacation." The auction description may tell you about luxury hotels, festive cruises, and exotic ports of call. Sometimes the scammer claims to be unable to use the cruise himself because of some conflict, health problem, or other reason. Other times, the scammer claims the slots have been unfilled in a desirable group trip, and so the tickets are being made available at a cheap price. You are the high bidder, send in the payment, and either receive nothing or only travel vouchers.[2]

Frequent Flyer Miles

In this fraud the scammer sets up an auction claiming that his frequent flyer miles are about to expire, and that he or she is willing to use them to buy a ticket to anywhere for the highest bidder. You win the bidding, send the payment, but get nothing in return. Sometimes, after receiving the money, the scammer sends an email stating that he just found out the airline won't let him transfer miles as planned and a refund will be sent to you. Of course the refund never arrives.[2]

Nonrefundable Ticket

A con artist claims that he has purchased a nonrefundable, but transferable, airplane ticket and was unable to use it for some legitimate-sounding reason. The individual then claims that he or she is willing to sell the ticket cheaply, possibly even losing some money on it. The ticket is for travel to a very desirable location, and naturally coincides with a popular holiday. Winning the bidding, you send payment but get nothing in return or only get a travel voucher.[2]

Contest

You unknowingly visit a fraudulent travel website where you see that a contest is going on and fill out an entry form. A few weeks later you receive an email stating you have won the contest—a fabulous Caribbean vacation for two. The vacation is discounted to only $400, and you can take it anytime in the next 18 months. You jump at the opportunity, call the number in the email, and give a credit card number to pay the $400. Unfortunately, every time you try to book the vacation you get a busy signal. You leave a message, but the "agent" never calls you back, or you are told all the slots are filled on that date. Soon the 18 months are up and the travel voucher is no long valid.[2]

Fake Website

In this scam you see an attractive website of a "travel agency" or receive an email referring you to the website, which offers great deals on package vacations. You pick out the package of interest and fill out the form—name, address, telephone number, email address, and credit card information. Your credit card is billed, but the tickets never arrive or do arrive but are fraudulent.

- **Trip to Maui.** Donna Copeland of Brighton, Colorado found what she thought was a great deal for her and her husband on the Sunscapes Travel website. Copeland paid $4,500 for round-trip airfare and hotel accommodations for seven nights on Maui. Although the trip wasn't scheduled to take place until May, Sunscapes demanded payment in full at the time of booking. A few months later Donna received the airline tickets and confirmation numbers for the hotel and car rental. She became suspicious after she emailed Sunscapes a question about her accommodations and never got a reply. When she went on the Internet, she was shocked to discover that the Sunscapes website had disappeared. Donna called the resort in Maui and discovered that there was no reservation in her name. She then called her credit card company to dispute the $2,100 hotel charge, even though the 60-day period for disputing a charge had passed. After she sent documentation to her credit card company proving that Sunscapes had gone out of business, the $2,100 charge was credited to her account. The Attorney General's office in Washington State filed a lawsuit against Sunscapes for failing to deliver more than $67,000 worth of travel services.[1]

TIPS TO PROTECT YOURSELF

Company. If you are not familiar with the company offering the travel deal, find out as much as possible, including their complete name, address, and phone number. Good sources are the Better Business Bureau or a local travel agent.[4]

Confirmation. Confirm the arrangements. If transportation and hotel are included in the travel package, ask how to contact those companies and confirm with them directly that the reservations have been made.[4]

Escrow. Ask if the company has an escrow account and get the number of the account and the name of the bank.[1]

Exaggerated Claims. Watch out for claims such as, "You have been selected to receive our spectacular luxury dream vacation offer." This doesn't mean you'll get a free vacation. It only means you may be offered an opportunity to pay for a trip that may or may not fit your idea of luxury.[5]

Free Trips. Be skeptical of offers for "free" trips. Airlines and other well-known companies sometimes do operate contests for travel prizes. However, there are also companies that offer "free" trips to try to lure people into buying their products or services. It's never "free" if you have to pay something or buy something.[4]

Good Deal. Realize that the deal may not be as good as you think. You may find that a travel offer requires you to make reservations through a specific company and that the costs are higher than they would be if you used your own travel agent or made the arrangements yourself. Or the offer may be valid only if you bring a companion along at full, and often inflated, fare.[4]

Hidden Costs. Know exactly what's included. A free or incredibly cheap trip may have hidden costs. For instance, the cruise may be free, but you have to pay to fly to the departure point and stay in a hotel at your own expense. Or you may have to endure a long, high-pressure sales pitch for a timeshare or travel club membership as part of the trip.[4]

Instant Agent. Watch out for "instant travel agent" offers where companies offer to sell you travel agent identification that will guarantee you discounted rates.[5]

Membership. Check to see if the "travel agent" is a member of ICTA (Institute of Certified Travel Agents), ASTA (American Society of Travel Agents) or ARTA (Association of Retail Travel Agents).[5]

Payment. Pay with a credit card. Fraudulent travel operators take the money and run, and even legitimate companies can suddenly go out of business. Credit cards are the safest way to pay for online purchases because you can dispute the charges if you don't get the services you were promised or if the offer was misrepresented.[4]

Pressure. Be leery of travel offers with phrases like "This is the last day to book" or "Offer expires at midnight," or

"Guaranteed discounted if you take immediate action." These kind of statements should be a clue to back off.[2,4]

Research. Do your own travel research. It's easy to get information from a local travel agent and other sources, such as newspapers, books, and the Internet. You may be able to get the trip you want for far less than the "bargain" price a company is offering.[4]

Restrictions. Be aware of restrictions. Often the best travel deals are only available for off-peak times, not during school vacations, holidays, or other popular travel dates. You may find it hard to get the promised price for the dates that you want to travel, or there may be no space available on those dates at all.[4]

Time Range. Be cautious if you're told that you have 18 months or more to take the trip. By the time you try to make reservations the company could be out of business. Many illegitimate firms will use stall tactics so your offer will expire before you can take a trip.[5]

Too Good to Be True. If it sounds too good to be true, it probably is. If the price is unusually low, get details on what is and is not included. Be sure to check all the details and conditions of the offer before committing your dollars.[5]

Unsolicited Emails. Unsolicited emails are often fraudulent. If you are familiar with the company that sent you the email and you don't want to receive further messages, send a reply asking to be removed from the email list. However, responding to unknown senders may simply verify that yours is a working email address and result in even more unwanted messages from strangers. The best approach to these is to delete the email.[4]

Website. Do not judge a company by its website. A fancy website with flashy streamers, videos, and stunning graphics is no guarantee that a company is financially stable. A website can be easily changed and provides no proof of what the offer was like when you first saw it. Not only that, a website can suddenly disappear.[5]

References

1. McKee III, Phillip C., Remarks to the Annual Conference of the American Society of Travel Agents, http://wvAv.fraud.org/news/1999/oct99/100899.htm, October 8, 1999.

2. Woods, Lynn, When Online Bargains Turn Sour - deals found on the Internet, Klipinger's Personal Financial Magazine, www.findarticles. com/p/articles/mi_m1318/is_7_53/ai_54882025?pi=cal, July, 1999.
3. San Francisco district attorney and attorney general crack down on unscrupulous travel agents, Press Releases, Office of the District Attorney, SFGov.com,
www.ci.sf.ca.us/site/uploadedfiles/da/press/1999/p031799.htm.
4. Travel Fraud, Internet Travel Tips, National Consumers League's Internet Fraud Watch, www.fraud.org/tips/internet/travelfraud.htm.
5. Twelve ways to avoid Internet travel scams, News and Resources, United States Tour Operators Association, www.ustoa.com/ consumernews/netscams_c.cfm.

Chapter 35

Viruses, Worms, Trojans, and Spyware

A contraction of *mal*icious soft*ware*, *Malware* interferes with normal computer functions or sends personal data about the user to unauthorized parties over the Internet. It includes viruses, worms, Trojans, spyware, browser hijackers, and dialers. Browser hijackers and dialers were discussed in Chapter 13. Viruses, worms, Trojans, and spyware are discussed in this chapter.

The Macintosh has fewer malware problems than Windows computers; however, Mac malware does exist, and the frequency of attacks on Macintosh computers is increasing.

VIRUSES, WORMS, AND TROJANS

While the words virus, worm, and Trojan are often used interchangeably, they are not the same. All three are malicious programs or pieces of computer code that can cause damage to your computer, but there are differences between the three, and knowing those differences can help you better protect your computer.

Viruses, Worms, and Trojans can get onto your computer's hard drive via email and malicious websites. More rarely these days, they can also get onto your computer from a floppy, CD or DVD disk, flash drive, or any media that is used to copy software or data from another computer.[1,2]

Viruses

A *virus* is a program or piece of code that is loaded onto your computer without your knowledge and runs against your wishes. A virus attaches itself to a program or file so it can spread from one computer to another, leaving infections as it goes. Viruses are spread by email attachments, floppy disks, CDs, DVDs, flash drives, or in material downloaded from the Web.

Email viruses are often labeled with intriguing subject lines such as "I Love You" or "Anna Kournikova Naked" to entice you into opening the attachment. When the attachment is opened, the virus is activated, and your computer becomes infected. Almost all viruses are attached to an executable file (.exe file), which is file in a format that the computer can directly execute. This usually means the virus may exist on your computer, but it cannot infect your computer unless you run or open the malicious program. People continue the spread of a computer virus, usually unknowingly, by sharing infecting files or sending emails with virus attachments.

The effect of a virus may be a simple prank that pops up a message on your monitor screen out of the blue, or it may destroy programs and data on your hard drive.[1,3,4]

- **Resume'.** A computer virus disguised as a resume' from a job hunter hit a number of corporate email systems posing a threat for computer users when they logged on after a long Memorial Day holiday weekend. The virus deleted computer files if it was activated by clicking on an attachment. The email carried the title "Resume'—Janet Simons," and appeared to be a letter from a job seeker. It was addressed to the head of sales and invited readers to click on an attachment to check the references. The attachment was labeled "resume'.doc" or "explorer.doc," as well as other names.[5]

Bomb

A *bomb* is a special type of virus that isn't activated by the computer user opening a program. Instead, it is activated by a trigger, such as a specific time or event. For example, the Michelangelo virus contaminates infected computers on Michelangelo's birthday. A bomb usually does something unpleasant when it "goes off." A bomb delivered in an email is known as an *email bomb*.[2,4]

- **Michelangelo Virus.** One of the biggest computer virus scares in the history of computer viruses was the Michelangelo virus. This virus was to activate on Michelangelo's birthday (March 6). Many people thought it was a doomsday virus. This particular virus destroys data by overwriting it when the computer is booted. It was an obscure threat until January 1992 when 500 personal computers contaminated with the virus were shipped from a major computer manufacturer in the United States. Within one week, another major manufacturer admitted to the accidental distribution of 900 floppy disks which were infected with the virus. In the frenzy that followed the media mistakenly reported that one out of four PCs in the U.S. would fall prey to the virus. The actual number of infected computers was estimated to be in the range of 10 to 20 thousand.[6]

Worms

A *worm* is similar to a virus by its design, and can be considered to be a subclass of a virus. Worms spread from computer to computer, but unlike a virus it has the ability to travel without any help from a person. A worm takes advantage of file transport features on your system, which allows it to travel unaided. One example of this is the ability of a worm to replicate itself and send a copy to everyone listed in your email address book. When the worm copies reach the computers of the individuals in your address book, the worm replicates again and sends itself out to everyone listed in each of those address books, and the process continues on down the line.

Due to the copying nature of a worm and its ability to travel the Internet, the end result in most cases is that the worm consumes too much system memory or Internet bandwidth, causing Web servers and individual computers to stop responding. In more recent worm attacks, such as Blaster Worm, the worm was designed to allow malicious users to control your computer remotely.[1,2]

- **Blaster (MSBlast, Lovsan) Worm.** Jeffrey Lee Parson, a 6-foot-4, 320-pound high school senior in Minnesota known as "Teekid," was arrested and charged with unleashing a computer worm that caused havoc on the Internet and in email boxes nationwide. He admitted to FBI agents that he had tweaked the original "Blaster" worm and used the variant to infect the computers of unsuspecting victims. Microsoft in Seattle, Washington was the main target. Investigators said the attack caused $5 to $10 million dollars in damages to that company alone. Parsons had even taunted Microsoft Chairman, Bill Gates, with an encoded message, "Billy Gates why do you make this possible? Stop making money and fix your software!" The worm was said to have affected 7,000 computers. Parsons could have faced as much as 10 years in jail and a $250,000 fine. Instead, he was ordered to pay Microsoft $497,546.55 in restitution.[7]

Trojans

Trojans are named after the mythological Trojan horse because they are full of deception. A Trojan enters a computer system from the Internet disguised as something else. And, although not a virus, it can transport viruses into your computer system. Those on the receiving end of a Trojan are usually tricked into opening them because they appear to be software or files from a legitimate source.

When a Trojan is activated on your computer, the results can vary. Some Trojans are designed to be more annoying than malicious (adding funny icons to your desktop) or they can cause serious damage by deleting files and destroying information. Unlike viruses and worms, Trojans do not replicate.

A *rootkit* is a type of Trojan that enables an attacker to have "root" access to the computer, which means it runs at the lowest level of the machine. It keeps itself, other files, registry keys, and network connections hidden from detection, therefore preventing its removal. The best-know example of rootkit intrusion is a Sony music CD that, in addition to music, also intentionally contained spyware that was kept hidden by a rootkit Trojan.[1,9]

Port Scanner

The *port scanner* hides on a system and scans the surrounding environment for Internet protocol addresses (address assigned to a specific computer so that it can be identified on the Internet) and opens software ports that it then makes available to malicious viruses or cybercrooks.[1,2,4]

- **Sub7.** Also known as Backdoor-G, Sub7 is a Trojan that comes hidden within a seemingly legitimate piece of software, either from an email, floppy disk, CD, or downloaded from the Internet. Executing the legitimate software does whatever it is supposed to do, while installing Sub7 in the background. Once installed, Sub7 opens a backdoor (port) and notifies the hacker that it is installed and ready to go. The hacker at the other end is able to do any of the following: (1) Add, delete, or modify your files; (2) log your keyboard keystrokes and capture things like your passwords and credit card numbers; (3) install things like other Trojans or DDoS applications; and (4) do almost anything else to your computer. Developers continue to modify, tweak, and improve Sub7, and with each subsequent release it is often just different enough to evade the antivirus detection designed to pick up the previous versions.[9]

SPYWARE

Spyware is a generic name for software that monitors or controls your computer use against your wishes. It may be used to cause popup ads, redirect your computer to websites, monitor your Internet surfing, or record your keystrokes, which in turn could lead to identity theft. Spyware is similar to a Trojan horse in that users unwittingly install the product when they install something else or visit a malicious website. Spyware installed when you visit a malicious website has become known as a *drive-by download*.

Spyware has eclipsed viruses as the fastest growing online threat. Sixty-one percent of U.S. computers are said to be infected with spyware.[10,11]

One way spyware and other malware gets onto your computer

is through manipulation of Active X controls in the Windows operating system. Active X checks the digital "signature" associated with a piece of software to be downloaded to be sure the creators of the software are who they claim to be. Attackers may try to disguise the popup messages to look like messages from Windows or make them appear to be generated by the website you are visiting. These messages usually prompt you to take some action immediately, such as clicking the "Yes" button to run a scan or download a program to repair a "problem."

Unfortunately, even if a dialog box pops up to alert you of an unsigned Active X control, clicking "No" doesn't always help. Some malware writers manipulate the dialogue box so that clicking on "No," or any other button, still downloads the software. To close these dialogue boxes without clicking on "No" or the "X" in the upper-right corner, press Alt-F4. This safely closes the window without allowing any downloads.

There are two ways to tell if you are visiting a secure website. First, the address in the browser bar begins with https rather than http. Second, you see a lock icon in the bottom-right corner of your browser.[11]

There are many types of spyware. The most common ones are keystroke loggers, adware, and some cookies.

Keystroke Loggers

A keystroke logger, or *keylogger*, is a program that captures and records every key depression on the computer keyboard and thereby monitors the computer's activity. A keystroke logger program does not require physical access to the user's computer. It can be downloaded unwittingly and executed remotely. The keylogger periodically uploads the information it has obtained to whoever installed the program. Therefore, a person with malicious intent could obtain passwords, user names, personal information, and anything typed on the keyboard.

Anyone with access to the Internet can purchase a legal spying keystroke logger. These tools are marketed to parents for collecting evidence about their children's Web activities.[10,12]

- **Needed a Patch.** A woman heard about a new Internet Explorer browser vulnerability and wanted to be sure her home computer was protected. Using a search engine, she found a website that offered information about the vulnerability and the option of having a patch for the vulnerability downloaded to her computer. She opted not to accept the download since she was leery of downloading information from an unauthorized source. Unfortunately, as she was reading information about the vulnerability on the website, the criminal who had created the website took advantage of the fact that her computer actually had the vulnerability. Unknown to her, a small keystroke logger was automatically downloaded and installed on her computer. The program was designed to covertly log everything she typed from that moment on and to send the information to the website owner. When she logged into her bank account, the keystroke logger recorded the name of her bank, her user ID, her password, and her Social Security number. He added her name and all of the associated information to a long list of other unsuspecting users and sold the list to someone who specialized in using stolen bank information to make illegal withdrawals. When the woman went to make a bank deposit several weeks later and asked for her balance, she was shocked to find that her bank account was almost empty.[13]

Adware

Adware can monitor and profile your Web use and direct popup ads based on your surfing habits. It comes bundled with many free programs, and you are only notified of this in the fine print of the End User License Agreement (EULA), if you are notified at all. It's simply another example that very few things in life are free; there is almost always some kind of price to pay. Adware is not as dangerous as other infections, but it can be incredibly annoying. And once installed it can be very difficult to remove, even for technically savvy users.[14]

- **MySpace.com.** More than one million users of MySpace.com and other websites were thought to have been infected with adware spread by a banner advertisement for the site www.deckoutyourdeck.com. MySpace.com is an online community with at least 70 million users. The ad exploited a problem in the way Microsoft's Internet Explorer browser handled WMF image files, allowing hackers to distribute a specially crafted WMF image through email, instant messaging links, and websites. If the image was opened, it downloaded a Trojan which caused infected machines to contact multiple websites and download, among other unwanted programs, advertising software from PurityScan, which then caused unwanted popup windows to appear. It also tracked a user's online activity.[15]

Unethical Anti-spyware Companies

Unfortunately, there are unethical anti-spyware companies out there. These fall into three camps: (1) Those that offer a free online scan, which turns up many more infections than you actually have in an attempt sell you their software to eliminate the bogus infections; (2) those that sell you anti-spyware software that doesn't work; and (3) companies that are responsible for downloading malware to your computer that does a number of extremely irritating things, including hijacking your browser, causing a frequent popup telling you that your computer is infected, and instructing you to click on the popup to fix the problem. If you click on the popup you are directed to the company's website where you can purchase their product to "get rid of the problem." Unfortunately, the program, if you purchase it, may not be a reasonably functioning anti-spyware program.

- **Buy Our Software.** According to the FTC, Entertainment Productions, Inc., Smartbot.Net, and Sanford Wallace used a variety of techniques to direct consumers to their websites where consumers had spyware downloaded onto their computers. Consumers received no notice that the spyware was being installed and did not consent to its installation. The spyware changed the consumers' home pages, changed their search engines, triggered a barrage of popup ads, and allowed tracking of the consumer's computer use. In addition, the spyware caused the CD-ROM tray on computers to open, and then a popup told consumers "FINAL WARNING!! If your

CD-ROM drive opens, you desperately need to rid your system of spyware popups immediately. Spyware programmers can control your computer hardware if you fail to protect your computer right at this moment! Download Spy Wiper now!"[16,17]

Spy Wiper sold for approximately $30.

Cookies

A *cookie* is information in a small text file some websites store on your computer. They are included in this section because they can serve as spyware in a very loose sense. Unlike spyware, however, they are not malicious in nature. Some advertisers use cookies to track your surfing habits while on their website, but it's important to note that unlike spyware, cookies cannot be used to track your surfing on other websites.[17]

Websites use cookies for several reasons, including collecting demographic data and personalizing websites.

Demographic Data

Cookies collect demographic information about who is visiting the website. Sites often use this information to track how often visitors come to the site and how long they remain on the site. Once a cookie is saved on your computer, only the website that created the cookie can read it.[18,19]

Personalization

When you personalize a website, like my.yahoo.com, by selecting components from a list, a cookie is stored on your computer so that when you return to the site Yahoo recognizes the cookie and automatically signs you in—your user name and password for the site have been saved. Also, if you have ever returned to a site and have seen your name mysteriously appear on the screen, it is because on a previous visit you gave your name to the site and it was stored in a cookie.

If you delete the cookies on your computer you will find that the next time you visit a website that you had previously personalized it won't recognize you. Not only that, you will find that all your saved user names and passwords for online accounts may have disappeared.

Another example of the use of cookies is the way some online shopping companies, like Amazon.com, make recommendations to you based on your previous purchases from that site. The server keeps track in cookies of what you purchase.[19]

INDICATIONS YOUR COMPUTER MAY BE INFECTED

Browser. Your browser is hijacked; that is, it takes you to a site other than the one you type into the address box. Your browser home page changes and you can't reset it. You are not able to access antivirus or anti-spyware websites.[20]

Error Messages. Random error messages begin to appear.[19]

Icons. New and unexpected icons may appear on the system tray at the bottom of your computer screen. Additional toolbars may be added to the browser. Additional webpages are automatically added to list of Favorites.[20]

Keyboard. Keys on your keyboard stop working; for example, the "tab" key might not work when you try to move to the next field in a web form.[20]

Link. Clicking a link does nothing or goes to a non-related website.[20]

Performance. Sluggish performance may occur when opening programs or saving files. The computer stops responding more frequently than normal. Poor performance occurs while browsing the Internet.[20]

Popups. A barrage of popup advertising windows appear when the browser is not open or appears over webpages that do not normally have popups.[20]

Search. Attempting to go to a search engine website, you go to a different webpage than intended.[20]

TIPS TO PROTECT YOURSELF

Active X Controls. Do not accept any software with an invalid Active X signature. Close the dialogue box without clicking on "No" or the "X" in the upper-right corner by pressing

Alt-F4.[11]

Anti-spyware Program. Be sure you have an anti-spyware program installed on your computer and that you keep it up to date. It should be running in the background to catch spyware as it attempts to install on your computer, and you should run it at least once a week.

Antivirus Program. Be sure you have an antivirus program installed on your computer and that you keep it up to date. It should be running in the background to catch viruses as they attempt to install on your computer, and you should run it at least once a week.

Bootleg or Pirated Software. Beware of bootlegged or pirated software. Virus and spyware writers take advantage of the large market for these to disseminate their creations across the Internet.[21]

Browser Settings. Minimize drive-by downloads by making sure your browser security setting is high enough to detect unauthorized downloads; for example, at least the "Medium" setting for Internet Explorer.[22]

Downloads. Download free software only from websites you know and trust. It can be appealing to download free software, like games, peer-to-peer file-sharing programs, and customized toolbars, that unfortunately may change or customize the functioning of your computer. Be aware that some of these free software applications bundle other software, including spyware.

Don't download and install any software without knowing exactly what it is. Take the time to read the end-user license agreement (EULA) before downloading software. If the EULA is hard to find—or difficult to understand—think twice about downloading the software.[22]

Email. Don't open emails from individuals or companies you don't know. If you do, don't click on hyperlinks, and don't opt out of receiving the emails. Simply delete them. And whatever you do don't open attachments.

Firewall. Install a personal firewall to stop uninvited users from accessing your computer. A firewall blocks unauthorized access to your computer and will alert you if spyware already on your computer is sending information out.[22]

Popups. "Congratulations you've won a free laptop," the popup says. Trust me; you haven't won anything but the right to download spyware on your computer. Don't click on any links within popup windows. Doing so may install spyware on your computer. Instead, close popup windows without clicking on "No" or the "X" in the upper-right corner by pressing Alt-F4. This safely closes the window without allowing any downloads.[21]

Spam. Don't click on links in spam that claim to offer anti-spyware software. Some links claiming to offer anti-spyware software install spyware on your computer. If you get a lot of spam, consider installing a spam filter.[22]

Update Operating Software. Update your operating system frequently. Ideally, have it set to update automatically. Your operating system (Windows, Linux, OS X) may offer free security patches to close holes in the system that spyware could exploit. Download and install them.[22]

References

1. The difference between a virus, worm and Trojan Horse?, Webopedia, www.webopedia.com/DidYouKnow/Internet/ 2004/virus.asp, October 29, 2004.
2. Viruses explained – protect your computer, Wiltshire, http://archive. thisiswiltshire.co.uk/2006/2/23/263293.html, February 26, 2006.
3. Definition of: virus, PCMag.com, encyclopedia, www.pcmag.com /encyclopedia_term/0,2542,t=virus&i=53963,00.asp.
4. Milhorn, H. Thomas, Cybercrime, In Crime: Computer Viruses to Twin Towers, Universal Publishers, Boca Raton, 2005, Pp 46-70.
5. E-Mail Virus Posing as Resume Spreads Slowly before Weekend, Technology, Reuters, http://partners.nytimes.com/library/tech/00/05/ biztech/articles/27virus.html, May 27, 2000.
6. Report on the psychology of computer viruses, Prevention is the best medicine, www.soc.hawaii.edu/leonj/409bf98/ginoza/report2 ginoza.html#10.
7. Becker, David and Matt Hines, FBI arrests MSBlast worm suspect, http://zdnet.com.eom/2100-1105_2-5070000.html, August 29, 2003.
8. Bradley, Tony, Sub7 Trojan/Backdoor, A brief overview, Internet/Network Security, About.com, netsecurity.about.com /cs/hackertools/a/aa032603a.htm.
9. Definition of: rootkit, PCmag.com, www.pcmag.com/ encyclopediaterm /0,2542,t=root+kit&i=55733,00.asp.
10. Edwards, Donna Johnson, Talking Tech, Richmond.com, www.richmond.com/business/output.aspx?Article_ID=2956723, April 13, 2004.

11. Conry-Murray, Andrew and Vincent Weafer, The Symantec Guide to Home Internet Security, Addison-Wesley, Boston, 2006.
12. Keylogger, SearchSecurity.com, Security Definitions, http://searchsecurity.techtarget.com/sDefinition/0,,sid14_gci962518, 00.html, June 8, 2005.
13. Cybercrime Stories, Symantec, http://sarc.com/avcenter/cybercrime/index_page4.html.
14. About Spyware, Adware, and Browser Hijacking Software, HP and Compaq PCs, http://h10025.www1.hp.com/ewfrf/wc/document?lc=en&cc=us&dlc=&product=59375&docname=c00206121#N400.
15. Kirk, Jeremy, Ad dishes up adware to over a million PCs, IDG News Service, http://news.yahoo.com/s/pcworld/20060720/tc_pcworld/126488, July 20, 2006.
16. FTC cracks down on spyware operation, Federal Trade Commission, www.ftc.gov/opa/2004/10/spyware.htm, October 12, 2004.
17. Mail Wiper and their "Marketing" Techniques, www.nomorespyware.50megs.com/mailwiper.html.
18. Understanding Cookies, Microsoft, www.microsoft.com/resources /documentation/windows/xp/all/proddocs/en-us/sec_cook.mspx.
19. Do cookies compromise security?, Webopedia, www.webopedia. com/DidYouKnow/Internet/2002/Web_server.html.
20. Spyware, Federal Trade Commission, FTC Consumer Alert, www.ftc.gov/bcp/conline/pubs/alerts/spywarealrt.htm, July 2005.
21. Computer viruses: How-to protect against computer viruses, www.how-to.com/Operations/how_to_protect_against_computer_ viruses.htm.
22. Spyware, Onguard Online, Your Safety Net, http://onguardonline. gov/spyware.html.

Chapter 36

Hoaxes

A *hoax* is an attempt to trick you into believing that something false is actually real. In cyberspace, hoaxes are propagated via emails. Although hoaxes are not illegal, and therefore do not fall under the heading of cybercrime, they can pose the threat of bogging down some Internet servers because most of the hoaxes request that people who receive them forward them to everyone they know, or at least everyone in their address books. And on rare occasions a hoax can lead you to do damage to your own computer if you follow the email's instructions.

HOAX CATEGORIES

Hoax categories include (1) celebrity hoaxes, (2) giveaway hoaxes, (3) hacked history hoaxes, (4) humorous hoaxes, (5) missing child hoaxes, (6) protest hoaxes, (7) scare hoaxes, (8) sympathy hoaxes, (9) threat hoaxes, (10) urban legends, and (11) virus hoaxes.[1,2]

Celebrity Hoaxes

Celebrity hoax emails usually report something bad happening to a famous person, such as being killed, arrested, overdosed, or in a coma. The following email falsely reports that Will Ferrell has died:

- "Los Angeles -- Actor Will Ferrell accidentally died in a freak paragliding accident yesterday in Torey Pines, Southern California. The accident apparently happened after a freak wind gush blew Ferrell and his companion towards a wooded area where they lost control before crashing into the dense foliage. Ferrell and his professional guide, Horacio Gomez of Airtek Paragliding Center, attempted the jump at around 2 in the afternoon. According to witnesses, the conditions were ideal for paragliding and the weather didn't pose a problem at all. The jump started normally as Ferrell and Gomez glided carefully across the vast area and seemed headed into the right direction just before a freak wind blew them off course, causing the paragliding professional Gomez to lose control. As horrified witnesses looked on, the duo headed straight for the dense woods near the jump off point and crashed at an estimated 60 mph, hitting the trees as they hurtled to the ground. Some friends who witnessed the accident immediately called 911. The paramedics vainly attempted to revive the two on their way to the nearby UCSD Thornton Hospital in nearby La Jolla. The duo suffered major injuries to the head and broken bones that caused their deaths. In an interview with Will's parents, Mary and Hubert Ferrell said their son died while doing one of the things he loved the most. Will was a graduate of the University of California where he obtained a Sports Information degree. Will was born on July 16, 1968. He was 36."[1]

Giveaway Hoaxes

Giveaway hoax emails go into great detail describing the prize you will receive from some big company if you just forward the message to everyone you know. What the email usually neglects to tell you is how the company knows you have sent on the message, let alone state the reason anyone would be willing to pay for forwarding the email.

A chain-letter hoax circulating the Internet since November 1997 claims to be from the office of the chief executive of Microsoft Corporation. Although there are a number of variants, they all claim to be from Bill Gates, and merely ask you to forward the letter to other people.[3]

- "FROM: GatesBeta@microsoft.com
  Hello Everyone,
  And thank you for signing up for my Beta Email Tracking Application or (BETA) for short. My name is Bill Gates. Here at Microsoft we have just compiled an email tracking program that tracks everyone to whom this message is forwarded. It does this through a unique IP (Internet Protocol) address log book database. We are experimenting with this and need your help. Forward this to everyone you know and if it reaches 1000 people everyone on the list will receive $1000 and a copy of Windows 98 (or some later version) at my expense. Enjoy. Note: Duplicate entries will not be counted. You will be notified by email with further instructions once this email has reached 1000 people. Windows 98 (or some later version) will not be shipped until it has been released to the general public.
  Your friend,
  Bill Gates & The Microsoft Development Team."[3]

Hacked History Hoaxes

Hacked history emails contain information about a real event, but the facts have been adjusted to fit someone's political agenda. These hoaxes tend to make someone appear prophetic, evil, or saintly, depending on how the information is stated. The changes from reality are generally small enough so that someone reading the account and remembering the event might be fooled into thinking the event really happened the way it is described.

Gold Star Mothers in the following hoax is an organization made up of women whose sons were killed in military combat during service in the United States armed forces.

- "Recently a delegation of New York State Gold Star Mothers made a trip to Washington, DC to discuss various concerns with their elected representatives. According to NewsMax.com there was only one politician who refused to meet with these ladies. Can you guess which politician that might be? Was it New York Senator Charles Schumer? Nope, he met with them. Try again. Do you know anyone serving in the Senate who has never showed anything but contempt for our military? Do you happen to know the name of any politician in Washington whose husband once wrote of his loathing of the military? Now you're getting warm! You got it! None other than the Queen herself, Hillary Clinton. She refused repeated requests to meet with the Gold Star Mothers. Now---please don't tell me you're surprised. This woman wants to be president of the United States and there is a huge percentage of the voters who are eager to help her achieve that.

Sincerely,

Cdr Hamilton McWhorter USN(ret)"[3]

This message obviously was started by someone with an anti-Hillary Clinton political agenda. The two mothers who went to visit Hillary did so without an appointment. The day they showed up, Hillary was not in the office, so of course she did not meet with them.[3]

Humorous Hoaxes

To no one's surprise, humor has made it to the inbox of your computer in the form of email hoaxes. These emails often take the form of presenting a scenario that sounds on the surface to have some degree of plausibility, until you actually give some thought to what the email is saying. Then it becomes clear that the email is a hoax. Consider the following "nuclear strike" email:

- "Symantec Virus Alert Center
  Hello Subscriber,
  As part of our ongoing effort to keep Symantec clients up to date on virus alerts, this email is being sent to all Symantec subscribers. A new, deadly type of virus has been detected in

the wild. You should not open any message entitled LAUNCH NUCLEAR STRIKE NOW, as this message has been programmed to access NORAD computers in Colorado and launch a full-scale nuclear strike on Russia and the former Soviet states. Apparently, a disgruntled ex-Communist hacker has designed a pernicious VBScript that actually bypasses the U.S. arsenal's significant security system and takes command of missiles and bombers directly. By opening the email, you may be causing Armageddon. Needless to say, Armageddon will wipe out your hard drive and damage your computer. ... Please forward this warning to everyone you can. Thank you for your attention to this matter,
Sincerely,
The Symantec Anti-Virus Team"[3]

Missing Child Hoaxes

Missing child hoaxes are all similar. A child is missing and a plea is made to help find him or her. A picture of a cute child is always included to give the email plausibility. Consider the following "girl from Philly" email:

- "Subject: Missing Girl from Philly
  We have a Deli manager (Acme Markets) from Philadelphia, PA who has a 13 year old daughter who has been missing for 2 weeks. With luck on her side she will be found.
  'I am asking you all, begging you to please forward this email on to anyone and everyone you know, PLEASE. My 13 year old girl, Ashley Flores, is missing. She has been missing for now two weeks. It is still not too late. Please help us. If anyone anywhere knows anything, please contact me at: HelpfindAshleyFlores@yahoo.com. I am including a picture of her. All prayers are appreciated!!'
  It only takes 2 seconds to forward this. If it was your child, you would want all the help you could get."[4]

Protest Hoaxes

Protest hoaxes always have a cause that appeals to a large number of people. You can almost envision the senders of the email along the side of a street carrying protest signs and yelling slogans. Consider the following "our gay Lord" email:

- "A disgusting film is set to appear in America later this year, which depicts Jesus and his disciples as homosexuals! As a play, this has already been in theatres for a while. It's called 'Corpus Christi' which means 'The Christ Body.' It's a revolting mockery of our Lord. But we can make a difference. That's why I am sending this email to you all. Will you please add your name to the bottom of the list at the end of this email? If you do, we will be able to prevent this film from showing in America. Apparently, some regions in Europe have already banned the film. All we need is a lot of signatures! Remember, Jesus said, 'Deny me on earth and I'll deny you before my Father.' Please don't just forward it!! Please copy this message, paste the text in a new email, then add your name to the list and send it to all your friends. When the list you sign reaches 500 names, please send it to: (Email address given) and then start again. Add the names of your family too. IF WE WORK TOGETHER WE CAN DO THIS. Thank You!"[5]

Scare Hoaxes

Scare email hoaxes tell stories about people, usually women or children, who have had something terrible happen to them, such as the following "poison perfume" email.

- "Seven women have died after inhaling a free perfume sample that was mailed to them. The product was poisonous. If you receive free samples in the mail, such as lotions, perfumes, diapers etc., throw them away. The government is afraid that this might be another terrorist act. They will not announce it on the news because they do not want to create panic or give the terrorists new ideas. Send this to all your friends and family members."[3]

Sympathy Hoaxes

Sympathy or charity hoaxes describe some person that has had something terrible happen to him or her, such as an accident or terminal illness. Every couple of years the "Little Girl Dying" hoax makes its rounds. Usually it includes a picture of a young child. Consider the following "brain cancer" email:

- "Please read this then forward
  If you delete this ... you seriously don't have a heart. Hi, I am a 29 year old father. My wife and I have had a wonderful life together. God blessed us with a child too. Our daughter's name is Rachel, and she is 10 years old. Not long ago the doctors detected cancer in her brain and in her little body. There is only one way to save her ... an operation. Sadly, we don't have enough money to pay the price. AOL and ZDNET have agreed to help us. The only way they can help us is this way -- I send this email to you and you send it to other people. AOL will track this email and count how many people get it. Every person who opens this email and sends it to at least 3 people will give us 32 cents.
  Please help us.
  George Arlington"[3]

Neither AOL nor ZDNET can track email and are not in the business of giving away money for chain letters.

Threat Hoaxes

Threat hoaxes promise that something bad will happen to you or your computer if you don't forward the email to a given number of people. Consider the following "living hell" email:

- "This is not a joke ... if you do not forward this email to 20 other people ... your computer will be a living hell thanks to one of our very own little ingenious viruses. I repeat, this is not a joke. This virus will come to you only a week after you open this piece of mail in a very indiscreet email. If you open this email after opening others it just might come as a letter

282

from your 'buddy' Watch out! You have one week, starting now. If this virus gets in, it won't come back out. It will slowly delete one file a day from system IRQ files, startup files, and win 95 kernels for registry address {1593338-489h985}."[4]

Urban Legends

Urban legends are hoaxes that have been with us for a long time and are likely to be with us well into the future. They are generally stories that are purported to be absolutely true by the writer, such as the following "Internet clean up day" email:

- "*** Attention***
  It's that time of year again!
  As many of you know, each year the Internet must be shut down for 24 hours in order to allow us to clean it. The cleaning process, which eliminates dead email and inactive ftp, www, and gopher sites, allows for a better working and faster Internet. This year, the cleaning process will take place from 12:01 a.m. GMT on February 27 until 12:01 a.m. GMT on February 28 (the time least likely to interfere with ongoing work). During that 24-hour period, five powerful Internet search engines situated around the world will search the Internet and delete any data that they find. In order to protect your valuable data from deletion we ask that you do the following:
  1. Disconnect all terminals and local area networks from your Internet connections.
  2. Shut down all Internet servers or disconnect them from the Internet.
  3. Disconnect all disks and hard drives from any connections to the Internet.
  4. Refrain from connecting any computer to the Internet in any way.
  We understand the inconvenience that this may cause some Internet users, and we apologize. However, we are certain that any inconveniences will be more than made up for by the increased speed and efficiency of the Internet once it has been cleared of electronic flotsam and jetsam. We thank you for

your cooperation."[3]

There is, of course, no such thing as a "cleanup day" for the Internet. If all Internet severs were shut down, there would be no Internet to clean.

Virus Hoaxes

The most common email hoax is the hoax virus. This usually consists of a message warning recipients about a new and terribly destructive virus. It ends by suggesting that the reader should warn his or her friends and colleagues, perhaps by simply forwarding the original message to everyone in the recipient's address book. The result is a rapidly growing proliferation of pointless emails that can increase to such an extent that they overload systems.[6] Consider the following Elf Bowling/Frogapult games email:

- "If you have received Elf Bowling or Frogapult games that have been circulating the Internet, or know anyone who has, they must be deleted before Christmas day. They contain viruses that are set to go off on Christmas day and will delete your hard drive. If you don't believe me, just wait and see. Our IT guy here just tested it on a non-networked PC and everything was wiped out. Make certain that every copy is off of your hard drive or any servers. Please spread the word. These games are very detrimental to your computing life."[7]

In 2002 an email circulated that instructed users to delete the file "Jdbgmgr.exe" because it was a destructive virus spread through MSN Messenger.

- "Hi, everybody: I just received a message today from one of my friends in my Address Book. Their Address Book had been infected by a virus and it was passed on to my computer. My Address Book, in turn, has been infected. The virus is called jdbgmgr.exe and it propagates automatically through Messenger and through the address book. The virus is not detected by McAfee or Norton and it stays dormant for 14 days before wiping out the whole system."

The email went on to give detailed instructions on how to delete jdbgmgr.exe. The truth is that jdbgmgr.exe should not be deleted. It is a standard Windows component included with Internet Explorer.[8]

HOW TO RECOGNIZE HOAXES

Neither you nor your computer is at risk from an email hoax, since they are usually just a nuisance. However, if you mistake one of these emails as being true it might cause you some anxiety and possibly even some loss of sleep. And rarely an email hoax may instruct you to do something that would damage your own computer. For these reasons you should learn to identify hoax emails. The following are some guidelines:

Debunked. Using one of the many search engines, check to see if the message has been debunked by websites that debunk urban legends and Internet hoaxes.[9]

Denial. Look for statements like "This is NOT a hoax." Such statements typically mean the opposite of what they say.[9]

Emotions. If the text seems aimed more at persuading than informing, be suspicious. Hoax emails are more interested in pushing your emotional buttons than communicating accurate information.[9]

Emphatic Language. Watch for overly emphatic language, as well as frequent use of UPPERCASE letters and multiple exclamation points!!!!!!![9]

False Claims. Read carefully and think critically about what the message says, looking for logical inconsistencies, violations of common sense, and blatantly false claims.[9]

Humor. Look for subtle or not-so-subtle jokes—indications that the sender is pulling your leg.[9]

Outside Sources. Check for references in the email to outside sources of information. Hoaxes don't typically cite verifiable evidence nor link to websites with corroborating information.[9]

Research. Research any factual claims in the email to see if there is published evidence to support them. If you find none, odds are you've been the recipient of an email hoax.[9]

Telltale Phrase. Look for the telltale phrase, "Forward this to everyone you know!" or some such phrase. The more urgent the plea, the more suspect the message.[9]

Unknown Information. If the message purports to impart extremely important information that you've never heard of or read elsewhere in legitimate venues, such as radio, TV, newspapers, and the Internet, be very suspicious.[9]

References

1. Christianson, Brett M., Email Hoax Archive – Email Hoax Categories, www.hoax-slayer.com/email-hoax-archive.html.
2. Full Hoax Index, HoaxBusters, http://hoaxbusters.ciac.org/ HBHoaxIndex.html, September 2, 2005.
3. CIAC Hoax Categories, HoaxBusters, http://hoaxbusters.ciac.org/ HBHoaxCategories.html, September 2, 2005.
4. Missing child: Ashley Flores, Urban Legends and Folklore, About.com, http://urbanlegends.about.com/library/bl_ashleyflores_ missing.htm
5. "Mockery of our Lord" protest, Hoax Slayer Forums, http://s12.invisionfree.com/HoaxSlayer_Forums/ar/t34.htm.
6. What is a hoax/chain letter?, Avira, www.avira.com/en/ threats/what_is_hoax.html.
7. Elf Bowling Virus, Scambusters.org, www.scambusters.com/urban-legends/elf-bowling.html.
8. Landesman, Mary, JDBGMGR.EXE virus hoax, Antivirus Software, Computing and Technology, About.com, http://antivirus.about.com/cs/hoaxes/a/jdbgmgr.htm.
9. Emery, David, How to spot an email hoax, Urban legends and folklore, About.com http://urbanlegends.about.com/cs/nethoaxes /ht/emailhoax.htm.

Appendix A: Where to Report Cybercrimes

Internet-related crime, like any other crime, should be reported to appropriate law enforcement authorities at the local, state, or federal levels, depending on the scope of the crime.

Federal Agencies

The federal law enforcement agencies that investigate domestic crime on the Internet include the: (1) Federal Bureau of Investigation (*www.fbi.gov*), (2) United States Secret Service (*www.secretservice.gov*), (3) Federal Trade Commission (*www.ftc.gov*), (4) United States Immigration and Customs Enforcement (*www.ice.gov*), (5) U. S. Securities and Exchange Commission (*www.sec.gov*) and (6) United States Postal Inspection Service (*www.usps.com/postalinspectors*). Each of these agencies has offices located in every state to which crimes may be reported. Contact information regarding these local offices can be found in your local telephone directories.[1]

Combined Agencies

To facilitate reporting, some agencies have been combined as follow.

Internet Crime Complaint Center. The Internet Crime

Complaint Center (IC3) is a partnership between the Federal Bureau of Investigation (*www.fbi.gov*) and the National White Collar Crime Center (*www.nw3c.org*). The mission of the IC3 is to serve as a vehicle to receive, develop, and refer criminal complaints regarding cybercrime. It gives the victims of cybercrime a convenient reporting mechanism that alerts authorities of suspected criminal or civil violations. For law enforcement and regulatory agencies at the federal, state, and local level, the IC3 provides a central referral mechanism for complaints involving Internet related crimes. If you have been the victim of a cybercrime, you can file a complaint at *www.ic3.gov/complaint*.[2,3]

Cross Border and E-commerce. In 2001, responding to the challenges of multinational Internet fraud, thirteen countries formed a joint effort to gather and share cross-border and e-commerce complaints. Such complaints can be filed at *www.econsumer.gov*.[4]

Specific Cybercrimes

Child Pornography. You can report child pornography online by forwarding the website address to the National Center for Missing and Exploited Children (NCMEC) at *www.cybertipline.com*. NCMEC will forward your report to the appropriate investigative agency for follow-up. You can also send an email to Operation Predator at *Operation.Predator@dhs.gov*. In addition, you can report child pornography to the local office of the FBI and IC3 (*www.ic3.gov*). If it is imported, also report it to U.S. Immigration and Customs Enforcement (*www.ice.gov*). If the mail is involved, also report it to the U.S. Postal Inspection Service (*www.usps.com/postalinspectors*).[1,5]

Copyright Violation. If you have been the victim of, or know of, copyright violation (software, movie, sound recording piracy) report it to the local office of the FBI and IC3 (*www.ic3.gov*). Additionally, if it is imported from or to another country report it to U.S. Immigration and Customs Enforcement (*www.ice.gov*)[1]

Cyberbullying and Harassment. Crimes involving cyberbullying or harassment should be reported to the local police and the local office of the FBI.[1]

Fraud. Report online fraud to the local office of the FBI, U.S. Secret Service (*www.secretservice.gov*), Federal Trade

Commission (*www.ftc.gov*), and IC3 (*www.ic3.gov*).
Hacking or Computer Virus. If your computer gets hacked or infected by a virus, notify your Internet service provider (ISP) and the hacker's ISP if you can tell what it is. Finally, file a complaint with the local office of the Federal Bureau of Investigation, IC3 (*www.ic3.gov*), and the Secret Service (*www.secretservice.gov*).[1,2]
Identity Theft. Forward spam that involves identity theft to *spam@uce.gov* and to the company, bank, or organization impersonated in the email. Most organizations have information on their websites about where to report problems such as spam using their names. You also can report identity theft email to *reportphishing@antiphishing.org*. The Anti-Phishing Working Group, a consortium of ISPs, security vendors, financial institutions, and law enforcement agencies, uses these reports to fight phishing. If you believe you've been scammed, file your complaint at *www.ftc.gov*, and then visit the FTC's Identity Theft website at *www.consumer.gov/idtheft*. Also file a police report.[1,2]
Illegal Alien Fraud. Report illegal alien fraud to the FBI (*www.fbi.gov*) and to U.S. Immigration and Customs Enforcement (*www.ice.gov*). You can send an email describing it to U.S. Immigration and Customs Enforcement at *CyberCrimesCenter@dhs.gov*.
Spam. Should you receive an email that you think may have a fraudulent intent, forward it to the FTC at *spam@uce.gov* and to the abuse desk of the sender's Internet service provider, as well as your ISP. Also, if the email is impersonating a bank or other company or organization, forward the message to the actual organization. If securities fraud or investment-related spam emails are involved, report it to the U.S. Securities and Exchange Commission. You can also send an email to *enforcement@sec.gov* Also file a complaint with your local Better Business Bureau.[1,2]
Spyware. If you believe your computer has been infected with spyware, file a complaint with the Federal Trade Commission at *www.ftc.gov*.[1,2]

References

1. Computer Crime & Intellectual Property Section, United States Department of Justice, Reporting Computer Related Crime,

www.cybercrime.gov/reporting.htm.
2. File a complaint, Internet Crime Complaint, www.ic3.gov/complaint.
3. File a Complaint, Onguard Online, Your Safety Net, http://onguardonline.gov/filecomplaint.html.
4. Econsumer.gov, www.econsumer.gov/english/contentfiles/report.html.
5. Montaldo, How to report child pornography, Crime/punishment, About.com, http://crime.about.com/od/childporn/qt/porn_report.htm.

Appendix B. Cybercrime Glossary

419 Fraud. A scam most often perpetrated by email. The sender requests help in facilitating the transfer of a substantial sum of money. In return, the sender offers a commission, usually in the range of several million dollars. The scammer then requests that money be sent to pay for some of the costs associated with the transfer. When money is sent, the scammer either immediately disappears or tries to get more money with claims of continued problems with the transfer. Also known as the Nigerian scam because it originated in Nigeria.[1]

Advanced Fee Fraud. Any scam that promises a sum of money but first requires an upfront fee. The 419 or Nigerian fraud is the most well known advance fee fraud.[1]

Adware. Software that periodically pops up advertisements on a user's computer. It displays ads targeted to the individual user based on key words entered in search engines and the types of websites the user visits. The marketing data is collected periodically and sent to the adware Web server.[1,2,3]

Anti-spyware Software. A computer program used to seek and remove spyware from your computer.[4]

Antivirus Software. A computer program used to seek and remove viruses, worms, and Trojans from your computer.[4]

Attachment. A file, such as a photograph or text file, that is sent attached to an email.[3]

Auction Fraud. Committing fraud by exploiting the Internet auctions conducted by the many online auction sites (such as eBay and Yahoo Auction) for monetary reasons.[5]

Back Door. An undocumented way of gaining access to a program, a computer system, or network. The backdoor is usually implemented by the creator of the program, and is usually only known to him. A backdoor is a potential security risk.[6]

Bandwidth. The rate at which information can be sent over the Internet. The greater the bandwidth, the more the information that can be sent in a given amount of time.[3]

Bank Fraud. Defrauding a federally insured financial institution, such as a bank, to obtain property or money. A federal crime.[7]

Black Hat. A term used to describe a hacker who has the intention of causing damage or stealing information.[3,6]

Bomb. Code that is hidden in a program or system, either maliciously or as a prank, which will cause something to happen later on, usually on a give date, such as a specific holiday.[3]

Bot. Used by search engines to crawl the World Wide Web and index sites/pages following the hyperlinks within the pages along the way. Also used in forwarding email and responding to newsgroup messages. Also called robot, spider, and crawler.[1,3]

Botnet. Army of zombie computers used by cybercrooks to do their bidding.[1,3]

Browser. The program that serves as the front end to the Web on the Internet. To view a website, you type its address (URL) into the browser's location field and the webpage at that address is downloaded to your computer.[2,3]

Charity Scam. A scam in which victims are duped into giving money to a bogus charity.[5]

Chat Room. An interactive, online discussion by keyboard about a specific topic that is hosted on the Internet. Chat rooms are available from major services, such as AOL, individual websites, and the Internet Relay Chat (IRC) system.[3]

Child Pornography. The illegal use of children in pornographic pictures or films. Can be spread via the Internet.[5]

Cookie. Information in a small text file some websites store on your computer. They are not malicious in nature.[2,3]

Copyright Infringement. The unauthorized use of copyrighted material in a manner that violates one of the copyright owner's exclusive rights, such as the right to reproduce or perform the copyrighted work.[8]

Cracker. A term sometimes used to refer to a hacker who breaks into a system with the intent of causing damage or stealing data.[3,6]

Cracking. Modifying a program to make it behave as the intruder wants it to behave rather that as its creator had intended.[1]

Cramming. The unauthorized addition of services to your telephone bill, such as charges for over-sea's calls you did not intentionally make.[1,3]

Credit Card Fraud. Unauthorized and illegal use of a credit card to purchase goods or services or the adding of charges to a card for goods or services not received.[9]

Credit Repair Scam. Bogus claim that for money someone can repair your credit.[10]

Crimeware. Software tools used in cybercrime. It covers a wide range of malicious software, including viruses, worms, Trojan horses, spyware, browser hijackers, and dialers.[1,3,12]

Cryptography. Converting information into a secret code to protect it or hide its meaning before sending it out over the Internet.[6]

Cyber. A prefix taken from the word cybernetics and attached to other words having to do with computers and communication.[11]

Cyberbullying. The use of email, instant messaging, and derogatory websites to bully or otherwise harass an individual or group through personal attacks. Usually applies to school-age children.[1]

Cybercrime. Any type of illegal scheme that uses one or more components of the Internet (chat rooms, email, message boards, websites, auctions) to conduct fraudulent transactions or transmit the proceeds of fraud to financial institutions or to others connected with the scheme. Also applies to generating spam emails, downloading viruses or spyware to your computer, harassing another through the Internet, child pornography, and solicitation of prostitution online.[6]

Cybercrook (cybercriminal). A person who uses computers and/or the Internet to perform illegal acts, such as fraud or hacking.[1,3]

Cyberextortion. A criminal offense which occurs when a person uses the Internet to demand money or other goods or behavior (such as sex), from another person by threatening to inflict harm to his person, his reputation, or his property.[3]

Cyber-harassment. Harassing another through the Internet. Usually applies to adults, whereas cyberbullying is the term used for school-aged children.[1]

Cyberhijacking. Hijacking someone's computer, browser, modem, or instant messenger. Also includes webpage hijacking.[6]

Cyberpunk. The stereotypical image of hackers—antisocial, socially inept, and burdened with anxiety or apprehension directed towards the real world which has been unfair to them.[2]

Cyber Snake Oil. Fraudulently using the Internet to sell such things as fake medications, unapproved test kits, and fake cures for such things as AIDS and cancer.[5]

Cyberspace. Refers to the electronic space created by computers connected together in networks to form the Internet.[1,3]

Cyberstalking. A series of actions that puts a person in fear for his or her safety. The act of stalking carried out with the aid of computers and the Internet. Done primarily through chat rooms and emails.[1]

Cyberterrorism. The use of computers and the Internet to cause harm or severe disruption with the aim of advancing the attacker's own political, religious, or other goals. Generally applies to governments and businesses.[1]

Dating Scam. A male or female makes contact with another person through an online dating agency and pretends to be looking for romance or marriage, but the only thing really wanted is money.[13]

Denial of Service (DoS) Attack. Repeated attack of a particular network or server until it is overwhelmed and is brought down.[6]

Diploma/degree Mill. Online "colleges" or "universities" which offer fraudulent or virtually worthless degrees in exchange for payment alone or for payment and or single "research paper."very minimal work, often a resume[5]

Distributed Denial of Service (DDoS) Attack. A multitude of compromised systems attack a single target, essentially forcing it to shut down and thereby deny service to the system to legitimate users.[1]

Domain Name. The textual name assigned to a host on the Internet; for example aol.com, bellsouth.net, and microsoft.com.[3,6]

Domain Slamming. Changing a person's website domain service company without his or her consent.[1]

Dotcon. A slang term for an online fraud. A take-off on .com.[14]

Drive-by Download. Spyware installed when you visit a malicious website.[1]

Dumpster Diving. The physical act of looking through trash containers for access codes or other sensitive information.[6]

Education Scam. Selling a worthless diploma or pretending, for an upfront fee, to be able to get you a grant of scholarship.[5]

Email Bombing/flooding. A denial-of-service attack that saturates the victim's email capability. Simple email bombing involves sending hundreds or thousands of messages to a person's email address.[1]

Email Chain Letter. A text in an email that advocates its own reproduction.[1]

Employment Scam. Unscrupulous persons posing as recruiters and/or employers offering attractive employment opportunities which require the job seeker to pay money in advance.

Encryption. The process of protecting information or hiding its meaning by converting it into a code.[3,6]

Escrow Service. An escrow service acts as a trusted third-party during an online transaction. It manages the payment process from start to finish, therefore protecting both buyer and seller. Used by online auctions such as eBay and Yahoo Auction.[1]

Firewall. A device designed to enforce the boundary between two or more networks, limiting access. Used to protect your computer from unwanted intrusion by hackers.[3,6]

Fraud. Intentional deception resulting in unlawful gain.[1,6]

Gambling Fraud. Consists of a number of online casino scams and sports betting scams.[15]

Geekfather. Slang name for organized crime member involved in cybercrime.[16]

Grant Scam. False guarantee of a grant, usually from the government, for an advance fee.

Hacker. Originally a term once used to describe a person who pursues knowledge of computer and security systems for its own sake. Now used to describe a person who breaks into computer systems with or without criminal intent. Purists want those who break into computers with criminal intent to be called "crackers" rather than "hackers."[3,6]

Hacker, Black Hat. A person who breaks into a computer system with the purpose of inflicting damage or stealing data. A bad guy.[1,3]

Hacker, White Hat. A person who is paid by the owner to break into a computer system and find vulnerabilities. A good guy.[1,3,6]

Hacking. Original term referred to learning programming languages and computer systems; now usually understood to mean the process of illegally bypassing the security systems on a computer system or network.[6]

Hijack. The process of taking over a person's computer, browser, instant messenger, or modem with malicious intent. Also applies to webpages.[6]

Hijackware. Browser hijacking software.[17]

Highjack, Browser. Malicious program that redirects a computer's browser to websites that often are of a pornographic nature or sell bogus anti-spyware software.[5]

Hijack, Computer. Turning computers into "zombies" that do whatever the botmaster instructs them to do.[5]

Highjack, Modem. Dialer program that downloads without your knowledge. It disconnects your computer from your ISP and reconnects it an overseas ISP so that you incur large, long-distance telephone charges.[1]

Hoax. Something intended to deceive. Not for financial gain.[1]

Identity Theft. Stealing the identity of others in the form of their credit card numbers, drivers license numbers, Social Security numbers, or other personal identification numbers.[1,3]

Illegal Alien Fraud. Fraudulently charging an illegal alien for paperwork and transportation into the United States, but not delivering on the promise after the money is paid.[5]

Instant Messenger. The transmission of an electronic message over a computer network using software that immediately displays the message in a window on the screen of the recipient. The recipient can then respond to the message in the same manner.[1]

Internet. An interconnected system of networks that connects computers around the world via the TCP/IP protocol.[1,6]

Internet Service Provider (ISP). A company, like AOL,

NetZero, or Comcast, that for a fee provides access to the Internet.[1,6]

Intranet. A privately maintained computer network that can be accessed only by authorized persons, especially members or employees of the organization that owns it.[1,3]

IP Address. Internet Protocol (IP) address is a unique number which is assigned to every computer connected to the Internet.[3,6]

IP Spoofing. An attack where the attacker disguises himself as another user by means of a false IP network address.[6]

Junk Email. See spam.

Keystroke Logger (Keylogger). A program that allows recording every character typed on a keyboard by a computer user.[3,6]

Laptop Theft. Physically stealing a laptop computer.[5]

Leapfrog Attack. Using a password or user ID obtained in one attack to commit another attack.[6]

Letter (email) Bomb. Massive amounts of email sent to a single person with malicious intent to overload the recipient's system. Letter bombing can cause problems not only for the targeted recipient, but also for other users of the networks involved.[11]

Loan Scam. Fraudulently pretending that for an upfront fee someone can get you a loan, regardless of your credit history.[6,8]

Logic Bomb. Code that is hidden in a program or system that causes something to happen when the user performs a certain action or when certain conditions are met. A logic bomb, which can be downloaded along with a corrupted shareware or freeware program, can destroy data, violate system security, or erase the hard drive.[1]

Lottery Scam. Scam emails tell the recipients they have won a sum of money in a lottery. The recipients are instructed to keep the notice secret and to contact an agent named in the email. After contacting the agent, the recipients are asked to pay money as fees—but they never receive any lottery payments. Another form of advance fee fraud.[1]

Malicious Code. Any code added, changed, or removed from a software system to intentionally cause harm or subvert the intended function of the system. Traditional examples of malicious code include viruses, worms, and Trojan horses.[6]

Malware. Malicious computer software that interferes with normal computer functions or sends personal data about the user to unauthorized parties over the Internet. Malware is commonly taken to include computer viruses, worms, Trojan horses, spyware, browser hijackers, and dialers. A contraction of *mal*icious software.[1,2,3]

Modem. A device for transmitting data over telephone wires by modulating the data into an audio signal to send it and demodulating the audio signal into data to receive it.[1]

Mouse-trapping. Websites are set up in such a way that users can't leave the sites by clicking on the "back" or "home" button. When they do so they may be connected to another pornographic site.[19]

Network. A system of computers interconnected by wires or other means in order to share information.[1]

Network Attack. An attempt to bring down a network so that it becomes almost totally unusable.[1]

Network Intrusion. Unauthorized entry into a network.[1]

Network, Wireless. Transmits data between computers and servers and other network devices without the use of a physical cable or wire.[1]

Nigerian Fraud. Also known as 419 fraud after the Nigerian code number for fraud (see 419 fraud).[1]

Online Sales Fraud. Generally takes the form of ordering and paying for an item online and then the item is never delivered.[5]

Organized Crime. Crime carried out systematically by formal criminal organizations.[1]

Overpayment Scam. Someone you don't know wants to pay you by check but wants you to wire some of the money back.[20]

Pagejacking. Webpage hijacking is stealing content from a website and copying it into another website to siphon some of the original site's traffic to the copied webpage.[19,20]

Password. A data string used to verify the identity of a user.[6]

Password Sniffing. The process of examining data traffic for the purpose of finding passwords to use later in masquerading attacks.[6]

Pedophile, Online. A person who is sexually attracted to children. May use chat rooms to try to meet them in person.[1]

Peer-to-Peer. File swapping systems that allow its users to share files, such as music and computing resources, over the Internet.[1]

Pharming. A form of identity theft. Cybercrooks obtain a legitimate website's IP (Internet Protocol) address and hijack Internet users as they attempt to go to a desired website, redirecting them to an identical-looking fraudulent website.[3,20]

Phishing. An Internet scam designed to trick an email recipient into revealing his or her credit card number, passwords, Social Security number, and other personal information to individuals who intend to use them for fraudulent purposes. The emails usually instruct the recipient to verify or update account information by providing the recipient with a link to a website where the information can be entered.[1,3]

Phracker. A person who combines phone phreaking with computer hacking.[6]

Phreaker. A person who hacks telephone systems, usually for the purpose of making free phone calls.[6]

Piggyback. Gaining unauthorized access to a computer system via another user's legitimate connection.[6]

Piracy. The act of illegally copying software, music, or movies that are copyright-protected (see copyright violation).[6]

Plagiarism. Presenting someone else's words as though they are your own.[8]

Ponzi Scheme. A swindle in which high profits are promised and earlier investors are paid off with funds raised from later ones. A pyramid scheme that involves an investment overtone.[1]

Popup. An unwanted advertisement that displays on your computer screen when you visit a webpage or have the misfortune of having adware running on your computer.[3]

Popup Blocker. A utility that prevents website popups from displaying. The challenge with this software is to distinguish a popup from a legitimate advertisement.[3]

Port Scanner. A piece of software designed to search a computer for open software ports. This is often used by a person who breaks into a computer system with the purpose of inflicting damage or stealing data.[1]

Predator, Sexual. A person who preys on people for the intent of committing a sexual assault crime. The most common means by which sexual predators contact potential victims over the Internet is through chat rooms, instant messages, and email.[22]

Prostitution, Adult. The act of offering one's self for hire to engage in sexual relations.[5]

Prostitution, Child. The sexual exploitation of a child for remuneration in cash or kind.[23]

Pyramid Scheme. A fraudulent scheme in which people are recruited to make payments to others above them in a hierarchy while expecting to receive payments from people recruited below them. Eventually the number of new recruits fails to sustain the payment structure and the scheme collapses, with most people losing the money they paid in.[1]

Ransomware. Software that is secretly downloaded to a user's computer and then holds that person's files hostage until a ransom is paid.[1,3]

Rootkit. A type of Trojan that enables an attacker to have "root" access to the computer, which means it runs at the lowest level of the machine.[3]

Script Kiddies. People, usually teenagers, who want to be recognized as dangerous hackers but lack the required skills. They use ready-made cracking programs, intending to cause damage and corruption of systems.[3]

Series of Events (Type II) Cybercrime. Consists of several events from the viewpoint of the victim: for example, the victim might be contacted in a chat room by someone who, over time, attempts to establish a relationship. Eventually, the criminal exploits the relationship to commit a crime.[24]

Single Event (Type I) Cybercrime. Consists of only one event from the viewpoint of the victim; for example, manipulation of data, hacking, and banking or e-commerce fraud.[24]

Server. A computer that is dedicated to a particular purpose and which stores all information and does the important functions for that purpose. On the Internet servers store webpages for ready access.[11]

Slamming. The unauthorized switching of your long distance telephone provider.[1]

Sniffer. A program designed to capture information across a computer network.[6]

Social Engineering. Term often used to describe the techniques virus writers and hackers use to trick computer users into revealing information or activating viruses.[6]

Spam. Unsolicited commercial email. Usually mailed out in batches.[6]

Spamming. The act of sending unsolicited email messages to many users at a time, possibly in the thousands, with the usual intention of advertising products to potential customers or defrauding them.[1]

Spoofing. The process of disguising one computer as another via a fake website or email address to send information through the Internet.[3,6]

Spoof Email. Claiming to be sent by well-known companies, these emails ask consumers to reply with personal information, such as their credit card number, Social Security number, or account password.[25]

Spoof IP Address. IP (Internet Protocol) spoofing is one of the most common forms of on-line camouflage. In IP spoofing, an attacker gains unauthorized access to a computer or a network by making it appear that a malicious message has come from a trusted machine by "spoofing" the IP address of that machine.[26]

Spyware. Programs that gather information about your Web surfing habits and sends this information to a third party, usually without your permission or knowledge. Spyware can change system settings, install keystroke loggers, collect and report your personal information, use computer processing capacity without permission, and deliver spam or ads without your notice and consent.[1,3,11]

Sweepstakes Scam. See lottery scam.

TCP/IP (Transmission Control Protocol/Internet Protocol). A protocol for communication between computers that is used as a standard for transmitting data over networks and as the basis for standard Internet protocols.[1]

Travel Scam. Victims are told by email that they have won a free or incredibly cheap trip. These trips often have hidden costs. Some cruises that are advertised as free don't include air far to the departure point or hotel stays. The recipient of the "free trip" is required to make these extra reservations through a specific company—and the costs are much higher than market price.[27]

Trojan Horse. Trojan horses (or simply Trojans) are computer programs that disguise themselves as useful software, but instead compromise your security and privacy. Trojans can allow hackers to take control of your computer or capture your keystrokes.[6,11]

Uniform Resource Locator (URL). Refers to the IP address of a particular website. Also known as website address.[2]

301

Usenet Newsgroups. A system of special interest groups to which readers can post messages. These messages are sent out to other computers on the Internet.[3]

Vishing. A form of identity theft. A scammer sends an email hoping to get the recipient to telephone a voice mail box to disclose personal information. Also known as voice phishing.[1,3]

Virus. A piece of computer code that hides within other programs or documents so it can spread from computer to computer, infecting as it travels. Viruses can damage your software and files. An action by the computer user usually is required to initiate a virus attack.[2,6]

Voice Over Internet Protocol (VoIP). A technology for making telephone calls over the Internet.[3]

Warez. Slang for pirated material (software, movies, and games) that has been modified by a cracker and made freely available to the public on the Internet.[1,6]

Worm. A computer code that is programmed to spread maliciously from one computer to another without any user interaction. Worms do not need to travel through a host program or file. They can travel alone and replicate themselves in great volume, slowing down computers and computer networks.[3,6]

References

1. Answers.com, www.answers.com.
2. Computer Definitions, http://ths.gardenweb.com/faq/lists/comphelp/2005011632014938.html.
3. Encyclopedia, PCMag.com, www.pcmag.com/encyclopedia.
4. Moritz, Robert, Protect yourself from cyber crooks, Parade, www.parade.com, June 28, 2006.
5. Milhorn, H. Thomas, Cybercrime, In Crime: Computer Viruses to Twin Towers, Universal Publishers, Boca Raton, 2005, Pp 46-70.
6. Cybercrime Glossary, TechTv, www.g4tv.com/techtvvault/features/35124/ cyberCrime_Glossary.html, November 30, 2001.
7. Bank Fraud, Wikipedia, http://en.wikipedia.org/wiki/Bank_fraud.
8. Milhorn, H. Thomas, Writing Genre Fiction: A Guide to the Craft, Universal Publishers, Boca Ratan, 2006.
9. Connelly, Jennifer, Colleen O'Reilly, and Darin Beffa, Credit card fraud online, www.pubpol.duke.edu/centers/dewitt/course/internet/fraud/ccfraud.html.
10. Credit Repair Scams, BCSAlliance.com, www.bcsalliance.

com/z_creditrepairscams~ns4.html.

11. High-tech Dictionary, Computer User, www.computeruser.com/resources/dictionary.

12. Crimeware: Bots, Symantec, http://sarc.com/avcenter/cybercrime/bots_page1.html.

13. Online dating scam, www.2beinlove.com/dating-agency-scam.htm.

14. Thomes, James T., Dotcons: Con Games, Fraud, and Deceit on the Internet, Writers Club Press, New York, 2000.

15. Online Gambling Promoter Craps Out - Industry Trend or Event, Newsbytes, www.findarticles.com/p/articles/ mi_m0NEW/is_2001_June_4/ai_75278265, June 4, 2001.

16. McCormick, Johan and Deborah Gage, Shadowcrew: Web Mobs, Basline: The Project Manager Center, www.baselinemag.com/article2/0,1540,1774393,00.asp, March 7, 2005.

17. HP and Compaq PCs - About Spyware, Adware, and Browser Hijacking Software, Hewlitt-Packard, http://h10025.www1.hp.com/ewfrf/wc/document?lc=en&cc=us&dlc=&product=59375&docname=c00206121.

18. The truth about advanced-fee loan scams, Facts for Consumers, Federal Trade Commission, www.ftc.gov/bcp/conline/pubs/tmarkg/loans.htm, May 2005.

19. US acts against 'page-jack' fraud, Sci/Tech, BBC News, http://news.bbc.co.uk/2/hi/science/nature/456287.stm, September 24, 1999.

20. Fake check scams, National Consumer Leagues' Internet Fraud Watch, raud.org/tips/internet/fakecheck.htm.

21. Webopedia, http://www.webopedia.com/.

22. Hughes, Donna Rice, Sexual predators online, www.protectkids.com/dangers/onlinepred.htm.

23. Glossary, www.polity.org.za/html/govdocs/white_papers/social97gloss.html.

24. What is cybercrime?, Symantec, www.symantec.com/avcenter/cybercrime/index_page2.html.

25. Spoof (fake) emails, tutorial, http://pages.ebay.com/education/spooftutorial.

26. IP spoofing: A tutorial, www.securityfocus.com/infocus/1674, March 11, 2003.

27. McKee III, Phillip C., Remarks to the Annual Conference of the American Society of Travel Agents, http://wvAv.fraud.org/news/1999/oct99/100899.htm, October 8, 1999.

Index

Index

www.ingramcontent.com/pod-product-compliance
Lightning Source LLC
Chambersburg PA
CBHW051045050326
40690CB00006B/603